A Cultural Mosaic: Thriving in Our East African Partnerships

By

Shawn Tyler

ISBN:

978-1-917505-39-0

Dedication

To my parents, Winford and Hazel Tyler, who would smile broadly to see this book finished, to my in-laws, Pat and Mildred Watkins, who supported us during our time in East Africa, to my children, Noah and Natalie, who shared many of the same experiences as me, and especially to my wife Linda who walked the same path with me and helped, encouraged, strengthened, and counseled me along the way.

This book is also dedicated to everyone who is reading it. May you experience the beautiful, loving people of East Africa the way we did. You will forever be changed.

Acknowledgement

I would like to acknowledge the contributions to cultural understanding that I gained from my coworkers as we labored together cross culturally. Specifically, my gratitude goes to my colleagues in Kitale, Kenya (Rolland and Jessie McLean, Kirk and Susan Hayes, Mike and Karolyn Schrage, and Dan and Traci Harrod), and in Mbale, Uganda (Sandi Piek, Ian and Danetta Shelburne, Philip and Laura Shero, David and Brenda Vick, Vince, and Joy Vigil) as well as a whole host of national coworkers in Kenya and Uganda – too many to name here. Yes, I must express my appreciation for some of my East African friend with whom I have worked closely for more than 30 years. These include Tom Ommemo, Dennis Okoth, James and Noeli Luchivya, David Bikokwa, Kennedy Obura, Richard Okwera, Peace Nanjala, and Stephen Masaba. From my work experience and coworkers, I discovered and refined numerous cultural insights that became the basis for this book.

However, I confess that the final content and format of the book you hold must be credited to my friend and first editor Myra Setliff Booth Reece. I initially approached her about an idea I had of selecting cultural insights from my more than 400 journal letters written over a twenty-year span. I believed they would be helpful for the newcomer to East Africa. Myra enthusiastically asked me to sift through the journal letters and come back with a list of important cultural lessons. I reread all my journal letters and returned to Myra with 104 letters. She praised my ability to narrow the topics knowing that each letter was precious to me. After many congratulations, Myra fixed her eyes upon me and said rather sternly, "PICK THIRTY." Shocked, I returned home and agonized, cried, and cut the number of letters down to fifty topics. Again, Myra praised my efforts, sympathized with my struggle, and then placed her gaze upon me and said, "PICK THIRTY." I wept and gnashed my teeth. It felt like I was having to choose favorites among my beloved children. I humbly returned to Myra with thirty-four topics. She smiled and said, "I think we can begin shaping and editing each topic now." With that announcement, we went to work. Myra asked me questions, forced me to refine my thoughts and goals for each topic and together we developed a format for many chapters. As she read, she eventually allowed me to add four topics back into the collection making the current 38 chapters. I share this simply to say that there is so much more I wanted to write and share. These 38 chapters are not comprehensive, but they do provide a solid foundation upon which to build your own cultural understanding of East Africa's lovely people. If this book does well, perhaps I can persuade Myra to let me add another 35 chapters in book two.

About the Author

Shawn Tyler and his wife Linda lived in East Africa for more than 30 years. Shawn continues to stay engaged in the work he helped start and he has visited annually since their return to the US. Shawn and Linda, with many coworkers, successfully established a children's home, primary school, clinic, university, churches, and a Bible school. Shawn's cross-cultural experience and insights in the personal, educational, non-profit, and government spheres provide valuable cultural lessons which enhance success for tourists, business, non-profit, humanitarian endeavors, and church related ministries. This book is a must for anyone going to visit, live, or work among the friendly people of East Africa. The cultural principles overlap significantly with the broader sub-Saharan African people groups.

Table of Contents

Chapter 1
How Can Something So RIGHT, Go So WRONG?

I don't remember her name or where she came from, but I do remember her story. She was a young American woman, of slender build, attractive, educated, from an above average economic social status, with red tear-filled eyes as she spoke to me. She said she wanted to make a difference. She wanted to help. She wanted to improve the lives of those less fortunate. So, she intelligently researched needs and decided to start a home for street children in Nairobi, Kenya. With a worthy project identified, she became an amazing advocate. She talked incessantly to her family and friends about it. She meticulously organized fund-raisers and, in a short time, raised $50,000 to buy land and to begin her street children's project.

She excitedly booked a ticket to Nairobi to look for the perfect place to begin the ministry. On her flights, she talked to her fellow passengers about what she was going to do. She handed out cards and solicited future donations from strangers now turned new friends. At the immigration desk at Jomo Kenyatta International Airport, she told the officer about her dream to help street children. While she waited for her luggage, an attendant approached her. He said he had overheard her plans to look for land and believed he could help. His brother was a government land officer for Nairobi, and he could help her identify available plots of land and even expedite land purchases. His guidance would be invaluable in navigating foreign laws. The young woman considered this meeting fortuitous and eagerly agreed to meet the next day at 2:00 PM.

At the appropriate time, a government vehicle met her at her hotel and drove her to view several pieces of land. The government official spoke excellent English and gave helpful observations about distances to schools, clinics, and markets at each location. He even had a city map on which plots were marked for sale. The officer knew some of the owners of several pieces and guided her away from some difficult people and toward friendlier faces. The official even offered to assist in the purchase should she find land suitable for her project.

The fourth piece of land she viewed was perfect. Not far from an upscale neighborhood shopping center, the land was lined with trees, flat and had a small stream running along the back of the property. She asked the price and found it to be $40,000. With legal fees, land taxes, and title processing, she could accomplish it all for $48,000, just under the amount she had in her pocket. She was elated and selected that site of all the ones she had seen. She believed the meeting, land, and price were providential.

The next day, she met the government official who had by now become a new friend, and they drove to the office of a lawyer he recommended, where a contract, copies of land surveys, maps, title deed, and the most recent tax receipts were meticulously scrutinized by the lawyer before pronouncing everything secure. She joyfully signed the documents, handed over the money, obtained her lawyer's receipt of payment, stamped in multiple places, and signed the land contract.

Arrangements were made to meet the government official the next day, and he would walk her through the process of obtaining her new land title deed. She went to her hotel and called her family to relay the exciting news. The project was beginning more quickly than she had anticipated. Everything was turning out so perfectly.

The next day, she waited anxiously at the entrance of her hotel. The official did not come. Something must have come up. She called him, but he did not answer the phone. Her disappointment turned to frustration, then alarm. Slowly, she began to have doubts. She never went to his office and didn't even know where it was. She never noticed the kind of vehicle or its license plate number. Nor did she remember where the lawyer's office was. Her doubts turned to fear.

After another day of waiting, she reached out for help through another lawyer and discovered the papers she had were neither original nor authentic. The receipt of payment was from an office and lawyer not on record in Nairobi. The truth hit her hard. She had been duped, and nearly all the money she raised was gone. She was ashamed of how easily she had been deceived.

As she told me this story, tears streamed down her face, and her voice quivered, "What am I going to do? How can I break this news to all my friends and family who helped me raise this money? I feel so foolish." I was unable to console her.

Her problem arose suddenly and bit her even before she was able to start her project, but sometimes problems only become evident later after much investment of time and money. I remember one young couple who moved in and successfully started a home for abandoned infants. Within a short time, they were caring for more than 100 babies, all under the age of five. They hired nannies, built a few brick homes to house all the infants, and had a well-designed website with ways to donate. It wasn't until a few years into the project that they realized a major oversight. They had not counted the cost of primary and secondary school education for all the children. School fees would eventually run over a quarter of a million dollars annually. They were short-sighted in their project and had no long-term or exit strategies. While this example might seem at first glance to be an organizational problem rather than a cultural one, in other countries, government officials would have demanded credentials, a project plan, proof of finances, and set guidelines on nutrition, health, and education. Yet, this couple began work in Kenya within a cultural context that allowed them to proceed without proper checks and balances. Instead, local officials were more interested in gaining some benefit from the couple's benevolent effort than in protecting the welfare of the children. The couple closed the project due to a lack of funds and parceled the children out to various homes that would take them, but not without facing some severe cultural and governmental upbraiding for having initiated something they were unprepared to maintain.

Over the years, these stories have been repeated, with variations, countless times. I have watched helplessly as the newest, most naïve, eager visitor arrives with grandiose plans, lots of enthusiasm, no ear for counsel, and zero understanding of the people or their culture. They figuratively strike up the band, gather local help to initiate their project, and parade the new initiative around for all to see.

But no matter how well-funded or organized the project is, cultural gaps in understanding and communication severely hamper progress. The naïve but confident visitor often cannot tell an honest person from a con man, a respected citizen from a troublemaker, or a hard worker from a thief. The newcomer is unfamiliar with the proper steps to obtain government permission to start a project, to register their activities, to identify good legal counsel, or to engage local leaders clearly and effectively. They either arrogantly or naively assume the teacher's role and instruct rather than listen. Misunderstanding develops, frustration turns to anger, and soon, all those engaged to help become major stumbling blocks for the project's progress.

Most of the time, after insurmountable problems bog down or doom the project, the naïve visitor abandons the undertaking and goes home defeated and bitter. To save face, some appoint locals to lead the project, and then the visitors leave, informing everyone that they have successfully "established" the project. They go home with no real plans to return. Only a minority stay long enough to figure out what went wrong and what mistakes they made. It doesn't matter whether the person represents a faith-based group, a non-profit organization, or a government position. They come with confidence, a measure of cultural superiority, and a whole lot of cultural naivety, and they often leave with emotional and psychological scars.

Creating a Cultural Mosaic

I lived and worked in East Africa for almost 40 years as a missionary and co-founder of multiple projects – including a children's home, primary school, dental clinic, orphans' project, Bible school, and LivingStone International University. I continue to make 6-8 week extended visits annually to reconnect with friends, check on school and orphan projects, visit refugee camps, interact with government officials, and teach in seminars. I have discovered that learning culture doesn't come in pre-packaged formats or step-by-step curricula. It is often messy, sometimes hurtful, unorganized, piece-meal, and varying in depth of insight. Immersing oneself in a new culture is much like creating a mosaic. Each event or piece, in and of itself, does not provide a complete picture, but as more and more experiences are collected, a larger, more nuanced cultural picture begins to form. The stories and topics in this book are "pieces" of a cultural mosaic. I have carefully selected each because they reflect important components of East African culture. The topic progression from superficial observations to deeper cultural truths serves as a tutorial for the Westerners who plan to visit East Africa or just want to learn about a different culture. By putting the big pieces of the mosaic together in this book, visitors who read and grasp the cultural principles receive a "pre-experience" advantage to understanding, living, and partnering with nationals who function in a culture very different from that of westerners. These stories reflect my own true experiences of life and events and my growing understanding and appreciation for the people of Uganda, Kenya, and South Sudan.

I write this book firstly from a tremendous love for the people of East Africa. I share a sense of home, and I have many dear friends who live there. Secondly, I realize my experience with various educational, medical, charitable, and missionary endeavors together with local and national governments provides a broad professional and institutional foundation for cultural acquisition. I have engaged and navigated within the East African cultures over many years, and I have served in many roles. The complex cultural and societal differences in East Africa furnish me with a wealth of personal and individual stories that illustrate cultural principles helpful for newcomers and visitors to more effectively engage and function with more knowledge, sensitivity, and benefit. Finally, I realize these insights and experiences from my now almost 40 years of work should be shared with those who are visiting or are moving to work or live there. The real benefit of this book can be validated by the new co-worker who joined our team six years after my own arrival. I was able to explain to him the invisible cultural structures and values that had made Kenyan responses so obscure to him. He and others noted that his grasp of culture and ability to navigate it was accelerated more quickly than if he had tried to learn everything on his own. This proves the wisdom of an ancient proverb that says, "Plans fail for lack of counselors, but with many advisers, they succeed."

I have in mind specific audiences that could benefit from my cultural experiences to avoid duplicating my mistakes while increasing their successful integration and achieving their endeavors.

To all tourists, this book introduces the culture and people of East Africa. It is not a list of restaurants and hotels or activities for a brief stay. Rather, it is a foundational understanding of a culture and people rich in history, complex in culture, nuanced in language, and very much worth learning about beyond the typical superficial "safari" experiences of a tourist.

To visitors who stay longer than casual tourists and who will experience the culture and people in deeper and more specific ways, the counsel on communication, finances, and relationships between East Africans is essential to accomplish a long-lasting objective that is not riddled with misunderstanding and enmity. This book will help you engage East Africans humbly and as a learner rather than haughtily as the Superhero who has come to save everyone.

To visitors who become long-term resident guests in East Africa, this book should help you dig deeper than the surface-level understanding of culture, language and people. So many visitors in residence think there is no need to learn more once they figure out how to drive, where to shop, and how to surround themselves with a few competent people. The truth is, surface answers don't always address the deeper, complex issues that are intricately intertwined with people who dwell within shame/honor, patronage cultures and particularly those which are also heavily tainted with poverty, corruption, and witchcraft. The deeper that you delve into cultural understanding, the better you will be able to address issues with comprehensive, longer-lasting goals and successes.

To the businesspeople who seek to develop or grow a market in East Africa, there are some important principles about money, business practices, relationships, corruption, patron societies, government interaction, and indirect communication that are necessary to increase their chances of success and avoid international disasters. It is a mistake to think that we are not that different because we can all communicate in English or speak of business models, products, and profits. It does not take long to discover that business practices can be radically different with unforeseen cultural obstacles that complicate what may look like easy transactions.

To the newly assigned diplomats who come to live and work in East Africa, what principles can one utilize to maximize international relationships? How should a diplomat manage the expectations of reciprocal time, appointments, gifts, hospitality, and generosity intermingled with government work and responsibilities? How does one negotiate or say "No" in a society that avoids negative responses because they highly value relationships? What is the real problem between two people accusing each other? How can bureaucratic red tape be overcome, and how does corruption play a part? Why are promises so easily and confidently made but follow-through so unpredictable? The culturally clueless diplomat may unwittingly do more harm than good and encounter more obstacles than necessary.

To the interested reader who may never travel to East Africa but seeks to learn more about different cultures, this book can unveil complex cultural principles in story form to expand knowledge and compassion for people groups very different from themselves. My personal stories and experiences illustrate cultural tensions and insights by providing a specific context, a problem, unexpected responses, and sometimes surprising results. The stories also act as a memory aid to make cultural truths and principles easier to retain and utilize.

To the students who use this book as a textbook or reading assignment, the cultural stories and principles introduced can open your eyes and bring a deeper understanding to the complexity of engaging people who are different from you. What are the contrasts between a Kenyan or Ugandan or Tanzanian? How do you distinguish between the dozens of tribal groups and languages within each nation, and how do the differences change your approach and engagement with those various groups? Each tribe's geography, history, culture, education, historical power, and interaction within each country with other tribes and outsiders creates a uniquely varied tapestry of smaller cultural differences within a single nation. To not see and appreciate the numerous differences within any nation is to overlook the rich heritages and cultures that make up that nation. A deeper understanding will shed important light on tribal tensions and government actions. Don't allow your assessment, responses, or actions to be based upon a surface national identity. Rather, dig deeper to learn the nuances of each culture within a single nation. These important East African cultural principles and practices would also greatly enhance understanding and smooth relationships between the various cultures in our own country. Though primarily an East African book of culture, this book can also provide cultural insights to better understand, value, and engage our culturally diverse neighbors in our own community.

Bridging the Cultural Gap

Let's use the imagery of a river to illustrate the cultural chasm that we must bridge. Moving to East Africa, or anywhere cross-culturally, to live and work is like moving to one bank of a large river. We can see the other side; we may even be able to communicate across the water, but our observations and understanding are distant and superficial. We must build a bridge of understanding across the river, the cultural divide that separates us. We can begin building on our side, but we must also find those on the other side who are willing to reach out to us to successfully span the river. How long it takes to construct a bridge will depend upon how large the cultural gap is, but more importantly, upon each side's willingness to immerse themselves in the other's culture. Of course, no cultural bridge can be built without diligence, cooperation, communication, and genuine love and interest in those on the other side.

Rather than relating dry or complex cultural principles and axioms, I chose to use my own cultural experiences about real people and events to illustrate new insights I gained that helped me expand my worldview. Every chapter in this book contains stories that represent immersion points that helped me grasp culture a little better and gave me skills to avoid future cultural mistakes. I believe we can learn culture more deeply when these cultural insights have a face, a name, a home, and a story. Included with each story are helpful suggestions, additional information, and African proverbs on how to utilize and maximize that cultural insight to increase successful cultural interchanges.

Moving to a new culture is a huge learning experience about a new place and people. It also provides critical reflection upon one's own culture and ways of thinking. This processing can be surprising, unsettling, and enlightening all at the same time. For example, after settling in East Africa, I was shocked to find a deep distrust, discrimination, lack of cooperation, and sometimes openly exhibited hatred existing between two tribal groups. I could not tell them apart, but they certainly could. My American culture tends to describe discrimination and prejudice within the context of racial differences. Yet, I witnessed a virulent tribalism that demonstrated deeper discrimination and repression than the "racial" bigotry that I observed in America. Having befriended Eastern Indians who escaped the caste system, as well as conversing with South Africans who shared with me about the tribulations of the mixed race "coloreds" of South Africa, I believe that culture also has a part to play in discrimination, prejudice and bigotry, and such attitudes are not limited to the color of one's skin.

Anthropologically, I define culture as a group of people who share a similar worldview. That worldview shapes their values and actions. It guides the establishment of institutions to serve that cultural group and produces artifacts, products, and art to accommodate them. Those living within a particular cultural group will see their way of life, values, actions, institutions, and products as "normal." Thus, anyone who engages in that cultural group and either refuses to integrate or rebels against the established "norms" of that group creates dissonance and cultural tension. It is a common human response around the world (though not necessarily benevolent) to reward outsiders who assimilate into the majority culture and to socially punish those who rebel against it.

Westerners set themselves up for social failure within their own countries if they insist on diagnosing discrimination and intolerance of a minority ethnic group as singularly a "racial" problem. Current social discourse is making headway in that cultural institutions that favor the majority culture are being identified and included in the dialogue for change. However, there are many more cultural factors that need to be included to find a more comprehensive solution to minority culture inequality. My broader cultural experience forces me to believe that cultural dissonance (often expressed through minority language, cuisine, dress, politics, education, business, family and social structures, economics, etc.) becomes a huge factor in developing majority prejudice that leads to discrimination. For example, our own American social problems will persist if we narrowly diagnose tensions as "racial" and not include the larger umbrella of cultural factors that create a significant number of societal differences. ALL these cultural differences must be identified, understood, and addressed to create true reconciliation and a more harmonious and equitable community. Part of the goal of this book is to illuminate principles of East African culture to provide understanding and tools to bridge the gap, reduce the cultural dissonance the visitor may initiate, and open avenues for mutual appreciation, friendship, and partnership.

Avoiding Cultural Mistakes

Disastrous cultural consequences are not limited to orphan projects, the naïve visitor, or even prejudicial discrimination. A lack of cultural understanding can significantly hinder sensitive diplomacy.

Rather than using threats and deadlines to force government action, more can be accomplished by a hospitable dinner invitation and a thoughtful gift.

A joint business venture may fail due to differences in handling accounting and receipts. Outlining financial procedures in advance improves the possibility of a successful business.

Humanitarian efforts that everyone could support may bog down if authorities are not properly recognized and "appreciated."

Educational initiatives may work well in Western countries, but are they adjusted to reflect the teacher/student relationships in shame and honor societies? Have such initiatives considered the lack of financial support or materials, or even if electricity is available in the classroom?

In the process of explaining objectives and dreams, can we speak without Western idioms and illustrations that only confound a local translator? Is it possible to include a local story or proverb that would drive the point home better than an hour-long speech?

Such cultural mistakes cultivate confusion and heighten suspicion between differing people groups. For example, how many Westerners understand the Arabic usage of the phrase "Israeli aggression?" While peace is highly valued, Islamic spiritual culture teaches that "aggression" by outsiders is a justifiable reason for going to war. This phrase becomes a cultural code with deep significance for Arabs that is only superficially understood by Western cultures. I wonder how many wars could have been avoided around the world had both sides been able to build a bridge of mutual understanding across the cultural gaps.

Engaging in another culture will incur numerous mistakes and embarrassing situations. That is unavoidable. There must be a time of trial and error. There is no way to understand another culture deeply without having first spent a lot of time immersed in it. Every experience within that different culture is a piece of learning that builds toward understanding. Individually each story in this book offers bite-sized pieces of cultural insights, but viewed together from an overall perspective creates a beautiful, intricate picture of another culture.

The variously humorous, sad, poignant, wonderful, complex picture of Ugandan and Kenyan cultures, specifically East African culture generally, ***can lay a foundation of understanding applicable to other diverse cultures all over the world*** and even within our American borders. These stories are not intended to be comprehensive but to prompt a deeper reflection of, and interest in, other cultures. There are many other stories to tell. I have only scratched the surface. I am still learning about the people and cultures that are very dear to me, including my own American homeland. Though I was born an American, having lived more than half my life in East Africa, I feel as though I am as much a son of Africa as any who were born after my arrival.

Finally, these prudently chosen stories are arranged to move from surface-level observations to the deeper, unseen, and often unexplained machinations of cultural interaction as they might be encountered naturally over the increasing course of time and exposure of the more extended visit. Do NOT read the first story and judge the entire book as shallow and one dimensional. Each progressive story will delve into more difficult issues as the chapters progress. It will get deeper and harder as the chapters progress. Referring to our metaphorical illustration, these stories help you construct a mosaic of cultural understanding that provides the principles and tools to bridge the gap between your home culture and your new East African host culture. You will navigate your visit or work more easily armed with these insights. The principles you gain will help you to be more successful. You will discover the beauty, wisdom, and richness of cross-cultural friendships and partnerships. These stories show that this undertaking is not an easy journey but one that is well worth the effort.

Chapter 2
International Travel: Checking My Bags and My Attitude

As soon as I turned the corner at Dulles International Airport in Washington D.C. and approached the ticket counter for Ethiopian Airlines, I became a minority in two ways. First, I was only one of a few passengers that had not been born in Africa. Second, I was the ONLY person I saw that was checking a single piece of luggage. The airline counter was awash in bulging suitcases, and I suddenly found myself in the middle of it. Every passenger seemed intent on bringing along all their earthly possessions on our flight. There were bags of all shapes and sizes. The lime green suitcase sat beside a smaller bag that had a world map printed on its side. Others were square-shaped heavy plastic suitcases that were so stuffed with clothes that they became giant beach balls on the floor. With each traveler so laden with bags, the clerks took a great deal of time sifting through the pile, weighing suitcases, and tagging bags. To my left was a bag too big to go. To my right, a suitcase was too heavy. The latter caused a gaggle of women to rush forward, unzip several other bags, rearrange items, put on some additional clothing, and eventually re-zip the bags and present them for a second weighing. They did not move out of the line, so no one else could be served until they were finished. Of course, this didn't seem to bother anybody else waiting to check-in. Anyone else around me would probably have responded the same way as these ladies.

The short, well-dressed Ethiopian lady right in front of me stood nonchalantly as this check-in chaos was going on around her. From the right, a tall airport attendant came walking up slowly to the counter carrying a car bumper wrapped in plastic on his shoulder. The bumper drew an immediate crowd of several men talking excitedly. They all examined the wrapping, taking special note of the Sunkist Orange cartons thrust on each end to protect the edges. The tall attendant waved the bumper around and shrugged his shoulders. Suddenly, they all pointed and called to someone to my left. A short fellow with no special uniform wearing black horn-rimmed glasses came over. He looked like another attendant for the airport. To my surprise, the fellow pulled out a radio and talked hurriedly into it. In a moment, he gave the OK sign for the bumper. With that, the men dispersed as the bumper went back behind the ticket counter.

A short young woman holding a toddler and pushing a cart with five monstrous bags approached the middle clerk at the counter. I was mesmerized by the load she was attempting to take with her. She began heaving bags onto the scale as her child played with a wheel on one of her many carry-on bags. The child, unfazed by the chaos, sang incessantly, loudly and off-key.

About this time, a guy in a white suit, wearing white shoes, a white shirt and a white tie, came strutting into the fray from around the counter. It seemed everyone knew him as he greeted numerous people in line. He would talk, then go away, and then return. He must have eventually gone through the line because I saw him later at the gate for the plane.

Suddenly, the guy with the bumper appeared again. Evidently, the car bumper needed to go through the metal detector. Off it went to my far left. The guy walked unhurriedly with his load.

More bags were unzipped and rearranged. As the line didn't seem to move forward and only grew longer behind me, two thoughts crashed into my brain at the same time. First, will the counter clerks ever be able to process all of us so that the plane could leave today? Second, is there really enough space on the plane for all these bags and passengers?

Then, the lady with the toddler became angry. The clerk informed her that she had too many bags – a fact that a blind man in a dense fog could ascertain. Yet this lady seemed honestly shocked by the revelation given by the kind but unmoved clerk. The clerk wanted money for excess baggage! This brought a new group of passengers and clerks to the counter with loud talking and waving of arms and pointing at the mountain of bags. Many in line just watched passively. A few waved arms and contributed to the discussion. I just stood fascinated by the communal effort to solve the problem.

A few passengers were slowly processed (because of the numerous bags), but the lady with the toddler became a permanent fixture at the middle counter. As I got closer to the front, the well-dressed lady in front of me with two small bags made a short phone call. Within two minutes, three large women, a porter, and a small mound of bags appeared magically by her side. One bag seemed large enough to enclose a small baby-grand piano. She had been "holding the line" for a large company of passengers. My hopes of getting processed sank into despair.

However, my attention was pulled back to the man carrying the car bumper. He had successfully x-rayed his package (yep, it was a metal bumper), and he walked slowly back, climbed though one of the slots in the counter and stood by the conveyor. It was then and there that it was determined the bumper would not make the corners in the conveyor. So, the man walked away to my right with the bumper on his shoulder – a pleasant smile on his face.

The middle counter clerk finally ordered the young lady to pull her bags off the scale and get out of line. By now I was close enough to learn that she claimed to have no cash and the credit card used for the flight was her husband's (who had just left). She was stranded and pleaded for leniency. Other passengers again joined the huddle at the counter.

I finally got a chance to approach the ticket counter. The weary-looking woman with a polite smile on her face took my passport and asked how many bags I wanted to check. I said I had only one. She stopped typing, looked at me, and then came around the counter to verify that I indeed had only one. Her eyes reflected disbelief. Her countenance brightened. She processed me in record time among the entire group. She even smiled large enough for me to see pretty teeth as I took my boarding passes and left.

Just as I passed, the young lady with the toddler realized that she was going to be tossed out of line and suddenly produced ANOTHER credit card to pay for the excess luggage. At this point, the staff and even some of the crowd let out a groan over the young lady's persistent haggling and waste of time. The clerk and attendants processed her bags with patience.

I left the chaotic area and was surprised at how quiet and calm it became just 100 yards away from the Ethiopian Airlines ticket counter. The walk and train ride to my gate was pleasant and lulled me into a sense of calm and relaxation. This was shattered as I approached my flight gate. There, I found another large mass of humanity crowded around the attendants' desk by the ramp to the plane. Two attendants were punching keys, pointing, waving, and talking excitedly to passengers in line. It became apparent that they were concerned over the massive mound of carry-ons gathered at the entrance to the plane. I don't know why, but I was shocked to see all the bags. I mean, how much stuff do these passengers need to take onto a plane? To the left of the attendants were two luggage trolleys stacked more than 6 feet high with bags that had been wrenched from the gripped fists of passengers. There was weeping and gnashing of teeth right in front of me! As I was asking myself what else the attendants could possibly pull out of the crowd, I looked around to see the guy with the car bumper walk up and enter the plane ramp. So, where did he put that bumper? Two guys appeared to roll the trolleys down the ramp. Surveying the growing passenger group, I figured they were going to need several more trolleys.

My ticket and seat were toward the back of the plane. So, by the time I got on board, the overhead luggage bins were already full. Items were stuffed under every seat and to each side. I thought to myself that the whole plane looked like a hoarder's garage. I found my seat, pushed bags out of the way and took my place.

I must include here that the Ethiopian Airlines attendants were patient, kind, and courteous. We left on time. I was served delicious food and attended to with promptness. If I poke humorous fun at any, it would be the passengers who obviously brought too much stuff to fly with. In fact, as I arrived in Malawi, we disembarked on the ground and walked to the airport terminal. During that short walk, my suitcase passed me and was waiting for me after immigration. Good job, Ethiopian Airlines!

International travel can sometimes be an exciting and chaotic experience even before leaving home. Traveling abroad introduces one to new people, dress, mannerisms, languages, and even strange behavior at what one would consider a normal task of checking in for a flight. Instead of personal expectations of how everything should work or go, be ready for the unexpected.

Visitors to East Africa will undoubtedly have some chaotic, scary, and amazing experiences as they travel through international airports. The throngs of different people and cultures will fascinate and frustrate you, and in turn, you may sometimes be the troublemaker for an attendant or counter clerk. Yet, in all the instances of flight delays, cancelled flights, lost luggage, and unexpected baggage fees, I would not trade my international travel experiences for anything. The best advice is to calm down and relax. There is no need to be anxious or in a hurry. Airport attendants know what they are doing and will get you where you need to be. Instead, take in the moment. Explore the airports and discover the different items for sale. Do not be content to eat food you are most familiar with. Try something new and exotic. Who knows? Perhaps your most favorite food has yet to be tasted. Do not ignore or resist, but absorb the world of cultures around you. Ask questions, grow in understanding and appreciation, and slowly, you will become a citizen of the world. J.R.R. Tolkien once wrote, "Not all those who wander are lost." Do not be so caught up in getting to your destination that you miss the adventure of the trip!

Proverbs

"One does not cross a river without getting wet" – Zulu South Africa
"A traveler to distant places should make no enemies" – Nigerian Proverb
"The road does not tell the traveler what lies ahead" – Bantu Proverb
"If you do not travel, you will marry your own sister" – Mozambique Proverb

Chapter 3
Stop and Listen – The Real Path to Wisdom

Many visitors come to East Africa and, without realizing it, bring their distinct cultural sounds with them. Some cultures are loud and aggressive. Others are not. To bridge the gap and learn East African culture more deeply, visitors must learn to be quiet and listen. Instead of making noises, absorb the sounds around you. Let East Africa speak to and teach you and woo you. Let her reveal her wondrous colors, smells, and especially her sounds. Listening may be the most important half of communication, and it is definitely a wise foundation for learning and understanding new people and cultures. To learn another culture, consider the wisdom of the African proverb that says, "The fool always talks and seldom listens. The wise always listens and seldom talks."

The Sounds of East Africa

It is a few minutes before 7:00 AM. I'm sitting on a balcony facing southeast, overlooking an inlet of Lake Victoria just a few miles south of Kampala, Uganda. The lack of a breeze gives a strange calmness to everything. It is cool but very comfortable in my short sleeves. It is mostly cloudy, giving a bluish-gray tint to the sky, but a brighter blue is poking through, as well as shades of pink to my right. A mist over the calm water is slowly distinguishing itself from the blue waters and the far-off hills. Ooh! A large orange sphere is just beginning to peek over the hills and lake to my right. It's now 7:04 AM.

Besides the differences in scenery, East Africa has its own sounds. For a city fellow, the first thing that impresses me is the absence of any motor noises. There is no highway close by. There are no horns, no trucks, and no airplane noises. In the absence of man-made noises, nature's sounds surge forth to push back the possibility of total silence. There is a profusion of bird calls – not all the same. There are many different bird calls, some very exotic sounding. Their total effect makes me realize that a massive number of living creatures share this part of the lake shore with us. A friend told me yesterday that some European birdwatchers recently identified over 120 different species in this area. This morning, they all seem to be chirping, cawing, hooting, and honking.

Yet the bird sounds aren't deafening. I can still hear the occasional sounds of roosters crowing from yards all around us. Dogs are barking, and somewhere close by, a turkey is gobbling in the morning. In the distance, a radio is playing a distinctively African beat, while downstairs, I hear the faint radio sounds of "Voice of America." Someone next door is sweeping with a straw broom. It's funny to think about it, but the straw gives off a different sound than the plastic bristles of Western brooms. Occasionally, a person calls out or speaks to someone else. A child shouts or laughs. There are many people close by who are beginning to stir. The faint engine sound that started up may be a motorboat or a pump running. It lasts only a few seconds before it fades away. To my far right, a motorcycle revs up and goes down the hill. It is 7:20 AM.

Slowly, the human sounds of activity begin – a gate opening and closing, pots and pans knocking together, doors closing, people talking, etc. They are crowding in on the bird calls. The man-made noises are not drowning out the birds; they are just competing for my ears' attention. The sun is up higher now, casting a bright yellow reflection across the water. The clouds seem to have receded, giving a hint that it will be a beautiful, sunny, hot day – though the air is still distinctly cool. It's a calm morning. It's a green and blue morning. It's a morning of bird calls. It is the sound of an East African morning.

A fish eagle is floating majestically overhead. As he looks for food, he reminds me that it is time for breakfast and time to start the day.

———————

I reflect on that morning and remember with fondness the "Sounds of Africa." That was only a single morning. My memory is full of many other sounds, some of which, when I hear again, take me back to a specific place and time. These sounds evoke powerful emotions and a sense of longing.

The cawing of an Indian House Crow reminds me of my first visit to Mombasa. The raucous sounds of the Pied Crow and Hadada Ibis remind me of Mbale, Uganda. Many mornings, I remember waking up to the cooing of the Mourning Doves and the Red Eyed Doves. The distinctive calls of the Woodland Kingfisher, Plantain Eaters (sounds like a laughing monkey), and White Browed Robin Chat enlivened our backyard in Uganda, especially on a warm afternoon as the sun set to my left. East Africa is a wonderful place to listen to the birds. My Kenyan friend Dennis Okoth reminded me that clans in East Africa believe certain birds represent ancestral spirits. He was taught that bird calls, depending upon the circumstances and time of the day, may be interpreted as a good or bad omen.

The people of Africa also make sounds. I smiled many times when I heard children laughing and playing. I laughed with the old men when they finished a story with an African proverb. There was a unique sound of women hoeing a garden or clanking metal cups behind the mud hut that signaled to me that hot chai was about to quench my parched throat. Men sitting in the shade and talking politics, a boy herding a few cattle to water, and an adolescent on a bicycle clanging his bell all bring precious memories and pieces of a cultural mosaic to mind.

East Africa's natural beauty has its own distinct sounds. There was always the fresh breeze that picked up and rustled the leaves of the trees just before a spring shower. The sound of rain on a tile roof could put me to sleep faster than anything. The rolling thunder of the northern plains of Uganda, the crackle of a fire, and the bleating of village goats put a faraway look on my face as I fall into deep contemplation of what is around me.

As for the more exotic, I remember the grunting sounds of hippos in the water, the trumpet of elephants near the water's edge, the laugh of hyenas, and the laughing growls of baboons.

Many in East Africa believe that every sound, irrespective of its source, is a message and has a meaning, and there are times when a sound is expected and when it is not. All these sounds and many more are lost upon the visitors who drive through the country with the windows up and the air conditioning on. Many of Africa's sounds are drowned out by city traffic or hotel music. If visitors would stop for a moment and listen, they would learn a lot. East Africa has much to whisper to those who would sit still and pay attention.

Cultural Insights/Principles

- Many visitors come with a list of things to do. They may see themselves as a teacher or expert in some field. Instead, they should open their ears, eyes, and hearts and take a learner posture if they wish to excel in bridging the cultural gap.
- Someone once said, "We have two ears and one mouth. Use them proportionally." This is "sound" advice for a learner of culture.

- Some tribal groups may express agreement by a sound rather than a word. Bukusu men may say, "Mmmm," to mean yes. Another may say, "Eeehhh". Or still, another may suck in the air quickly to express the affirmative. If one hears nothing, look at their face to see if they are raising their eyebrows to express a "Yes."

- Being loud while living close together is not intended to be rude. It is a community effort to say one has nothing to hide. Someone walking down the street loudly at night wants everyone to know he is passing and has no ill intent. It is the thief who moves quietly.

- Playing music loudly, talking loudly, and banging pots and pans are all signs of friendly communication.

- Two people may stand in the street and shout loudly and wave arms at each other. Listen carefully, their tone and expressions can help one discern if they are angry or engaging in friendly banter.

Proverbs

"There is no loser if all can listen to each other" – African Proverb
There is more wisdom in listening than in speaking" – African Proverb
"The ears that do not listen accompany the head when it is chopped off" – African Proverb
"Advise and counsel him; if he does not listen, let adversity teach him" – African Proverb

Chapter 4
Greetings As An Important Demonstration of Friendship

Being a fellow from Texas, I found it very uncomfortable the first time my Yakobo (my Kenyan male host) grabbed my hand and shook it vigorously but then did not let go of it. After greeting me, he intertwined his fingers with mine and led me toward his house. What I would have interpreted as a romantic handhold was nothing more to him than a real sign of East African friendship. I fought the urge to pull my hand away, which would have been a disastrous start to our friendship. Instead, I walked awkwardly beside my host until he guided me to a wooden chair in his sitting room. Only then did he let go of my hand. Right then, I had to start adjusting my cultural understanding of greetings and holding hands.

Visitors will discover that handshakes vary a little between the tribes of East Africa. Those same visitors also interpret the enthusiastic greetings of East Africans as merely a sign of friendliness and miss the deeper meanings and cultural signals included. African greetings are much more prolonged and elaborate than Western cultural greetings, and many visitors miss important clues built into East African greetings, which, if understood, can have a significant impact on communications and relationships.

Greeting Michael Isanji

It often takes an experience or two before someone picks up on the importance of something. Such has been the case for me concerning greetings. Oh, there is no doubt that greetings are important in East Africa. Greetings are often loud, demonstrative, and lengthy and can be accompanied by lots of handshaking, hugging, smiles, ululation, and laughter. I remember on several village visits ladies would line the small path to the meeting place and sing and clap hands until we entered. One time, while visiting a refugee camp in northern Uganda, the refugees met us about a quarter of a mile from the building and insisted we get out of the car and walk in a parade of singing. We definitely felt welcomed by our hosts. Sometimes, on joyous occasions, hosts can complete the greetings and then even start all over and go through the handshakes again. On other occasions, the host may not let go of your hand for some time, leading you where to go or sit. From the first day getting off the plane in East Africa, I realized greetings were a big part of meeting someone. Still, I did not comprehend the depth of its importance. It took a couple of epiphanies to help me understand the deeper significance.

The first epiphany came through frustration. I had developed a seven-lesson series that I was conducting at Namutokholo, about 30 minutes south of Kitale, Kenya. A small group had agreed to host the course in their building and invite local friends and neighbors. Still, our gathering was small, and by the sixth week, I knew everyone attending. Yet even though I knew everyone, and they all knew each other, we still spent the first 30 minutes of our scheduled time each week going around the room and letting each person stand up, tell their names, what position they held in the community or organization, and give a short talk before sitting down. By now, I was really frustrated with this "waste of time" before we got to the "really important" reason for coming together – my lesson. Unfortunately, I was evaluating the greeting time through my American lens. I judged greetings to be a cultural tradition that only delayed our important scheduled activity. I believed the repetitious introductions were needless since we already knew each other, our positions, and our responsibilities.

In the previous months of living in Kenya, I learned how to introduce myself in a culturally acceptable way, even in such a way as to make everyone smile or laugh. Still, I thought greetings were one of those cultural obstacles we had to hurdle before getting to more important stuff. Yet, during the sixth week of my series, it dawned on me that perhaps there was another purpose to our greetings that I was missing. If everyone knew each other already, then what was the "real" reason for standing up and "introducing ourselves?" Could there be a significant cultural value that was eluding me? For the first time, I began to rethink why greetings were insisted upon before starting any meeting. As I continued to reflect on that, another incident happened.

The second epiphany came through embarrassment when, one morning, I was late for a village visit. I stuffed my things into the truck and quickly started it up. I backed up, preparing to head for our compound gate. As the truck engine turned over, Michael Isanji, a gardener, dropped his broom and ran for the gate to open it for me. I whirled the truck around the yard and ran up to and through the opened gate. Then, I stopped abruptly at the roadside to check for traffic. Michael closed the gate behind me and started walking back to his broom. It was at that moment that I noticed I had accidentally picked up some papers my wife Linda needed for the day. I grabbed them quickly, jumped out of the car, and raced back to the barred gate. I called to Michael, who turned and ran back to me. I stuck the papers through the bars of the gate and said, "Would you please give these papers to Linda? She will need them for her work today." Michael reached out his hand but did not take the papers as I had expected. Instead, he passed up the papers and stuck his hand through the bars of the gate, looked me in the eyes, and said, "How are you today?" It only took an instant for me to realize my numerous cultural blunders. First, I had run out of the house and gone immediately to my truck, not even acknowledging his presence in the yard. I passed him as I went through the gate and again did not stop to greet him or say thank you for his help. Then, when I got out of the truck and spoke to him, I skipped the greetings and immediately went straight to business. All of these were just too much for Michael to overlook. In a quiet, unassuming manner, Michael reminded me of the importance of greetings. I was focused on the tasks at hand. He was focused on our relationship. I stuck my hand out for business. He extended his friendship. I kicked myself for not realizing what I had done.

So, I pulled the papers back, stepped inside the gate, and began to greet Michael. I apologized for not greeting him earlier, then I asked how he was. I asked about his family. I asked about his brothers and about his extended family. I asked how his work was going and if he needed anything to complete his duties. As I focused on our greeting and even extended it beyond the norm, I saw a smile grow on Michael's face. I demonstrated to him that his friendship was meaningful to me. In fact, my delay showed him that the village appointment could wait a moment. *Michael was more important to me than keeping time.* He understood that and appreciated my effort to express it.

As I returned to the truck, I realized that greetings are deeply ingrained in the giving and receiving of respect and honor, which in turn reflects a high value of communal relationships. At Namutokholo, no one assumed a stranger had arrived and needed to be introduced. For them, greetings were an opportunity for every person to be acknowledged and to participate in the meeting. Everyone who greets and is greeted, who gives and receives honor, receives proof that they are a valued member of the group. Without proper greetings, a meeting and its agenda are doomed to fail. Older people who embrace this value of greetings will demonstrate this emphasis when they encourage young children to greet everyone in a large assembly.

The importance of greetings can most clearly be seen in unusual circumstances. When I drove my car to the mechanic, he would come out with grease-covered hands but feel compelled to greet his honored customer. So, he would clench his right fist and stick his arm out toward me, encouraging me to grab his wrist and shake. He completed a greeting with me but showed extra respect for me by not getting my hands dirty. Once, during a cholera epidemic, people found a hygienic way to greet each other. They would clench their fists and bend them down to bump each other's wrists, avoiding any part of the other's hand. They would do this in a playful way to reduce the awkwardness of the sickness while underscoring their friendship.

It took even longer for me to realize how greetings played a significant role in identifying the most honored within a hierarchal society. To successfully bridge the cultural gap, it is important to note how greetings are conducted. In formal settings, the host most often introduces the local people first, with their group leaders last. Then, the host will move to local leaders from the community who may have attended. The host moves up the honor scale by introducing and greeting those who have traveled the farthest. He will give them an opportunity to introduce themselves, beginning with the least and ending with the person who is scheduled to talk or bring news. Sometimes, if the host does not know how to provide a "pecking order" among the visitors, he may request one of the visitors to introduce the group. Then, the responsibility of arranging them goes to another, allowing the host to avoid embarrassing someone or inadvertently dishonoring an important guest.

In East Africa, relationship trumps schedule or responsibilities **EVERY TIME**. Work can wait if a visitor arrives. A trip should be delayed if a neighbor needs help. **EVERYONE** must greet each other before any meeting can begin. There is **ALWAYS** time to greet and underscore the importance of friendship. How much emphasis you put on greetings can completely change the outcome of important meetings.

Cultural Insights/Principles

• The longer or more expressive the greeting, the more honor is demonstrated in that relationship.

• Extended greetings may include questions about the status of one's children, cows, goats, bones, and potatoes, often drawing a smile from the guest.

• Greeters will often give a slight bow to older or honorable guests.

• Two hands are often used in greeting. The right hand is extended to grasp the visitor's hand, while the left hand may touch the back of the visitor's hand, their forearm, or the host may touch his own forearm, keeping both hands in view.

• Older people, or people in positions of authority, may greet others with one hand.

• Traditionally, women tend to look down or away from a man when greeting him as a show of respect. To maintain eye contact throughout the greeting could be considered dishonoring or even suggestive.

• Young girls may curtsy as they greet a visitor.

• In Eastern Uganda, some women and girls may kneel to greet a visitor. If they are in the field, they may even stop hoeing the garden and kneel and greet from a distance.

• Not greeting someone is a sign of a troubled relationship.

• When entering a person's compound, the guest must call out to let the host know they are present. Then, the guest must remain passive and allow the host to initiate the greetings. The host may greet lightly outside but take even more time to greet once everyone is seated.

- In traditional greetings, mothers-in-law would not shake hands with their sons-in-law as a show of respect (also to observe traditional sexual taboos). The same was true for daughters-in-law and their fathers-in-law.
- Titles and honorific names, positions, or deeds are mentioned during greetings to add esteem to special guests.

Proverbs

"Honor a child and he will honor you" – African Proverb

Chapter 5

Hospitality – A Mark of Reciprocal Friendships

It was a hot, dusty day when we sat down for a meal in a small village beyond Endebess in Western Kenya. I took with me Larry Stephens, a friend and mentor and an experienced missionary of more than 13 years at the time. We ate a normal meal of chicken and ugali (cornmeal cooked into a play dough consistency) but were surprised by an after-lunch snack of fresh, cold apple slices. Both of us sat up with wide eyes as the red, juicy slices were placed before us. As Larry put his fourth apple wedge into his mouth, he turned to me and asked, "Do you get apples a lot?" With a straight face, I said, "Yeah, I get so tired of eating apples all the time." Jealousy sprung up in Larry's eyes. Then I started laughing. "Actually," I said, "I have never been served apples before." We discovered that the village was next to one of the only apple orchards in all of Kenya. There was a cold storage house not far, and a young man had ridden a bicycle over to get a few apples for us. They were delicious!

Almost everyone who visits East Africa testifies to the wonderful hospitality of the warm-hearted, generous people. Yet, not everyone understands the full meaning of hospitality in East Africa and how accepting hospitality obliges one to reciprocate in unexpected ways.

Mama Dina's Hospitality

Mama Dina is a short, squatty lady with a confident walk, a sharp, discerning eye, and a beaming smile. But what makes her stand out even more is her voice. She possesses a booming voice and laugh. She doesn't just talk; she barks out commands with a confidence that reflects her expectation of obedience. When she shouts, the dog winces, the chickens scatter, the cows in the pen jump, and her daughters-in-law break into a run. She manages her house well, and if truth be told, the houses of her sons. In fact, if Kenya was not a patriarchal society, I suspect Mama Dina might just run it all. Mama Dina's initially perceived rough exterior hides a very tender heart.

Visitors do not fit into the same category as Mama Dina's kinfolks. Instead of her iron-fisted rule, on numerous occasions, we enjoyed her lavish hospitality. I always enjoy visiting her home in Nangili, just north of Bungoma in western Kenya. The worship service nearby is always lively, the people love to laugh, family and friendship ties are strong, and hospitality overflows upon all who enter. When our long teaching session is finished, I get excited when I see our escort ushering us toward Mama Dina's house. The tables are always covered with cloth and bulging with metal dishes of ugali, chicken, beans, rice, ripe sweet bananas, cooking bananas (called matooke), and especially chai. Mama Dina's chai is the best of any home I visit. She uses well or river water that is brought to a boil in a large aluminum pot, and then she adds freshly squeezed raw milk with all its cream. This mixture is brought to a boil again before she adds tea leaves and an ample portion of locally grown sugarcane (often grown on her farm). She stirs the mixture with a thick wooden spoon over a wood fire, perfecting the hot, sweet, milky, smoky, flavored tea. Mama Dina brings the chai to a sun-surface heat that is somehow handled in metal cups without mittens. But there is one more ingredient Mama Dina adds that I have almost never experienced. As she cooks the chai, she will step outside her kitchen hut and pull a few blades of lemon grass, crinkle them up, and add them to the boiling concoction over her well-stoked fire. The lemon flavor is a special treat and always tastes superb. Perhaps the lemon grass is especially flavorful because it is well-fertilized by the chickens that run free range around the house. It doesn't matter, the added lemon grass is my favorite way to drink chai.

Recently, our meeting let out on a late Sunday afternoon, and I found Mama Dina standing in the middle of her compound in front of her house, barking directions to the running maidens. Chairs and stools were carried to the freshly arranged tables. She pointed to a young boy and shouted something in Bukusu. He ran off on a bicycle to an unknown place and returned later with a sack of sodas. We were positioned around the tables inside the living room as we listened to the clinking sounds of bowls, plates, and pans outside by the separate kitchen. Mama Dina was in fine form, orchestrating the entire reception committee. In came mounds of ugali, a platter of bananas, bowls of beans and rice. The meal was so hot the steam rose above the plates in the darkened light of the room. A second wave of huge metal cups appeared, dangling off every finger of a young girl who very carefully positioned a cup in front of each guest. She stopped and adjusted each cup and moved them again as though she couldn't quite get the exact placement (later, I learned this fastidiousness was to demonstrate a heightened attentiveness to guests – a sign of great respect). When all the food was placed, a basin was brought in, and warm water poured over each visitor's hands. Cold water is for neighbors and frequent visitors. Warm water is for special guests because extra time and wood was used in heating the water over the first. When all have clean hands, Mama Dina barked something to a young girl standing nearby, and she immediately bowed her head and prayed over our food. (The women who prepare the food most often pray over it). Then, as we lifted our heads in a loud voice, Mama Dina shouted in English, "Eat." All of us obediently dug in… and enjoyed our meal. As we ate, Mama Dina stood by the door.

Sometimes, Mama Dina sits on a stool near the door. She will sit and talk to us while we eat, never tasting the food she has spent hours preparing. In fact, I can't remember ever seeing Mama Dina eat while we were at her house. Occasionally, her eagle eyes spotted an almost empty cup, so she would yell out for someone to come in and refill our metal cups with more hot chai. Eventually, we slowed down and sat satiated with food and drink.

Then came the puzzling part of culture that, for years, eluded me. She would stand up and almost snap at us to eat more. Some of the more learned visitors had turned the handles of their metal cups away from them, signaling they had finished drinking tea. But Mama Dina would look exasperated, grab the metal cup, turn it around, and order more tea to be poured. She would insist we eat another banana, more rice, and drink more tea – to the point of being uncomfortable.

Here is where Bukusu hospitality extended beyond my realm of understanding. To me, a normal host would offer food and drink but would be especially attentive to the desires of the guests. When they finished, that would be it. But for Mama Dina, the guests had little say in when they were finished. She would force more food and drink down us to the point we would waddle out to the truck and then painfully bounce our way home with full bladders on potholed roads.

Most visitors see Mama Dina as lavishing extravagant hospitality upon us. This is true. However, there are other cultural factors involved in hosting guests. To many in East Africa, real friendship is demonstrated by the exchange of resources. If I need something, I borrow it from my neighbor or friend. They can borrow from me when they need to, and this exchange confirms our friendship and positive status within the community. To withhold from a neighbor would be a shocking sign that something is very wrong with the relationship. So, Mama Dina's hospitality is expertly maneuvering through a very important cultural demonstration of relationships. She not only provides us with food and drink, she prepares more than we can possibly eat (to eat it all would be shameful to our hosts) and then presses us to eat more than we can comfortably hold – not because she is concerned with our appetites, but because she is demonstrating the high value she feels in our relationship.

There is an obligation in this hospitality that visitors to East Africa often miss. If Mama Dina stuffs us with food when we visit her house, then she will culturally expect reciprocity in some measure when she visits our house. By eating her food, we have confirmed our relationship and extended to her the possibility of seeking something in return. Mama Dina may not want a meal; after all, she is surrounded by vegetables, chickens, milk, and bananas (matooke). She may request from me school fees for her niece, or assistance with a hospital bill for her daughter. The opportunity for reciprocity will come in some form, and I need to be keenly aware of how I respond when it happens. To refuse medical assistance or not help Mama Dina when she asks may severely hinder our future interaction. The visitor may eat their fill and assume Mama Dina is the queen of hospitality. The wiser visitor will understand that lavish hospitality is also an opening step for a reciprocal relationship.

Additionally, neighbors will not ask for more than they can give in return. The expectation that a neighbor will come and ask for something in kind limits how each will fashion their request. Thus, there is a balance to reciprocal relationships. However, the unknowing Western visitor often does not understand or participate in East African reciprocal relationships. So, East Africans may ask for help often and extravagantly without fear of the visitors seeking something in return. Because they do not understand the dynamics of East African hospitality, Western visitors may feel manipulated or unfairly pressured. Once visitors understand and fully participate in reciprocity, the asking will balance out.

Do not misunderstand me. Hospitality is a major cultural value in East Africa. Let us all enjoy it. However, there is also a deeper and more significant cultural dynamic happening than just eating a meal.

Relationships are being forged, and the visitors should be keenly aware of the friendship dynamics being constructed around them. A Ugandan proverb illustrates this point quite well. It says, "Brotherhood is eating. He who goes away hungry will never return." Do not foolishly think that this proverb is talking only about food.

Cultural Insights/Principles

• The guest is expected to remain passive after announcing his/her presence. The host, usually the man, will come out and provide directions on where to sit and what to do.

• It is not uncommon in pleasant weather for visitation to take place outside. In some East African traditions, visitation was done under a designated tree or under the eaves of a house.

• The host will initiate and direct greetings.

• When pots and plates are moved numerous times on the table in front of you, that is intended to show honor because of how much attention is being placed on making everything just right.

• East African culture is patriarchal, so all hosting reflects on the man and how well he receives, feeds, and honors his guests. Traditionally, hosting also reflected the man's wealth and how well he was able to provide for his own house.

• Though the culture is patriarchal, the women tend to oversee the cooking, washing of hands, serving, praying, removal of plates and cups, and cleanup. At a neutral site (not at home), a man may pray over the food and help serve the group.

• Modern food hospitality may lean toward a buffet style with many pots and plates of food for the guests to choose from. More traditional food hospitality may bring already prepared plates of food.

- If a sink is not available for washing hands, basins and water will be brought to allow guests the opportunity to wash their hands before eating.

- If eating utensils are brought, washing hands may not be necessary.

- It is not uncommon for meat dishes to be prepared for special guests while other guests eat beans or vegetables.

- Traditionally, when serving chicken, the gizzard is served to an honored guest.

- Occasionally, the chicken's back and feet may be included in the serving bowl. Visitors are not expected to eat them. They are presented to respectfully show how large of a chicken is being given to the guests.

- Hospitality concerning food varies among tribal traditions. One tribal group may feed guests with several local visitors. Another will place all guests in a room with food and then leave, believing it is rude to watch them eat. Still, another tribe may leave a single designated host in the room with visitors to direct outside servers.

- It is disrespectful to talk badly about or even refuse to try food offered by the host.

- Often in the village, visitors may also go home with a chicken, a stalk of bananas, or some other kind of gift to accentuate the honor of the guest.

- When you visit someone unexpectedly, and they have not had time to prepare food, they may insist upon you staying long enough for them to prepare something. However, since your visit was unannounced, they may not be prepared to feed a guest. So, the guest can help the host by explaining why he must go without something so that the host can be "talked out" of preparing food. This allows the host to free his guest without any food and preserve his honor and relationship. This process is for the highly skilled in culture who knows when and how to balance resistance and yielding to food.

• A wise visitor will spend less time watching the food and more time noting who is sitting with the visitors and who has not been invited. This kind of social pecking order will provide counsel about whom one should walk with and work with.

Proverbs

"It is an offence against hospitality to open your door and darken your countenance" – Traditional Proverb.
"Warning: Protect your friendships for a close friend can become a close enemy" – African Proverb
"A guest who breaks the dishes of his host is not soon forgotten" – African Proverb.
"A home is a home only if it is visited" – Zulu Proverb from South Africa
"Do not eat by yourself" – Bukusu Proverb from Kenya

Chapter 6
Food! – Are You Going to Eat That Fish Head

Vince Vigil and I were escorted into a small mud hut west of Soroti, Uganda, to have a snack before our meeting. We were served a plate of boiled cassava sticks and a small bowl of black goo that looked like it had tiny sticks or splinters in it. We asked what it was, and our host cryptically said it was a sauce to dip our cassava sticks in. When we hesitated, he said the sauce was sweet. I picked up a cassava stick and put it into the dip. When I tasted the goo, it was surprisingly sweet and made the cassava very palatable. I was on my fourth stick, which I had slathered with the black goo, when my host returned and asked how I liked the sugar ant sauce. I stopped chewing when I realized I had been eating crushed ants. I was momentarily repulsed, then realized they were tasty. I shook my head, decided the sauce was good, and kept eating.

Moving to a different culture means different food. Some Western visitors may struggle with the changes. If possible, every visitor should go into a cultural food experience with the idea that maybe their most favorite food in the whole world has yet to be discovered. On the other hand, if you just cannot eat something, there are polite ways to circumvent the experience.

Fish Heads and Other African Meals

A few years ago, fellow missionary Ian Shelburne and I visited two islands in Lake Victoria just off the Ugandan shore near Lwanika. To get there, we had to climb into a 20-foot-long, wooden, hand-made boat with a small outboard motor. We were not the only passengers. Others carried huge bags full of food, clothing, and other small items to be sold in island shops. Our boat was so full the top edges were just inches above the water. The first island, called Yuwe, lay about an hour away. While we baked in the equatorial sun, Ian and I admired the tropical scenery that covered the shores we passed. Occasionally, we would encounter various fishermen in a small wooden boat. One fisherman paddled while another other stood and threw a large circular net into the water. Weights would cause the net to sink, and then the fisherman would pull on a long rope to draw the net closed and bring it back up. Local markets brimming with Tilapia and Nile perch proved the success of this net-throwing method. Water birds like the Cormorant, Pied King Fishers, White Backed Pelicans, and African Darters were numerous and colorful. The most majestic were the African Fish Eagles, which glided on the winds high above the waters.

At Yuwe, we gathered in a small house briefly to make plans for an evening meeting before climbing back into the boat and traveling to a neighboring island called Lufu. On Lufu, we gathered information about the life and needs of the fledgling community. We discovered that Lufu had no clinic, elementary or secondary school, no churches, no mosques, no running water or electricity and no phone service. In fact, Lufu had no tarmac roads or even a single brick building. The citizens of Lufu spoke of a hard life cut off by a lack of transportation, communication, and sufficient goods. They were surprised that we had come to their island, and they wanted to know how we could help them.

It was in Lufu, with a population of about 600, that I had a very memorable lunch. Nearly all the inhabitants were fishermen. They would fish all night, bring in their catch by morning, and sell to merchants who were waiting in boats to carry their purchases to the mainland. Then, the fisherman would sleep during the day. They literally worked with, rested by, and ate fish. The island smelled of fish. So, it was not surprising that when lunch came to us, it was fish.

There were ten of us who gathered around a long rectangular table for lunch. Ian sat three people to my left. Several communal bowls of ugali were brought and spaced out among the guests. Then, a smaller bowl came to each person. As they put my bowl down, I found myself staring at a huge fish head that was staring back at me. Its mouth was open to the right, and it seemed to me that the fish had a surprised look on its face. As I poked it with my fork, the head seemed to curl upward as though it was being hurt by the puncture. I immediately stopped and took a moment to realize I was just reacting badly to a well-cooked fish head.

I looked down toward Ian and noticed he had a huge piece of what looked like a two-inch-thick fish fillet. I secretly coveted his fish fillet while crying inwardly about my unblinking fish head. I ate as much of the meat as I could, pulling it gingerly away from the mouth, gills, and eyeballs. To my right, a fellow dug the eyeball out of his fish head first and popped it into his mouth with a gleeful look on his face. At one point to my left, a fellow had a fish lip halfway in his mouth, and he was chewing on it. I thought to myself, "What is there to eat from a fish lip?" As I finished my plate, I saw another fellow who had completely devoured his fish head and had collected two fish lips, some gills, and a tiny skull beside his bowl. Now, that fellow knew how to clean his plate.

Later, I confessed to Ian that I had coveted his fish fillet. He started laughing. He said he had been served a fish head also. His fish head was just looking the other way. He had glanced at my bowl and thought I had received a fish fillet. Ian had been coveting my "fish fillet" lunch.

The truth is my being served a fish head is a rare occurrence. Stories like this are usually just told to scare visitors to East Africa.

Modern hotels and restaurants fill the capital and tourist areas. Menus are full of Italian, Chinese, Indian, Ethiopian, Arabic, American, and local dishes. Supermarkets import all kinds of products and spices so that any visitor can prepare nearly anything from their own home culture. Eating in East Africa is not difficult by any means. In fact, it offers quite a tasty, international selection of dishes.

However, I would encourage everyone to try local cuisine. Kenyan and Ugandan food varies a little by tribe, but essentially, ugali or rice or matooke (in Uganda) are the major dishes served with meat. Ugali consists of white cornmeal mixed into boiling water and cooked to the consistency of thick playdough. In some village settings in Uganda and western Kenya, it may be wrapped in banana leaves or heated in tin bowls and plates by the fire, giving the outside a crispy covering. Smaller dishes are served to everyone which often contain a piece of chicken or small beef cubes in a broth. Bowls of beans, greens, or cabbage may also accompany the meal, depending upon the time and year. Often, the meat and vegetables are cooked with spice mixes that can be traced back to Indian cuisine that accompanied the first Indian immigrants to East Africa in the late 1800s. If no food has been prepared, then chai is offered by itself or with mandazis (fried bread like a Mexican sopaipilla) or chapattis (like thick flour tortillas). If chai accompanies the meal, it most frequently comes afterward rather than during the meal. In Uganda, matooke is more commonly served with a savory dish. Matooke is the Bagandan word for plantain bananas or cooking bananas, which are hard, peeled with a knife, and either cut into chunks or mashed like potatoes before being served. A slightly more extravagant lunch may include sodas or bottled water.

If no food has been prepared, then chai is offered by itself. Many Western visitors may be familiar with chai, but not in the way it is prepared in the village. Most often, it is served in metal cups that accentuate the heat of the fire and can burn the fingers of the novice visitor. Traditional rural chai is a must-try item in East Africa.

Perhaps the best-kept secret, though, is the lightly fried chapattis. Every morning, by the roadsides across East Africa, men and women rise early to mix an entire bag of flour, baking powder, water, and margarine (Blueband) and roll it into small balls of dough. Once the wooden table is covered in small dough balls, each one is carefully rolled out flat and cooked with a little oil on a flat iron griddle over a charcoal fire. A chapatti is thicker than a tortilla and heavier than Indian naan. A freshly cooked chapatti with its buttery, greasy outside coating may be the most delicious food item in the entire region. Chapattis ready for sale are stacked up on the tables and sold to passersby as they hurry to work. Upon request, an egg may be broken and cooked under a chapatti, which can then be rolled up as a takeaway breakfast.

A Western visitor may not leave the larger cities and get to experience traditional food items. They may spend the entire time eating in restaurants with foods familiar to their home culture. One would have to travel to the more remote areas to experience local foods. Through the years, I have been served fried termites, rehydrated fish, cow intestine, camel, clabbered milk, chicken heads and feet, goat, turkey, duck, pork, numerous kinds of greens, and lots of fruit such as mangoes, passion fruit, bananas, papaya, and pineapple (the sweetest tasting on the planet).

Village food is overwhelmingly tasty. Even the most difficult to eat can become a favorite over the years. The best advice is to try everything. Eating together builds friendships and memories. Refusing to even taste the food or expressing outright disgust is very disrespectful to the host, especially for poorer village hosts who have put much effort and resources into providing a feast for their guests.

I now live in America, but every morning, I drink Ugandan coffee. I have East African spices in my pantry, and occasionally, we eat East African food. When I eat, I remember my second home and my dear friends who are just a phone call or a Facebook message away.

Cultural Insights/Principles

- For any cross-cultural travel that includes food and water, it is wise to carry some stomach medicine because such changes upset many travelers and short-term workers.
- Offering food and drink is an important sign of hospitality. It is very important to at least try the food and drink offered.
- If possible, eat a fair amount, but never eat everything offered. It is important for the host to feel as though they offered more than the visitors could consume.
- Most East Africans understand dietary restrictions such as no sugar, allergies, eggs, etc. A visitor can politely inform the host of these diet limitations. However, the host may insist upon preparing something else for you to show hospitality.
- Always take bottled water with you – it is understood Westerns prefer bottled water.
- Carry a few snacks, nuts, energy bars, or other such items in your backpack. However, be sensitive about eating it in front of everyone.
- Do not offer snacks or sweets to children without asking permission from the host.
- The Western visitor may visit a village numerous times. He can praise the food he enjoys and remain silent on the food he does not like. The hosts will learn what he prefers and alter their cooking to accommodate him.

•   Some foods may take a while to acquire a taste for, but they can become a favorite over time.

49

Proverbs

"The mouth that eats does not gossip" – African Proverb
"An onion shared with a friend tastes like roast lamb" – African Proverb

Chapter 7

Public Transport and The African "System" of Getting Somewhere

There are over seven billion people on earth. Of those, around 800 million can drive a vehicle. Not all of those own the vehicles they drive. So, it should not be surprising to learn that most people in East Africa are unable to afford their own vehicles. Thus, public transport is widely used. While not always noticeable, there is a loosely organized system for traveling long distances, carrying things, getting around town, and even sending small packages to other places. Any visitor, short- or long-term resident, or even businessperson may find themselves in need of public transport. Following are some much need principles one should learn before attempting this dangerous adventure.

My First Ride in a Taxi

Can you believe it!? I lived in East Africa for 13 years before taking my first ride on public transportation. Part of the reason was that we had our own vehicle. A bigger reason was that public transportation had a very bad reputation for being slow, overcrowded, and dangerous. Because of this reputation, if I couldn't go in my own car or borrow one, I just didn't go. So, for 13 years, I missed the public transportation experience.

However, that changed as soon as I moved from Kenya to Uganda. We flew into Entebbe, Uganda, to begin our new assignment, but our car, an Isuzu Trooper, was stored in Kitale, Kenya. I had to figure out a way to get to Kitale and drive the Trooper back.

Greg Carr, a friend of mine in Kampala, offered to ride with me in a public transport van to Jinja, Uganda, about an hour from Kampala. There, we would spend the night with some new friends before I set off on my own the next morning for the Kenyan border.

To begin our journey, Greg and I were dropped off at the taxi park in downtown Kampala. It was a huge dirt parking lot where hundreds of white vans, all looking alike to me, were crammed together in some unknown but evidently semi-orderly fashion. Thousands of people were milling about between the vans, looking for transportation or hawking small items of food, kitchen utensils, beauty lotion, etc. Drivers stood around outside their vehicles and shouted out the destination they were planning to reach.

Greg and I mingled around for a minute and stepped up to a white van going to Jinja. We purchased two seats in the back of the van. There was already a large lady sitting there with two huge bags in her lap, so the three of us totally filled the back seat, especially with the addition of our own luggage. It was then that the conductor said four were supposed to ride on the seat. Greg looked at me and said, "I don't think so." He called the conductor over and purchased the remaining phantom seat on our bench so that just the three of us could occupy it.

The rest of the taxi van was organized by having two seats on one side and a single seat on the other side with an aisle between. Then, on the edge of the two-seater was a fold-down seat that was pulled down as the back filled up. Each row of seats was filled from back to front. During our wait, several business transactions were made. For example, the back door of the van immediately behind us was opened, and a goat with its legs tied was shoved under our seat and pushed against our legs. The goat protested loudly to this indignant handling and cramped quarters. We also bleated out our complaints, which fell on the deaf ears of the van's conductor, who had just become richer for adding the goat. Then another man approached with three large groups of chickens all tied together at their feet. The chickens hung upside down passively as the customer talked. Eventually, the chickens were tied up on top of the taxi, where an already full luggage rack was fastened to the top of the van. We could see the chickens hanging off the back of the van, occasionally flapping their wings and resettling themselves. Not only were we a public van, but we were also a traveling barnyard!

When the van was almost full, the final passengers materialized quickly out of the mass of people. I learned later that most taxis depart and return on a time schedule. Passengers purchase their tickets and then walk around until time to leave to avoid the heat and crammed condition of the vehicle. Of course, a taxi is never full. The motto for the taxi's conductor is, "There is always room for one more," even if it means hanging onto the outside of the vehicle. We had not sat in the van for more than five minutes before we were off. In a way, the whole public taxi system impressed me as being efficient in gathering customers, using limited space in the taxi park, and maneuvering through the maze of vans.

The driver ably maneuvered between other taxis, missing some of them by inches and eventually headed out of town – at least that is what I thought. No! He had to stop first and put gasoline in the van. Why had I assumed he would have filled it before coming to the park? After getting petrol ("gas" is a term used for cooking gas, not fuel for a vehicle), we lurched out into traffic and, through several roundabouts, snaked our way to the eastern outskirts of town. As we sat in traffic at various points, I noticed a goat staring at us from the back of another van. Evidently, he was untied and standing up. I guess he wanted to know where he was going, and maybe he paid for the added privilege. Our taxis traveled together for several miles before we separated.

For the first two-thirds of the trip, we did not stop. During that time, I realized that the back of the van felt the hardest impact when jumping over speed bumps or hitting potholes. I also discovered that my seat had the thinnest layer of foam ever made. That whisper of a cushion was all that protected a rather personal part of my body from a hard board that became even harder the further we traveled. However, I must say the driver navigated the road, the spiked barriers of the traffic police, motorcycles, bicyclists, pedestrians, cattle, goats, and other moving obstacles skillfully and less recklessly than I had expected. I was impressed.

As we neared Jinja, people started calling out names of local destinations along the road where they wanted to get off. As one passenger departed, the driver and his conductor would look for someone else to fill in the vacancy – often with the van door open and the conductor hanging out, calling out our intended destination. Why leave a seat empty when it could bring in money? I observed a system for this seat switching. If the passenger was from the back, another passenger going all the way to Jinja was instructed to sit further back, leaving the front two rows for those getting off early. I feared we would lose a lot of time doing this all the way into Jinja, but I was surprised at how little this seat switching there really was.

An unusual event occurred at one of the stops for a passenger. A young boy of about seven years old, sitting in the seat directly in front of me, started hopping up and down and moaning. At first, I thought he was sick, but then I realized he needed to go to the bathroom – badly. His mother reluctantly got up and helped him out of the van. She walked around some nearby small shops, followed by the boy hopping up and down. We waited and waited. Then she returned without the boy. Finally, the boy came around the corner and climbed up into the van. His entrance brought the strangest reaction to everyone. As he climbed back to his seat, every person by a window would groan, throw open the window and stick their head out. When he got back to me, I discovered why. He hadn't made it to the bathroom in time. He had gone in his blue suit. Even the goat under our seat seemed to complain.

At first, the mother made him stand up as if he were to do that until we reached Jinja. Any time he tried to sit down, she would hit him. She did not want him to ruin the taxi seat. Finally, after hearing plenty of instructions from the other passengers, she barked out something, and the kid began peeling off his clothes. Mom pulled more clothes out of her lap luggage together with a plastic bag. (There are many good reasons to carry plastic bags on journeys in East Africa.) The kid eventually undressed completely, showing evidence to anyone looking exactly where the problem was. Mom used some of his extra clothes to clean him up, making him put the soiled clothes into the plastic bag. Eventually, he put on some short trousers ("pants" in East Africa is a term used for underwear) and a clean shirt. By the time we reached our destination, the young boy was dressed again, and the aroma had all but dissipated. I wondered how the boy felt having to strip. Was he humiliated? Did he think anything about it? It was probably more embarrassing for him to remain in soiled clothes than to strip and change.

Nearing Jinja, another van with chickens tied to the top luggage rack passed us. I saw a string of chickens slowly sliding down the back door toward the bumper. Evidently, the rope had become loose, and a group of chickens were flapping around as they went down. The van rushed ahead of us so that all of us could witness a group of about six chickens fall off the back of the van. The driver did not notice and continued driving down the road. The chickens lay in the road and began to separate. Pedestrians along the road ran out to scoop up a chicken and run off before the driver and owner returned. This whole incident made me glad I had nothing on the top of our van.

For me, the ride provided an interesting first experience. We arrived in Jinja safely and reached our friends' house in time for a supper of chicken and dumplings. As I sat there among many friends in a well-lit room and nice smelling food, I couldn't help but wonder where that little boy was and what additional humiliation he was suffering as his mother pulled him out of the public eye. I wondered what happened to the lost chickens and where the goat finally ended up. I was reasonably sure that I was not eating one of the chickens. Not bad for my first public transportation experience.

Traveling around in public transport (vans called taxis) has allowed me to scrutinize public vehicles and drivers and make an astute observation that will help me in the future to choose the right taxi. Firstly, you must understand that on any given road made for two cars to pass comfortably, four taxis will vie for position. This means that taxis often pass within inches of each other. Crowded conditions are normal to them. It is nothing to sit in a monstrous traffic jam, windows down, and be able to touch the driver of a car going in the opposite direction on the shoulder with your arm extended. It gets really personal in heavy traffic. A taxi may climb up onto a sidewalk to gain an advantage or to pass a stubborn truck driver trying to cross a road.

Secondly, there is nothing orderly about public transport driving. On one occasion, I remember our taxi having to stop for a train to cross the road. It was a long train, and it took several minutes. As we waited, other taxis ran up the shoulder of our lane to the front of the line to get ahead of everyone else. Within seconds, we had two lanes going forward. The train stopped and started backing up. So, more taxis ran up in the lane for vehicles coming from the other direction. Then, still, more taxis ran up on the far shoulder of the road. Within two minutes, we had created four full lanes of traffic on a two-lane road, completely blocking the road off for oncoming traffic. I thought to myself how much the other side would be surprised when the train finally passed. When the train moved away, we found ourselves staring at four full lanes of traffic facing us. My heart almost stopped. I thought we were going to spend the night there unraveling this traffic mess. All the taxis jumped forward onto the train tracks, honking horns and waving their arms. They inched, nudged, and drove into the small spaces between vehicles. It was chaos. But within five minutes, we were completely cleared out and traveling again. I really don't know how the taxis did it. These kinds of incidents make me think our African taxi drivers are part magicians in getting through difficult places.

To help move about in such conditions, some vans have placed mirrors on the front and rear corners facing down so that the driver can tell if the bumpers are close to touching anything. Such mirrors are an indication that the driver is prepared to drive in extremely close conditions. This driver doesn't think in meters. He thinks in centimeters! But my question is, "Why should I want such a driver?" I would rather have a driver who seeks to avoid such close encounters. So, when I see the van with mirrors on all four corners, I let him pass and take the next one.

Let me share one final observation gained through personal experience. On one taxi, I jumped in and sat by the window, thinking I would enjoy the fresh air. The road was so rough on our journey that I banged my head on the metal window frame numerous times. I determined that fresh air was less important than a comfortable ride. One Ugandan laughingly suggested I sit in the middle of the bench between two large women. Since personal space is almost non-existent, I could bounce off the two ladies without offending and have a more cushioned ride. It works! It was the best advice I ever received about public transportation.

Cultural Insights/Principles

• Taxi prices are negotiable! The price will change depending on the distance you want to travel and the amount of luggage you are carrying. If possible, listen and learn the price structure before attempting to bargain.

• There may be a main taxi park for most taxis. However, many towns have a specific spot where taxis gather to go to specific destinations, i.e., east, west, north, or south. These may be the fastest way to get out of town and to a specific destination.

• The best place to sit in a taxi is in the front seat next to the driver.

• Many taxis to villages do not run all night. Often, the taxis "sleep" out in the village and make an early run to town before businesses open. They often make their last runs out of town between 7:00 PM and 8:00 PM.

• Private hires are available for around town or to a specific destination if you wish to avoid the cramped quarters and frequent stops along a route. They are more expensive, but you can enjoy air conditioning and a comfortable seat.

• In buses where passengers stand up, be careful of pick pockets. Crowded spaces where people are always bumping into each other is a perfect place to lose money or a wallet. It is best not to place money or wallets in trousers or coat pockets or in a big bag. Instead, use a neck pouch inside the shirt with the strings hidden.

• Public transport will be most crowded at rush hour times for going and coming from work.

• Never leave baggage unaccompanied.

• Dotted along the roads are motorcycles for hire. They can zip through traffic jams, but they are often involved in accidents.

• Large buses are often the cheapest way to travel across the country. Overnight buses travel from Nairobi, Kenya, to Kampala, Uganda, or from Nairobi to Mombasa.

- Taxis have a system for communicating with each other about where police stations are set up on the road. If the driver spends a lot of time communicating, he may be in violation of some traffic laws and could cause major delays and headaches for his passengers if he is caught.
- Overnight trips on public transport can be cold. Take a coat or jacket to stay warm.
- There is a train service from Nairobi to Mombasa and from Kampala to Nairobi.
- Most larger cities will have a location where one can hire a small truck, a dump truck, or a small car for a variety of tasks. Find out ahead of time what the average charge is for a day or for a certain distance before you begin to bargain.
- In renting vehicles, building a relationship with the driver is important to prices and service.

Proverbs

"If you want to go quickly, go alone. If you want to go far, travel together" – African Proverb.
"Go slowly and you will reach far" – Ugandan Proverb
"Hurry, hurry, has no blessings" – Kenyan Proverb

Chapter 8
My Holidays, Their Holidays, Our Holidays!

It was February and the Super Bowl, the American Football Championship game, was being televised live in East Africa. The only problem was we were eight hours ahead of game time. This meant we had to get up at 2:30 AM for the game starting at 3:00 AM. Since we were not the only ones interested in watching the game, we invited friends over to have a Super Bowl party. Kids came in pajamas and fell asleep in front of the TV. Adults sat around and cheered or booed the performances of their team. In preparation for the game night, I purchased 2 kilos (4.4 pounds) of beef fillet with the intent to grill it outside, in the dark, by flashlight, during half time at 4:30 AM. My wife was incredulous. She said, "No one is going to eat a heavy meal so early in the morning." I said, "Trust me. This is football. At least all the guys will be eating and snacking throughout the game. It won't matter what time it is." So, she prepared snacks, and I grilled meat. When the game was over, I looked at the empty pans and then at my wife and said, "I told you so." It seems strange for anyone new to living in East Africa to get up in the middle of the night to watch American sports, but it is just the way of life. Special events are like holidays. They get mixed up because the climate, time zone, and geography are different from that back home.

Without realizing it, a significant part of an individual's learning of their home culture comes from his/her way of celebrating holidays and the climate associated with them. Once we move to another culture, we surprisingly find ourselves in tension with what we expect or want and what is happening around us. The greater the dissonance in climate and holidays, the greater the culture shock we experience.

Thanksgiving in a Hot, Dry East Africa

Perhaps no American holiday is more wrapped up in family and food than Thanksgiving. Our extended family, for years, gathered at my grandparents' home where turkey and dressing, giblet gravy, pecan pies, sweet potato casserole, fresh rolls, and a generous helping of cranberry sauce would vie for spots on the dinner plate. Often, I would have to put a spoon full of fruit salad or green beans on top of the meat just to keep from going back a second time. Having been born and raised in Fort Worth, Texas, meant we enjoyed an afternoon Dallas Cowboys football game as well.

Thanksgiving is not just about family and food. It signals a change of the seasons. The leaves turn colors and fall off the trees. There is a chill in the air. Lawn care slows down, and there is talk of winter freezes at night and instructions on bringing potted plants inside. Department stores decorate for weeks before Thanksgiving, and special foods not seen all year pop up in advertisements and TV commercials. We annually complain about how the retail stores invade our Thanksgiving planning and celebrations with Christmas decorations, music, and gift specials. It is not time for Christmas yet! It is THANKSGIVING! The days become shorter, and we start pulling out our winter clothes.

You can imagine our surprise when much of this did not happen after moving to East Africa. Instead of the autumn, when leaves turn colors and fall, we experience the end of the short rainy season. In Africa, many trees stay green all year; very few lose their leaves. Maize harvest is in full swing, and farmers work long hours. After the rains, East Africa begins its dry season, which is also the hottest time of the year. The grass slows in growth and becomes brittle and brownish in the harsh sunlight. Gardens stop producing unless watered. The dirt roads turn dusty, and bushes along the road collect a thick dirt coating that does not wash off until the first rains in late March or early April.

East Africa did not decorate for Thanksgiving. There were no special foods in the supermarket, and the fourth Thursday of November was a workday like every other one. The entire holiday atmosphere was non-existent. There was no external holiday spirit evident. It was business as usual.

Still, we wanted to observe Thanksgiving, a strong personal cultural tradition. So, to prepare our own special Thanksgiving, we had to plan in advance to purchase some of the decorations and food items. Having been in America during the previous "summer," my wife Linda purchased cranberry sauce and packed it in our suitcases for the trip to East Africa. Working off a list of food items not available in Mbale, Uganda, Linda spent weeks in advance purchasing everything she could in Kampala, Uganda or on one of our trips to Kitale, Kenya. Part of the household goods that we shipped with us were holiday decorations. I complained about packing them but enjoyed them immensely when we pulled them out for the holidays. Linda told me all the food items had been purchased except the turkey. No supermarket, open market, or local butchery had turkeys for sale. She looked at me and said it was my job to find a turkey. I knew instantly that the success of our Thanksgiving meal depended upon me.

A few homes in town and most in the villages keep chickens. Village butcheries, if the clientele is large enough, will butcher a cow every day and perhaps a goat. Dehydrated fish from Lake Victoria can be found in a small corner of any market. There is no need to ask where. Just follow your nose. Live chickens are sold in the market, and customers are expected to take the chicken home and kill it themselves. Sometimes, a person at the market will butcher the chicken if the customer requests it. Until recently, there were no frozen chickens for sale.

Turkeys are rare, expensive, and not raised by many farmers. So, I had to do some real searching to find out what to do. I learned that some Ugandan farmers brought turkeys once a week to a market about 20 miles south of Mbale. On the appointed day, I drove down to the market area and found a crowd of people along the road selling all kinds of livestock. My presence created a stir, and several people came up, offering to sell me a chicken. When I said I was looking for a turkey, they looked perplexed.

After a brief search of the market, I found live, gobbling turkeys for sale. Twenty or thirty male turkeys (Toms) were strutting around, gobbling and puffing out their feathers. Is there any bird that characterizes pride more than a turkey? Their puffed-out feathers and strutting made me laugh. I was also shamefully reminded of politicians.

Now, what was I supposed to look for in selecting a turkey – especially one that doesn't have a label on it sitting in the freezer? Several sellers surrounded me immediately, pointing out the weight and age of their birds. No one mentioned good looks. Turkeys are ugly birds! Standing in the middle of a bunch of turkeys in Uganda, I asked myself, "Why did Benjamin Franklin want a turkey as the national bird of the United States? Could he have been thinking about politicians also?" I was glad Franklin lost that proposal and that our Founding Fathers chose instead the bald eagle.

I finally selected a large turkey and negotiated a price. This took me about ten minutes of some serious haggling, where I explained my poor circumstances, and the seller listed his multiple personal financial problems. The final price came out to about $11.50.

However, before I could congratulate myself on purchasing a turkey, I was approached by a man identifying himself to be a veterinarian. He claimed to have inspected all the birds for sale, and he was demanding a 20-cent charge from me for the turkey I was holding. He also claimed 20 cents from the seller. To both me and the seller, the veterinarian reminded us of the government's obligation to keep diseased birds from the market. I was sure the seller and I both thought an opportunist had found us. I reluctantly paid the 20 cents, thinking I had just been scammed.

Before I could leave, another person blocked my departure and informed me that I had to pay another 20 cents for a transportation permit. What? I was sternly told, almost scolded as if I should already know this, that every chicken, turkey, or cow sold in the market must obtain a government permit for transport. I just stared at this unidentified "official" in disbelief. I almost asked out loud if they really collected this from everyone in the market. Or was I just a special customer and an easy mark for extra money? Instead, I said nothing and paid up. After I dropped the money into his palm, I almost ran to the car, hoping that no one else pressed me for another permit or fee.

It was on the trip home that I, a city fellow, learned an important lesson about tying turkey legs. To take the turkey home, I was given a small sisal string and instructed to tie the turkey's legs. That way, they said, he would lay passively in the back of the car. Tying the legs of a live turkey is difficult enough at any time. When you are in a hurry, it is even harder. The turkey flapped around and tried to get loose. I kept a tight hold on the legs because I didn't want to go back and face those officials again. Yet, I was in a hurry. So, I tied its legs, jumped into the car, and drove off. For about two miles, I heard nothing and almost forgot I had a turkey in the back of the car. Then, it gobbled very loudly and flapped around, causing me to jump nervously and hit a series of potholes in the road. I gained control of the car again and said some not-so-nice things to the turkey.

I discovered that a turkey's gobble in an enclosed, small car is really loud and annoying. I could not fathom how a turkey hen could be attracted to a male turkey's gobble. Maybe they get irritated at the sound like I did? A few more miles down the road, my turkey started flapping wildly and scraping his feet. The next thing I see is a head poking up behind the back seat. The turkey was standing up! I thought about pulling over to re-tie the legs but decided I could make it home while the turkey was loose in the back. As I swerved to miss some more potholes, the turkey gobbled again and flapped its wings. When I looked in my rearview mirror, I saw the turkey perched on top of the back seat, staring menacingly at me. I have not been around turkeys very much, but this one looked mad.

I drove quickly, partially surveying the road but mostly watching the turkey in the mirror. I reached home without bodily harm but with frayed nerves. Our yard was fenced, so I let the turkey out of the car to run around the yard during the day. I knew he would be butchered later in the evening. One unexpected glitch in my turkey plan arose. My children found the turkey in the yard and thought it was cute. My daughter Natalie would not leave the turkey alone. She followed him everywhere. By evening, the turkey was no longer a Thanksgiving meal but a family pet. My children pleaded for the turkey's safety to no avail. They were traumatized that the turkey was slaughtered and spent the night in the freezer. Considering all the problems that turkey caused me, I enjoyed eating him a little more than I usually enjoy a Thanksgiving meal. That turkey may have been short on personality, but he was tasty.

Cultural Insights/Principles

- Research the climate ahead of time and purchase clothing appropriate for your visit or stay.
- Rainy seasons can be long and muddy, so purchase sufficient jackets, shoes, and umbrellas.
- For long-term residents, consider packing decorations and special canned foods for your holiday celebrations.
- Adapt your holiday traditions to your new host culture.
- Learn and observe local holidays.
- Businessmen need to plan trips around East African holidays as offices will be closed.
- Many offices are empty, and government paperwork is hard to complete between December 15 and January 5.
- Surprisingly, Valentine's Day has become quite popular in East Africa.
- Most East Africans do not eat turkey. They believe turkeys are wild and difficult to raise. If a farmer does raise them, it is primarily for commercial purposes only.
- Because turkeys are expensive, they are sometimes valued more highly as part of the bride price negotiations instead of chickens.

Proverbs

"There is always room for one more at the supper table" – African Proverb.

Important East African holidays to consider include:

East African Public Holidays

Kenya

1 Jan – New Year's Day; **1 May** Labor Day; **1 June** – Madaraka Day; **20 Oct** – Mashujaa Day; **12 Dec** – Jamuhuri (Independence) Day; **25 Dec** – Christmas Day; **26 Dec** – Boxing Day

Uganda

1 Jan – New Year's Day; **26 Jan** – Liberation Day; **Feb 16** – Archbishop Janani Luwum Day; **8 Mar** – International Women's Day; Easter Sunday; **1 May** – Labor Day; **3 Jun** – Martyrs' Day; **9 Jun** – National Heroes' Day; Eid al Fitr (End of Ramadan); Eid al-Adha (Feast of the Sacrifice; **9 Oct** – Independence Day; **25 Dec** – Christmas Day; **26 Dec** – Boxing Day

Rwanda

1 Jan – New Year's Day; **1 Feb** – Heroes' Day; **7 Apr** – Genocide Memorial Day; **1 May** – Labor Day; **1 Jul** – Independence Day; **4 Jul** – Liberation Day; **15 Aug** – Assumption Day; **1 Oct** – Patriotism Day; **25 Dec** – Christmas Day; **26 Dec** – Boxing Day

South Sudan

1 Jan – New Year's Day; **9 Jan** – Peace Agreement Day; Easter Sunday; **1 May** – International Labor Day; **16 May** – SPLA Day; **9 Jul** – Independence Day, Eid al Fitr (End of Ramadan); **30 Jul** – Martyrs' Day; Eid al-Adha (Feast of the Sacrifice); **25 Dec** – Christmas Day; **26 Dec** – Boxing Day; **28 Dec** – Republic Day

Tanzania

1 Jan – New Year's Day; **12 Jan** – Zanzibar Revolution Day; **26 Apr** – Union Day; **1 May** – Labor Day; **7 Jul** – Saba Saba Day; **8 Aug** – Nane Nane Day; **14 Oct** – Nyerere Day; **9 Dec** – Independence and Republic Day; **25 Dec** – Christmas Day; **26 Dec** – Boxing Day

Burundi

1 Jan – New Year's Day; **5 Feb** – Unity Day; **1 May** – Labor Day; **21 May** – Ascension Day; **1 Jul** – Independence Day; **15 Aug** – Assumption Day; **13 Oct** – Anniversary of Louise Rwagasore's Assassination; **21 Oct** – Anniversary of President M. Ndadaye's Assassination; **1 Nov** – All Saint's Day; **25 Dec** – Christmas Day

Additional Resources

Mama Panya's Pancakes – A children's book

The Night Before a Ugandan Christmas

(A variation on a familiar Christmas poem by Clement Moore)

I wrote the following poem after experiencing a very ugly encounter during our Christmas season.

Twas the night before Christmas, and all through our house,

All manner of creature was stirring - even a mouse.

The stockings were hung but no chimney is there,

In hopes St. Nicholas will come - does he dare?

The children sleep in mosquito netted beds.

With visions of Legos and dolls in their heads.

And Mama in her gown and I in my all

Had just settled down after the last phone call.

When out on the lawn there arose such a clatter,

I sprang from the bed to see what was the matter.

Away to the window I fell over my jeans,

The windows stayed closed because of the screens.

When what to my wondering eyes should appear,

But an electric truck and a driver with gear.

With a bill in his hand and smirk on his face,

I knew St. Nick wasn't visiting my place.

More rapid than eagles his accusations they came,

And he whistled and shouted and called me by name;

You're behind on your bills and I'll turn off your electricity,

And you'll be in the dark unless you have something for me.

To the top of the porch, to the box on the wall,

I'll pull out the fuses, I'll pull them out all!

No wait, I said, there must be a mistake,

I have all my receipts for goodness sake.

His eyes - how they twinkled! His dimples, how merry!

His cheeks were like roses, his nose like a cherry!

His droll little mouth was drawn up like a bow,

That fact he had been drinking was not hard to know.

A wink of his eye and a twist of his palm

Soon gave me to know he expected an alm(s).

He spoke not a word, but went straight to his work,

I stopped him with a gift and thought, what a jerk!

He returned to his truck, to his team gave a whistle,

To the next house they flew, like a heat-seeking missile.

But I heard him exclaim, ere he drove out of sight,

Happy Christmas to all, and to all a good night.

Chapter 9
Avoiding Embarrassing Bathing Moments in the Village

Bathing is an essential daily task. However, with frequent power and water outages in East Africa, one may find oneself in an awkward situation, unprepared, and not knowing exactly how to proceed. The following stories provide a humorous insight into traditional bathing experiences as well as some helpful hints on how to be prepared for all circumstances.

Avoiding Embarrassment While Bathing in the Village

I traveled about 75 miles northwest of Mbale, Uganda, to Aparissa to teach a three-day seminar. I took a tent and bedding to control mosquitos, and I carried my special first-aid kit, which consisted not of medical supplies but snacks and sodas that would supplement my local diet. The one thing I could not control was how or where I was going to bathe.

I pitched my tent in the compound of William Eboyu, a tall, slender man of mid 60's with a quick smile and a humble but forceful nature that made him a natural leader in his community. Most compounds, like William's, are traditionally demarcated by trees or bushes and often have a planted hedge that provides some privacy and shade around the main house. William graciously found a flat place near his house that was protected from the African sun by trees he had planted years before.

As dusk approached, William Eboyu came to my tent and informed me that bath water was ready and that he would show me where it was. William led me to the traditional place behind his house, not far from the latrine. There, I found a newly constructed cubicle about four feet wide and five feet long. Four wooden poles marked the corners, and trimmed tree branches provided the frame into which fresh maize (white corn) stalks were woven. Evidently, it had been a bad year for maize because the stalks were not close together, leaving gaping holes in the walls that supposedly shielded me from the outside world. The holes were the least of my worries.

The entire structure was only about five feet high. Since I am six feet tall, I was able to stand inside and have a grand view of the countryside. I was also able to see a group of ten men who were sitting under a Flamboyant Tree about 30 yards away to the left of the house. They were talking but also curious about me taking a bath. Obviously, I was the evening's entertainment. I made a mental note to bend over when I washed under my arms lest people think I was waving to them, and they come to see what I needed.

I discovered inside the cubicle that there were no shelves for placing my soap, towel, or other toiletries. I found some protrusions on the branches poking out of the wall and used them to hang my clothes. I took my towel, trousers, and shirt and hung then over the wall in places where the gaping holes were the largest. Obviously, there was no mirror, light, or bathmat. This kind of bathing facility was not for the timid or bashful.

To make this bathing cubicle accessible for his guests – men or women, William fittingly constructed it right off the path from his house to several of his neighbors' homes. Even more conveniently, he made the door of the cubicle facing the path. I shouldn't say, "Door." I should say, "Opening," because there was no door to the cubicle. This allowed me to greet anyone coming down the path as they passed, which several did. One guy rode by on his bicycle, clanging the bell on his handlebars. I looked up, and he waved at me. I waved back as he passed the open door, saying, "Hi. How are you? Yes, nice to SEE you too." He pretended not to look, but he immediately ran off the path into high grass and fell off his bicycle. I suppose it isn't every day you see a naked white guy bathing. I wondered how many times he would tell this story to his friends. I was also able to greet a couple of women who walked like snails past the door carrying bundles on their heads. Yes, I was the entertainment for the evening.

The floor of the bathing cubicle was dirt that became mud as soon as water was spilled. For my convenience, William had placed a large flat rock about 18 inches across for me to stand on. The basin of water was sitting on the ground beside it. I was supposed to stand on the rock and splash water onto myself, avoiding the mud. This would have been easy for me if the bottom of the rock had not been curved slightly, causing me to have to do a balancing act while bathing. At least twice, I lost my balance and stepped into the mud. Did I hear a slight chuckle go around the group of men under the Flamboyant Tree?

I found warm water in my blue plastic basin. Most of the time, such water in the villages is cold, but on special occasions, I get warm water. The water is usually cold because it is brought from the river or possibly a well, and heating uses precious firewood. Two gallons of warm water is a treat, and that is all the water I had to clean myself. With the blue basin on the ground, I had to stoop and splash water up onto myself. I discovered from previous bathing experiences that it helps to have a washcloth available.

As I tried to balance myself on the rock and then stoop for water, I wondered how many of my friends had ever done this. The showers back home use, on average, 17+ gallons of water that can be set to a desired temperature. Could they bathe with only two gallons of water in a maize cubicle?

While I was bathing, a black chicken came to the open door and stuck its head inside. It cocked its head sideways and stared at me. It blinked several times before turning away. I guess it was not used to seeing a white fellow bathing in his yard, either.

As I bent over to wash my hair while balancing on my wobbly rock, some of the soap got into my eyes. My eyes clinched tight because of the stinging. It was in this delicate position, with my rear end up in the air and pushed against the maize stalks, that I was startled to the point of fright and flight. Without me seeing him, a huge 200-pound pig had walked up quietly behind me and was looking around for something to eat. The fresh maize stalks looked good to him, especially the ones right by my rear end. When the pig started grunting and squealing and took a big bite of the stalks by my rear, I shouted out and almost tore the rest of the maize stalks off the frame to escape the cubicle. In a split second, I was standing outside, pointing at the beast and announcing to everyone in a high girly voice that there was a pig by my bath.

This time, I heard laughter from underneath the Flamboyant Tree. I gained control of myself and stepped back into the cubicle and onto the slippery wet rock with my muddy feet and continued my bath. From then on, I was a chameleon. I had one eye on my bath and the other on that pig or what other kinds of animals might decide to visit. After that incident, every time I started to take a bath in Aparissa, I took notice of where that pig was.

Bathing in such places is not the kind of experience men or women visitors generally look forward to. Rather, it is approached with great uneasiness and apprehension. Yet, after finishing, everyone feels like they have bragging rights. Stories are swapped among the experienced bathers about the smallest cubicle, lowest walls, biggest holes in the walls, least amount of water, muddiest floor, coldest water, the greatest number of visitors, etc.

The truth is bathing in the village can be an awesome experience. Some of my favorite memories of staying in the village revolve around bathing. After hours of hot, sweaty walking, after the sun has beat down on us all day, and dehydration is very close, the coolness of water splashing on my skin brings a curious sense of relief. Often, baths are done in the evening with only a canopy of stars for light. I distinctly remember one place on the slopes of the Rwenzori mountains in Western Uganda where the bath cubicle overlooked a breath-taking view of the valley. With the stars as my ceiling and a gentle breeze brushing across my wet skin, the bath was invigorating. Nature is overwhelming in such instances where crickets and night sounds provide the background music for bathing. The openness and stillness of the night provide a relaxing calm that is missed under the yellow dimness of light bulbs and the reverberation of wooden walls. I am not suggesting we all start bathing outside, I am, however, suggesting there can be some amazing experiences in a maize cubicle in the East African bush.

I must include one other embarrassing bathing adventure in Nimule, South Sudan. I was staying in a brick house about a mile east of the Nile River on a hill that provided a beautiful view of northern Uganda. When evening came, bath water was prepared, and I was led to a small cement room about four feet square. The cement floor sloped gently to the corner, where a small hole allowed the water to drain outside toward the garden. A pair of slippers (flip flops) were provided for me to wear so that I didn't have to stand on the wet cement. Since my hosts had no electricity and it was dark in the room, a small wooden table about 18 inches high was placed inside, and a candle was lit. My host allowed a few drops of candle wax to fall onto the table, and then he stood the candle up in the hot wax. I thought that was a clever way to provide lighting.

I was not used to bathing in a very small cubicle by candle. As I was washing, I became aware of my shadow on the wall. I began noticing how fat I was and that I needed to lose some weight. I started sucking in my stomach and striking muscle poses. In playing with the shadow, I accidentally splashed some water onto the candle. Instantly, I was in the dark, naked, wet, and soaped down. I realized I didn't have a match to re-light the candle. My options were to embarrassingly call for help and get a match or to manly finish my bath in total darkness. I chose the latter and came out of the room disheveled but clean, with my dignity intact.

For any visitor to East Africa, there is a strong chance one may find themselves stuck in an awkward situation while bathing. I have been in a luxurious hotel that had to bring me five gallons of warm water to use for bathing and in homes when the water stopped in the middle of my shower. I have bathed by candlelight, lantern light, flashlight, and under the stars. I have been in grass, maize, and banana leaf cubicles, and one time just standing under a tree, in the dark, with the basin between the gigantic roots. The key to such experiences is to remain calm, laugh at the situation, and figure out how to make your disastrous bathing experience into a really good story for your friends. Anyone can bathe in a modern bathroom, but how many can tell a wonderfully embarrassing bath story like mine?

Cultural Insights/Principles

• Traditionally, when a woman is happy with her husband for some reason, she will express that by providing him with some warm water for bathing at home. However, generally, he gets cold water.

- Modesty is gauged differently in East Africa. It is not uncommon to find children or adults bathing in a stream by the side of the road. Additionally, women may breast feed their babies in public meetings or hoe gardens stripped down to their waist. Yet, they will not show their legs above the knee. While tight jeans are becoming more common, modest women avoid any clothing that accentuates their thighs and buttocks.
- Men and women may bathe just outside their back door late in the evening.
- Near lakes, it is not uncommon for people to go down to the shore and bathe or even walk into the water a short distance to bathe. Passersby are expected to look the other way.
- Small village children stand in a basin while the mother bathes them.
- In desert areas, I have seen a mother lay an infant in her lap, gathering some water in her mouth to warm it, and then squirting water through her teeth to wash and clean the child.
- Because of the general tendency to bathe outside by a stream, lake, or out-of-basin behind the house, there are few shower stalls around the home. The only reason for building a shower area is for guests who may be staying for a few days. Hence the reason they are always makeshift in construction.
- It is not uncommon to find in hotel bathrooms one or two pairs of slippers (flip flops) and a plastic basin leaning against the wall. These are not accidentally left behind by a previous customer or the cleaning staff. They are intended for customer use in case a more traditional way of bathing is preferred. Traditional belief is latrine, and porous cement floors of bathing cubicles are dirty.
- It is wise to carry a large towel and wash cloth for village stays.
- If preferred, slippers (flip flops) are good to carry also (remember the dirty floors).
- Purchase a small flashlight or head lamp and put it in your toiletry bag.

- Women in East Africa always carry a Lesso/Kitenge/Kanga for bathing purposes. It is a large piece of cloth about four feet wide and up to six feet in length. It is lightweight and used to wear, carry a baby on the back, or mop up something that has spilled. It is perfect for a bath covering. It can also be used as a mobile door to the bathing cubicle.
- Plastic bags or containers may be useful for storing wet soap, wash cloths, scrunchies, or other toiletries.

Proverbs

"A child while bathing only scrubs its stomach" – African Proverb
"Fishing without a net is just bathing" – African Proverb

Chapter 10
Toilets, Pit Latrines, and Little Round Holes in the Floor

I hesitate to mention the sensitive topic of toilet facilities. Some may feel uncomfortable with this subject. Yet, every visitor to East Africa will, at some point, need to use a toilet! Under normal circumstances, most people dread finding a restroom while they are away from home. It is an inconvenience. We may not know where adequate facilities are, and it interrupts our activities.

It was very shocking to us upon moving to East Africa that we found it common to see men urinating along the road. In fact, buses would often pull off the highway to allow dozens of passengers, men and women, to get out and find some bushes to alleviate themselves before continuing their journey. With lengthy stretches of road void of adequate stopping places for toilet facilities, visitors may find themselves in need of a bush or two.

In fact, this practice may become such a common occurrence for Westerners that children who have grown up in East Africa become accustomed to relieving themselves outside. It is also embarrassing to have your own kids do this in the front yard in America and have the neighbors stop by and report it to you.

The Joys of Pit Latrines

Without the luxury of indoor plumbing, most people living in the rural areas of East Africa bathe outside and build pit latrines to relieve themselves. A pit latrine is normally constructed by hiring someone to dig a deep hole, usually three feet wide, six feet long and as deep as one can go. Such work is done by a pick, a shovel, and a bucket on the end of a rope. To descend and climb up out of the hole, notches are cut into the sides of the wall, and the digger executes his Spiderman abilities without the benefit of a net. A price is agreed upon for each foot of digging, and a rope hung on a rod laid across the hole to the bottom will determine how many feet were dug.

Once the hole is made, small tree trunks are split in half and placed over the pit with cutouts for the intended holes in the floor. A wooden structure is erected over the pit with two or more compartments. The walls are mudded, and a grass or tin roof is placed on top. Wooden doors are hinged to a small frame, and a sliding latch is fastened to the inside and outside for opening and closing the doors.

The floors are most often mudded, then cow manure is spread over the floor to harden the dirt and keep it from being dusty. Nicer pit latrines may cement the floor and put in a PVC plastic pipe, starting beneath the floor going through the roof to help ventilate the latrine. A few may even have a wooden lid that sits over the latrine hole. Pit latrines come in all sizes, shapes, and conditions.

Since it rains a lot in East Africa, traditional construction of grass roofs comes low to the ground to protect the mud walls from washing away. This means many latrines have short doors requiring those entering to stoop down low. Sometimes, the doors are not very wide, forcing larger individuals to bend and turn sideways to get inside. Such gymnastics is not easy, especially when there is an urgent matter to attend to.

Sometimes, I have stepped into a grass-roofed latrine only to find gigantic spider webs just above my head filled with the largest spiders I have ever seen. Other times, I have stepped inside only to have the floor sway up and down as though it was about to collapse.

In most circumstances, I find a hole in the floor to be about the size of a golf ball. Most Westerners used to sitting on toilets may not be so… *adept*… at hitting such small holes. Additionally, I almost never find toilet paper anywhere close to the latrine. In some latrines, hosts may pile fresh leaves on the floor, or some old newspaper is lying around. Generally, you are on your own. I must confess that many pages of my teaching lessons have been, in a crisis, crumbled up and used for other purposes than academics.

Daniel, a Kenyan friend who is short in stature but long in funny stories, once tried to describe the tremendous love his heavenly Father had for him. He was at a loss on how to adequately explain his heavenly Father's willingness to love and encourage him even when he made so many mistakes. Then his eyes brightened, and he began his latrine story (we all have a story).

Daniel looked down sheepishly and began with a big smile on his face. He said once he was visiting a friend in the village and had to use the latrine. He found a small round latrine in the back with a grass roof and a maize sack covering the door. He stepped inside and completed his business. When he was finished, he said he stood to pull up his trousers when suddenly he saw his billfold fall out of his pocket. He said it was like watching in slow motion as his wallet hit the manure floor, bounced around, and then fell into the hole in the floor. Daniel stood horrified for a moment; his mind was racing with questions about what to do. At first, he thought about just leaving it and considering everything inside the wallet as lost. Then he remembered all the important documents that were in his wallet and the amount of money he would lose. Finally, Daniel decided to try and rescue his wallet.

Borrowing a flashlight, Daniel peered into the dark hole of the latrine. After his eyes adjusted, Daniel was able to see his wallet. It was about 15 feet down and partially submerged in the sewage, the top of which was crawling with maggots. His heart sank. Daniel thought his task was impossible. Then, he hit upon an idea. Looking around the pit latrine, Daniel noticed a stand of canes nearby. He borrowed a knife and cut a long cane. He also borrowed a wire clothes hanger, which he tied to one end of the cane and fashioned a hook. Walking back to the latrine, Daniel realized he would have to take the grass roof off to utilize the cane pole. After about 30 minutes of work, Daniel and his friend removed the roof.

Stepping inside again, Daniel lowered his cane with the wire hook into the pit latrine hole. Yet, with the sunshine falling around him, he was unable to see into the hole to maneuver the hook. So, Daniel pulled the cane out and used a rubber strap to tie the flashlight just above the hook on the pole. Again, he sent it down into the hole. Daniel touched the wallet. Then missed it. He hooked it a little and moved the wallet around on the top of the sewage. One time, he hooked the wallet and got it halfway up before it fell back down. Finally, Daniel knew how he had to hook the wallet to get it all the way up. After more than an hour of work, Daniel was able to pull the wallet up out of the latrine hole.

We laughed as he made faces about how badly the wallet stunk, how filthy it was, and how he didn't even want to touch it. He talked about washing it off and rescuing all the documents and money inside. Our eyes were filled with tears from laughing so hard at his story. Then he silenced us all. He said as he held up that prized wallet in all its filth and smell, and he was so flooded with joy that it was then and there that he realized his own poor choices and mistakes probably made him look like that wallet to his heavenly Father. However, his Father's love would not allow him to leave Daniel in such horrible, filthy circumstances. His Father continually pulled Daniel from the sewage of poor choices. It is an illustration of spiritual and parental love that I will never forget.

I must include another admonition about using pit latrines that came from my friend Josh. He spent a year in South Sudan building a clinic in the middle of the bush back when independence still had not been obtained from Sudan. During his time, he became quite accustomed to using a pit latrine and bathing with a basin of water.

One day, Josh had quickly squatted over the tiny hole in the latrine but had neglected to consider the climate of his surrounding area. Because it was hot and dry, all kinds of creatures were attracted to the dark, damp, cool hole of the pit latrine. Thus, when Josh, a rather large man who filled up the room, stepped in, rattling the floor and squatting over the hole, all manner of creatures jumped and stirred at the noise and vibration.

As Josh's rear end dangled only inches above the latrine hole, an 18-inch blue-bodied, orange-headed lizard jumped out of the hole and attached itself to Josh's exposed thigh. While still using the latrine, Josh jumped up, shouting loudly, dancing around in circles, and swatting at whatever had clawed his leg. The shocked lizard crawled around a second and then let go, fell to the floor, and ran out underneath the wooden latrine door. Josh collected himself and finally finished his business, first inspecting the hole closely before squatting over it again.

For weeks afterward, Josh refused to tell his coworkers why he had screamed in the latrine, and he would not explain why the walls were inexplicably wet after his departure. Josh, with a calm, thoughtful look, told me, "After that, I always stomped on the floor and looked around inside the hole before squatting over it." This sounded to me like sage advice from a man of great pit latrine experience.

Since floor-level latrines are the more traditional way of going to the bathroom, it is not surprising then to find that flushing toilets in many public buildings are also floor-level. East Africans call them Asian toilets. Each floor toilet comes with its own bowl of water fastened higher up on the wall, usually with a chain hanging down the right side. After completing one's business, you are expected to yank the chain and flush the toilet. Some floor-level toilets may have enough water pressure that water will come out onto the floor. It is always wise to stand back a little.

Some hotels, malls, and other public shopping areas are beginning to install Western-style toilets. The cleanliness of such places has really improved over the years. Long ago, it was wise to avoid using public toilets. It would be better to return home if possible. Today, many places are nice. However, it is always wise when traveling to ask the driver to stop where there is good food and where there are clean toilets.

There is no need to be fearful of public toilets. Just be prepared. Don't carry a lot of things into the toilet area with you so that your hands are free. Yet, be sure to take some toilet paper, sanitary wipes, and hand gel so that you can be ready for any kind of toilet conditions you encounter. For women, it is a good idea to purchase a large East African cloth called a gitenga or lessos that can be used as a wrap around the waist, a cover, a hand towel, a floor blanket, or especially a cleanup cloth. Armed with these accessories, any tourist is ready for public toilets. What may be an uncomfortable experience can become a great story later. So, eyes open, don't slip, be prepared, and let the stories begin!

Cultural Insights/Principles

• Traditionally, most tribal groups believe that relieving oneself outside is being generous to nature. It is a way of giving back to nature through various "bush encounters."

• Most toilets in remote areas are just for visitors and are hardly used by the family on a regular basis. This explains the lack of maintenance on latrine construction.

• Take a roll of toilet paper with you wherever you go!

• Take sanitary wipes with you everywhere!

• Don't carry personal items into the toilet with you. There may be no place to put them except on the floor.

• If you must assume a squatting position, make sure there is nothing in your pockets that could fall out.

• Some toilets in public places may require a fee to use it.

• Rarely, a toilet may have a small water hose and sprayer connected next to it instead of toilet paper.

• Latrines are often set on fire in the hole underneath to "burn" or "smoke" to reduce (destroy) waste.

• It is not uncommon to find footprints on Western-style toilets in public places since most village folks are unfamiliar with Western-style toilets and are more used to floor-level toilets.

Proverbs

"If you've never been to a pit latrine, you will never know that a cockroach can be a chief" – African Proverb.
"An Elder does not break wind in public, but in a latrine" – South African Proverb.

(It is shameful to break wind in public, but the culprit seldom acknowledges it, and others politely ignore it – except for the children who may laugh.)

Village Toilet Score Card

Numerous times, women traveling with me have had to use a pit latrine out in the villages. They have no experience with village latrines. They don't know what to expect, and they often come back with hilariously embarrassing stories. It is not surprising, then, that latrine stories can become a funny topic for evening discussions among tourists and short-term workers. Several gathered one evening and, poking fun at themselves, developed a kind of rating system for village latrines.

Let me interject that since no latrine contains all the items below and that some ladies value one condition over another, the rating system just gives a point for each condition included. The women who put this rating system together want me to emphasize that NO pit latrine has a perfect score according to their cultural lens!

A pit latrine receives a point*:*

- If it has 4 walls
- If it has 4 *solid* walls
- If it has 4 *tall* walls
- If it has a roof
- If the roof does not contain such a variety of spiders and bugs that National Geographic would want to do a special on it.
- If there is any semblance of a door
- If the door actually covers the opening
- If, after closing the door, there is still enough light to see what you are doing.
- If the hole in the floor is bigger than a golf ball
- If there are some raised rectangular steps on both sides of the hole (to correctly position the user and to keep one's feet higher than the potentially wet floor)
- If there is some kind of path out to the latrine so that you don't have to wade through waist-high stickers to reach it
- If there is no smell inside. (Hint: choose a latrine with a PVC pipe sticking out of the roof.)
- If there are no flies congregating inside
- If toilet paper is present, this is a big bonus point if you haven't yet figured out which leaves can be used.
- If the door (or opening) doesn't face the main road so that, you must greet everyone who passes by
- If you don't have an audience
- If the latrine is at least somewhere close to the house, (The sudden urge to go in the middle of the night is scary to contemplate.)
- If the doorway is wide enough that, you can go inside without having to turn sideways and duck.
- If the floor is solid, this is a **very big** bonus point and offers LOTS of peace of mind while inside. (Have I heard of someone falling through the floor before? YES.)

Chapter 11
Language Learning As An Exercise in Humility

The old man came to me in the dark sitting room of the house. I was visiting a new place called Nabing'eng'e, and no one really knew me. He stopped about three feet away and looked at me. I felt like a bug under a microscope for a moment. I stood up to show respect but waited for him to initiate the greeting. He leaned toward me and held out his hand, and I leaned toward him, grasping his bony hand lightly with both of my hands (a sign of more respect). He spoke slowly, enunciating every syllable of a Swahili greeting. He assumed a teaching role as though I did not know how to greet him. I responded clearly and correctly. He cocked his head and smiled. He asked how home was. I answered in Swahili again. He shook my hand vigorously as his smile became huge. Then I surprised him by asking in his native Bukusu language how he was. His eyes brightened. He laughed loudly and let go of my hand to raise his hand up high and then slap my hand and shake it in a more traditional Bukusu greeting. He continued laughing while he looked around the room. In that moment, I moved from a foreigner to a friend all because of my greeting skills.

Nothing builds friendships or opens doors better than learning the local home language. As a visitor to East Africa, gaining language skills communicates an interest and investment in those with whom you are engaging. It is a way of honoring your host and bridging a significant obstacle of the cultural gap. Language learning brings smiles and opens hearts. It makes every friendship, business transaction and project easier. Language learning also enhances a deeper understanding of the values and thought processes of the host culture.

I was nervous. I was young, inexperienced, had recently moved to Kitale, Kenya, and was about to stand up in front of a small group of Kenyans and speak for the first time. Even though I had gone through three and a half months of Swahili language learning in Nairobi, I was still far from producing a riveting lesson in Swahili. Instead, I stood there totally dependent upon a cocky translator who had all the mannerisms of a TV evangelist (a fellow who didn't work very long with us) who seemed to provide additional commentary on my choppy English lesson sentences.

Not knowing the culture well, I chose a basic Bible story, hoping to draw out some basic principles that would be trans-cultural. If I spoke too long or used difficult English words, my translator would ask me to repeat myself. If I formed short sentences, I struggled to present my point forcefully. So, the translator and I performed a speech dance where sometimes I led, and most of the time, he led. I am sure it was whimsical to watch and distracting to follow.

I remember we were in a small primary school classroom on the north side of Kitale. Linda was sitting in the front row of desks along with Beatrice, our newly hired house worker. (Hiring a house worker was strongly suggested by trusted friends to help us learn the language and culture and manage the house cleaning and market shopping.) Beatrice was strong in strength and opinion and not at all shy in demonstrating both. She was slightly older than us, and she considered it her job to help us learn about living and speaking in her country. She was overprotective, and perhaps that is why she did what I am about to describe during my lesson.

As my translator and I awkwardly danced through my speech, I was drawn to Beatrice's face. At first, I thought she was completely focused on my lesson. She did not take her eyes off me. She almost seemed to ignore the translator, who moved about more freely than

I did. As I spoke, her eyes widened, and her brow wrinkled as though she was hearing some newly discovered truth. Her attentiveness was so severe and so outmatched by everyone else in the room that she became distracting to me. As I continued to speak, she suddenly jerked back and pulled her hands up, guarding her chest with eyes wide open. I quickly thought about what I said and wondered if I had made a cultural mistake. As I plunged into the next sentence, Beatrice forcefully grabbed Linda by her arm and began shaking her and pointing at me. Linda looked at Beatrice, who looked at her and then at me and began whispering in Swahili, something Linda didn't understand.

Others in the room noticed Beatrice. The translator finished his long soliloquy and looked at me for my next sentence. I distractedly began my next point when suddenly Beatrice literally rose up out of her front row desk, pointing at me, and in a loud voice began shouting "Doodoo, Doodoo, Doodoo"! I stopped in mid-sentence. I didn't know what to do. I had never had anyone interrupt my speaking before by standing and shouting. I certainly never had anyone yell "Doodoo" at my teaching before. My mental train of thought went off the rails and crashed. Beatrice continued pointing and shouting, "Doodoo, Doodoo."

As Beatrice was standing and shouting, the "TV evangelist" looked over at me and noticed the reason for Beatrice's behavior. At some point during my teaching, a praying mantis had flown into the room and landed on my right coat sleeve. Beatrice had noticed it land, but she could hardly contain herself as it slowly walked up my arm onto my shoulder and began moving toward my exposed neck. The translator, with half-closed eyes and absolutely no concern for me on his face, looked at me, reached up with his left hand, and deftly brushed the praying mantis off onto the floor. He said nonchalantly, "You may continue," and then he turned back to the audience, awaiting my next sentence.

I stood there for a moment, collecting my wits and thoughts. Okay, I thought, so my lesson is not Doodoo. She was not judging my speaking abilities. Beatrice was reacting to an insect crawling up my coat. Still, my words were lost. My train of thought was off the rails. I stumbled forward, trying to compose myself. The rest of the crowd seemed nonplussed. The translator moved smoothly into the next act of his show. Beatrice settled down. Linda regained some blood and feeling in her arm after Beatrice's tourniquet grip was released. We eventually finished.

I don't remember the lesson I gave that day. I don't remember the translator's name or exactly how many people were in the room. All I remember that morning is that I learned a new Swahili word. The general word for "bugs" in Swahili is "dudu" (pronounced doo-doo). It is on every can of bug spray in the supermarket. However, I learned it first in public, during my teaching session, thanks to the attentive watch of Beatrice. Yes, she taught us a lot during the time she worked for us. However, some might say secretly that my speaking abilities never recovered.

Don't Be Afraid to Make Mistakes

There is no way to learn a language without making mistakes. We must learn how to think and express ourselves in another language. Often, we must learn a completely new way to form sounds for words or put sentences together in a different sequence than in English (i.e., adjectives are after the noun instead of before it, putting the plural on the front of a noun instead of behind it, or building verbs with different prefixes and suffixes and infixes – a direct object marker placed between the verb tense and the verb stem). And most importantly, we must learn how to laugh at ourselves. We must be bold and try. We laugh and learn. Our mistakes will become great stories later.

The Best Language Learning Techniques

While there have been fads on how to learn language, the best approach still includes **learning as much vocabulary as possible and immersing yourself into situations where you are forced to use what you know**. Practicing outside of the classroom and without the tutor is essential.

"Oh, He Speaks Like One of Us"

Not long after moving to Kenya, one of our sponsors came to visit. During a side conversation with a Kenyan, the visitor asked how I and my coworker were doing with language learning. The Kenyan replied, "Oh, Shawn's coworker knows Swahili very well. His grammar is perfect. He has developed a large vocabulary. He knows how to connect all of his adjectives to the nouns correctly. He is progressing very well. Then, the visitor asked how I was doing. The Kenyan quickly replied, "Oh, he speaks like one of us." This was a compliment in his eyes in that I had been there long enough to speak like them. There is a point in language learning where you begin to pick up local accents and phrases that may or may not be grammatically correct but are distinctive to that particular people group or area. If one stays long enough, he/she will be able to distinguish tribal accents and even what part of the country someone comes from.

As an example, a few years ago, Linda and I visited Zanzibar and were speaking Swahili to a local vendor. He looked at us and said, "Your Swahili is not from here in Zanzibar. It is not from Tanzania or coastal Kenya. Are you from Nairobi?" We replied, "No, we are from Western Kenyan." He was trying to place our Swahili accent.

"All We 'Like' Sheep"

During my first year in Kenya, I got myself into trouble with my translator while preaching in a church. I used a passage from Isaiah 53:6 but quoted it in a King James Version phrasing – "All we, like sheep, have gone astray." My translator, who was not very proficient in English, struggled with the wording. After he translated it, I noticed the people looked at me strangely. So, I thought I might try to clarify before going on. I said, "We have gone astray, become lost, like sheep." My translator, once again, struggled with the wording, and the audience began to grimace and look thoroughly confused. In the back, Linda realized what was happening. My Kenyan helper translated "like" as "love." In essence, the translator was telling the audience we had sinned and become lost because we love sheep. Fortunately, we were able to correct the mistake, much to the relief of everyone in the room. After that, I became more attentive to the words used by my translators.

A Taco is not a Tako

When learning a language, it is easy to discover that words sounding the same in two different languages can have very different meanings. A Peace Corps volunteer once learned this when a Kenyan man asked him about his favorite food to eat in America. The volunteer thought for a moment and said confidently, "Without doubt, I will always choose a taco." The Kenyan's eyes widened in shock. The volunteer, interpreting the Kenyan's expression as interest, added more description. "Yes, when I get back to America, I will run and get me the biggest taco I can find, one that is so big it takes two hands to hold. I don't want a hard one. I want one that is soft and chewy. And I will put lots of sauce on it." The Kenyan was speechless. Come to find out, the Swahili word "tako" (pronounced the same way) means a butt cheek. You can only imagine what the Kenyan man was imagining about the Peace Corp Volunteer!

Stages of Language Learning – What Does "Being Fluent" Really Mean?

Based upon my own experience of learning Swahili over an almost 40-year period, let me illustrate some of the stages I recognized in my own language acquisition in becoming "fluent." Without a doubt, everyone learns language at different rates and in a different order than I list. It is not so much a length of time as it depends more upon how much a visitor engages in the language. These are my personal identifying markers for language learning.

- **Stage 1** – Greeting and giving brief introductions
- **Stage 2** – Bartering in the market, asking for directions
- **Stage 3** – Giving a brief talk (with lots of notes)
- **Stage 4** – Engaging in simple conversations
- **Stage 5** – Identifying contractions and idioms (recognizing all the words in a phrase but realizing they mean something else)
- **Stage 6** – Identifying accents (distinctive tribal vocabulary and phrases) or bad grammar
- **Stage 7** – Understanding and using humor
- **Stage 8** – Dreaming in the local language
- **Stage 9** – Teaching concepts and incorporating local proverbs and stories
- **Stage 10** – Speaking well enough to move others emotionally
- **Stage 11** – Praying and worshipping in the local language as well as you do in your own native language
- **Stage 12** – Understanding all the words on TV or radio (one learns vocabulary connected with his/her line of work. TV and Radio will use words from a broader spectrum.)

- **Stage 13** – Going months before hearing an unknown word

Cultural Insights/Principles

- Many linguists say East Africa functions in three languages: a heart language (one spoken in the home from childhood), a trade language (a common language used among tribes for business, i.e., Swahili), and an official language (for East Africa, that is English).

- Any western visitors can move about and function in English, but they will be seen as outsiders. Speaking Swahili deepens friendships. Speaking the "heart" language will connect the visitor most deeply to his/her target audience. However, there is a significant complication. Such deep focus identifies the speaker with one tribe and may hinder relationships with other tribal groups. Be careful in selecting a language to study.

- East Africans see English as the language of academics and used by educated citizens. They may prefer to speak in English even if the long-term visitor knows the trade or heart language.

- It is not uncommon for a long-term visitor to finally succeed in learning Swahili and then have their host switch to a heart language for sensitive conversations in their presence.

- About 15% of Swahili comes from Arabic. Often, the Arabic word becomes Sawhili when changed slightly by adding a vowel at the end. Kalam/Kalamu (writing pen); Ishirin/Ishirini (20), Thelethin/Thelethini (30), etc.

- All Bantu languages in East Africa give only one sound to each vowel, and each vowel makes its sound in every word (diaeresis). There are no short AND long sounds for vowels, and two vowels will not combine to make only one sound (synaeresis).

- Almost always in Swahili, pronunciation emphasis is placed on the next to the last syllable. If there is an exception, it may be a word borrowed from another language.

- Many languages in East Africa will use double vowels like "oo" or "uu" as a way to express an extended vowel sound. Words like "choo" (for bathroom) or "kuu" (pronounced "coo" and meaning supreme or main) can trip up speakers if they don't catch the extra time in pronunciation.

- As in many languages, a slight rise in voice at the end of a sentence may signal a question.

- Learning language takes practice. So, immerse yourself in situations where you have to use it.

- Don't depend on translators but seek to learn without them present.

- Not all translators are created equal. Depending upon their tribal background and education, they may have a strong accent or use poor grammar. Seek advice from local leaders or schoolteachers who teach English and the language you seek to learn!

- The visitor may like the translator, but if that person has a poor reputation or is not liked by the audience, it will greatly hinder the speaker's message and influence. Be wise in selecting with whom you travel and eat.

- A great first step is learning an extended introduction for yourself and family or friends and to explain why you are there.

- Learn how to ask questions for directions or what a word means.

- Build vocabulary for everyday things, but especially for your project, work, or task at hand.

- Do not be afraid to make mistakes. Expect them. Embrace them. Tell stories about them!

Proverbs

"If you want people to understand you, speak their language" – African Proverb.

"Kindness is a language which the blind can see, and the deaf can hear" – African Proverb.

"If you talk to a man in a language he can understand, that goes to his head. If you talk to him in his language, that goes to his heart" – Nelson Mandela of South Africa.

"There are many teachers who do not hear themselves" – African Proverb (This is similar in meaning to an American proverb about "Do as I say, and not as I do." African wisdom observes that not all who teach live by the principles they expound.)

Additional Resources

Language Apps

Duolingo is a great app that is free and can help in learning Swahili. The lessons are short and will automatically return to difficult words to reinforce learning. Duolingo features a Swahili that is more Tanzanian than Kenya or Ugandan. However, it is worth trying. Another good app for language learning is Babble.

Informal Instruction

While language schools are available in most East African countries, I have found it better to hire a personal language tutor who comes to the house daily rather than find meals and lodging near a language school. An "at-home" instructor provides personalized tutoring for less cost, greater flexibility, and less disruption to the entire family. There is also a greater chance to integrate language learning into daily and work life. However, this approach takes discipline to not let life push language lessons to the side. For the less disciplined, a language school may be the better approach.

Chapter 12

Driving in East Africa – A Road Test You Must Pass To Live

It was the rainy season, and the roads were muddy slick, and ruts were full of water. There was no way of knowing how deep the potholes were, so every motorist drove slowly. Heading out to a village, I left the tarmac (pavement) and the nicer murram (all weather dirt) roads and found myself driving down a trail with lantana bushes scraping both sides of my vehicle. As I turned a corner, I found a bicyclist riding in front of me, going in the same direction. He followed a singular track in the mud that had been beaten down by pedestrians and other bicycles. I drove up close behind him, thinking he would hear the engine and pull off to the side to let me pass. Instead, he put his hand down to one side and gave a sign for me to wait and be patient. He kept pedaling along. I became frustrated that a bicyclist would hinder a vehicle on the path. So, I honked. Again, he waved his hand at me, this time more forcefully. He was in the lead, and he refused to yield. I went from frustration to anger. I trailed along behind him for several hundred yards while he passed up numerous opportunities to pull over to the side. Instead, he stayed right in the middle of the road. Finally, we turned another corner and there in front of us was a mud hole filled with water about 40 yards long covering the entire road. The trail the bicyclist took swerved to the left side embankment about a foot higher than the road. I gunned the engine and lurched forward to pass him. As I entered the water-filled mud hole, a wave of dirty water over six feet high splashed the bicyclist, drenching him and his bicycle. My passengers inside the car erupted in laughter despite themselves saying he should have let us pass earlier. Perhaps fate was dispensing a splash of poetic justice. I felt a twinge of guilt but realized there was little I could do. I must admit that over the decades, I have been guilty of many drive-by "baptisms" – some unintentional, others more calculated.

Visitors may be spared the thrill and challenge of driving in East Africa. However, long-term visitors may not be able to avoid the pleasure. The following humorous list provides key examples of "obstacles" that one faces while driving. Learning to expect, identify, and navigate these obstacles will greatly improve one's safety.

Driving Rules and Observations

Ugandan traffic seems to have its own rules and expectations. I know the British built modern roads and set up traffic laws (especially driving on the left side of the road), but any visitor can easily see that East African traffic functions differently than is expected in other countries. Let me give some examples.

The emergence of a **pothole** changes all road rules. The habit of driving within a marked lane is abandoned if a huge pothole large enough to instantly remove your engine is looming ahead of you. Traffic in both lanes (coming and going) will make allowances for the pothole and alter their lanes so that vehicles can miss it. This is especially unnerving to a visitor when he sees huge trucks (called "lorries" in East Africa from British influence) pull over into oncoming traffic to avoid a pothole. Ugandan drivers do not panic. They simply alter their lanes to accommodate the pothole… and do so without ever slowing down. Staying in your designated lane makes no sense at all when the pothole is large enough to go swimming in.

The construction and placement of **rumble strips** and **speed bumps** are certainly an enigma to visitors. However, if you put on your East African hat for a moment, you will realize how practical they are. First, they are overwhelmingly made by folks who do not own a car or drive one. They possess a "pedestrian" mentality and think of vehicles as menaces to people crossing the road. So, the sharper or higher the bump and the slower the car must go to crawl over it, the better. That means pedestrians will be safe. I shouldn't call them speed BUMPS. Most of them are a good 14 inches high, more than six feet wide and stretch all the way across the road. They are often unmarked and placed in shady spots, making them difficult to see, though more effective in slowing traffic. I still remember the first night at the Mayfield Guesthouse in Nairobi after some speed bumps were installed on Ngong Road during the late afternoon. All night, I could hear cars screeching their tires to slow down just in time to hit the new BUMPS hard. That explains why most high bumps have scrapes across their tops where transmissions were unexpectedly removed and oil pans shifted to the back bumper. Many shock absorbers have lost their lives on late-night rides in Nairobi, where roads are "under construction." Coming from the Nairobi airport is a road sign that warns motorists of "rumble strips" as they merge onto highway A104. Visitors take the sign to mean there are small bumps in the road to slow traffic. What "rumble strip" refers to is the new sounds your car acquires after experiencing Kenyan speed bumps. Of course, with such dangerous speed bumps that bring traffic almost to a standstill, small cars veer off the road to avoid them. This puts cars together with pedestrians again. Oddly enough, I have been in small market areas where the cars drive in the ditches, and the people stand in the road – all because of the speed bumps.

Pedestrians are a wonder to behold. They take two steps into a road before looking either way. Sometimes, they don't look at all. When they do look and see you bearing down upon them at a high rate of speed, they look surprised, as though a car should not be on the road at all. This suggests to me that they come from that village where the cars drive in the ditch, and the people walk in the road. Then, immediately following the surprised look, the pedestrian regains his composure and casually steps out in front of you, forcing you to step on the brakes to avoid hitting him. It seems that pedestrians, bicycles, motorcycles, goats, cows, chickens, dogs, guys pulling carts, tractors, and crazy naked people (yes, seeing crazy naked people is more common than you can imagine simply because there are no institutions to care for them) all have the right of way on roads. A motorist gets into terrible trouble when he accidentally hits, bumps, or touches one of them. Rural pedestrians are more dangerous than city pedestrians. Rural folks may not spend much time in a car, so they are generally unaware of how quickly a car can traverse a certain distance and how much time is needed to stop. That explains why an old woman will saunter into the road in front of a car traveling 60 miles an hour and then look surprised as it passes by just behind her with the mirror gently caressing the back of her dress. On the inside of the vehicle, the motorist stops screaming, tries to swallow his heart and regains his composure. Such road hazards are a good reason for drivers to avoid using their cell phones while driving.

I call the principal about driving past pedestrians, the "chicken rule." When goats and cows are walking or running across the road, they will always continue in the direction they are headed. So the motorist can swerve behind them fairly safely. The pedestrian, however, is more like a chicken. They may stop and stare or jump to either side. There is no safe guess as to which way they are going to run – same as chickens. In multiple-choice situations, it is even harder. My wife Linda once ended up hitting a cow because she wanted to avoid the man chasing it.

Motorcyclists must have their own honorable mention. Though I have no hard proof and have heard only a few private confessions, I believe most motorcyclists have never taken a course in driving in their lives. Their cousin's brother works at the office where driver's licenses are produced. They go in, drink tea, pay some money and come out with a driver's license. I was even able to "somehow" obtain a driver's license for a motorcycle when I don't own one, nor have I ever taken lessons on one. I also noticed that there is a box to tick on the driver's license form for obtaining a license to drive an armored personnel carrier. I have thought about going in, drinking some tea, paying some money, and coming out with a driver's license for an armored personnel carrier. I mean, how hard would it be to drive one? I bet I could get it over the speed bumps! Anyway, the motorcyclists drive as though they are oblivious to traffic rules. They will carry people the wrong way on roads, cut in between vehicles in traffic, run up the middle of roads narrowly missing cars, and cut across flowered medians to get to their destination. I have even seen a motorcyclist cut in between two vehicles going around a roundabout, with the first vehicle pulling the second. The motorcyclist drove up by the towing chain, made the corner, and then sped out to his destination. The guy in the second car didn't even raise an alarm about it. Of course, he was not really watching the motorcyclist since he was talking on his cell phone.

Occasionally, it goes badly for the motorcyclist and his passenger. I witnessed one motorcyclist running up the outside of a line of traffic only to reach a car just as the car's passenger opened the door to get out. The door was smashed outward, and the driver and passenger on the motorcycle fell off, moaning in the dirt. While no one was seriously hurt, I had to leave before I could see the end of the huge argument that developed over who was in the wrong. In Sudan, I heard about two drunk soldiers, both driving motorcycles in the opposite direction at dusk, who hit each other head-on and stood there for two hours arguing over who had the right of way on the dirt path. I think they should build some speed bumps on those dirt paths. Oh wait, they already did that!

Then there are **accidents** and **breakdowns**. Linda and I once rounded a corner on the highway at 60 miles an hour and found a huge 18-wheeled truck loaded to the sky sitting exactly in the middle of the road with tree branches in front and behind it for 100 yards. Any learned driver in East Africa knows that tree branches in the road mean a stalled vehicle is lurking up ahead. Road accident signs are expensive and don't last long, whereas a tree or bush is always growing nearby. I have seen engines drop on the side of the road with the mechanic working underneath the vehicle – his feet sticking out into the road. Yet, no one would hit his legs because he had taken out a gigantic spare tire and placed it in the middle of the road to alert traffic of a problem. While motorists slow down to navigate the tire, they can miss their legs. It works! I have never yet seen a mechanic with a leg cast.

I can understand when a truck turns over in a sharp curve, but why do they wipe out in a straight stretch? Recently, while traveling to Nairobi, we came upon two huge, over-laden trucks, both sprawled out on their sides along the road. As we slowed down to miss the tree branches, we discovered the reason they wiped out. Just in front of us was a pothole the size of New Hampshire. It had a drop-off of 18 inches hidden from view from their side. I guess they didn't know the road well enough to miss it. Anyway, by the time we came back, the trucks were gone, and a small mountain nearby had been removed and put in the pothole to make a new series of speed bumps. We slowed down anyway because the tree branches were still in the road.

"Right of Way" may be a familiar phrase for Western drivers, but it is an unknown term here. The vehicle that pulls out in front of you instantly has the right of way. And if the driver does not look at you, then it can't be his fault for causing you to stomp on the brakes and swerve. Large trucks carrying heavy loads have the right of way in any lane. Buses that speed along at 80 miles an hour have the right of way on any road they traverse. Of course, the donkey pulling the cart trumps all of these and can make a full dump truck swerve. Once a visitor learns these rules, they will be able to navigate safely through any traffic in East Africa.

Oh, and watch out for those police checks. They are haphazardly placed throughout the country. Often, the police are sitting under a shade tree, but trucks don't dare pass without stopping first. That is because the police have perfected the best traffic control device yet. It is an eight-foot-long metal speed bump that bristles with metal spikes. Have you ever seen one of those spikes stuck to a truck tire flopping around under the chassis? Not a pretty sight at all, and think about how much trouble it will "cost" the driver to get that set right with the police.

Anyway, I have learned how to drive very skillfully in East Africa. Only occasionally, when I carry visitors fresh off the plane, do I realize how much I have adopted Ugandan driving skills. The quick intake of breath or the slightly muffled cry from the passenger seat alerts me to the fact that I have just hurdled the gap between Western motorist etiquette to a Ugandan driver mentality. Still, I think it is a bit over-reactionary for my visitors to jump out at the end of our journey and kiss the ground.

Cultural Insights/Principles

- Most countries in the world drive on the right side of the road, so all instincts to look and react are OPPOSITE to what is needed in East Africa.
- If there is a chance one might drive in East Africa, then purchase an International Driver's License in your home country. These usually may be obtained through AA and are good for 1 year

in over 200 countries. This helps visitors avoid the bureaucracy of trying to obtain an official driver's license in East Africa.

- A pedestrian waving their arm up and down quickly with their palm toward the ground is a request for you to stop or slow down.

- Big lorries or trucks may use turn signals not only as an indicator that they are turning but also if it is clear to pass. A left turn signal means it is safe to pass. A right turn signal means to wait until it is clear to pass. So, check to see if there is a road up ahead, if not, they are giving you a signal about passing.

- If the big truck is flashing lights at the oncoming vehicle, it is warning the coming vehicle that he is intruding into the truck's lane.

- If a big lorry breaks down on the road and it is loaded with goods, it will not be left unattended lest it be looted. There will always be someone watching it.

- Motorcycles are limited to two people only by law. However, many times, a visitor may see three or more passengers with the driver smashed up close to the handlebars.

- East African speed limits are based on the kind of vehicle. Private vehicles are generally 100 kilometers per hour (Kph), which is about 60 miles per hour. Buses and large trucks may have a speed limit of 80 Kph (50 mph). Trucks pulling trailers may be 60 or 50 Kph. Speed limit signs are used right before town centers where 50 Kph (30 mph) is usually posted. Otherwise, few speed limit signs will be found on the open road.

- Avoid giving your home country's driver's license to any policeman on the side of the road. If you have an International Driver's License, give it instead. Traffic police cannot force you to give your home country's driver's license.

- Traffic police are not supposed to ask you for your passport or immigration paperwork.

- Traffic police are legally not supposed to stop a motorist unless there is a suspicion of a problem of some kind. However, many traffic police stop vehicles anyway and may ask questions about the point of origin and destination.

• In a pinch, it might be wise to carry bottles of water that can be given as a gift to traffic police – especially if you are supposedly in trouble for something.

• Occasionally, police may threaten to arrest you. They can do so legally and hold you for several days without charging you for any crime. However, any police officer doing this may be looking for some kind of financial gain rather than jailing you.

• Traffic police cannot legally ride in your car or leave their post by the roadside.

• Always be polite to traffic police and other officials along the road.

• Drivers of taxis may flash their lights at you to ask if traffic police are behind you. As the driver, you may give a hand signal to go on and that the way is clear. A driver using one finger pointing down and going in circles means a police car is behind them. Sometimes, they may point two or three fingers up and down to show how many police are behind them. If they point down, they are near. If they point up and back, they are far.

• Be careful. Drive slowly and watch for pedestrians.

Proverbs

"Smooth seas do not make skillful sailors" – African Proverb.
"Do not look where you fell, but where you slipped" – African Proverb.
"Every path points in two directions" – African Proverb.
"Better to reach late than to fail to arrive" – African Proverb.

Additional Resource

Link for an International Driver's License – https://international-permit.com/en-us?gad_source=1&gclid=CjwKCAjwuJ2xBhA3EiwAMVjkVI7BKYSrq8wHVwrI8c8S3ni7k6cTbOg6zr8-vwUL3YOKAH0L4Jb2_BoCiuwQAvD_BwE

An East African Driving Test

We have been able to humorously approximate what the driving test given to new drivers in Uganda might be. Test yourself to see if you are ready to drive in East Africa. The answers are listed at the end of the test.

This first section has questions about common things that are seen on the road. The driver is supposed to recognize the items and know their meaning.

1. There are branches with leaves lying on the road. This means:
    A. A herd of elephants just crossed the road
    B. A heavy windstorm just blew through
    C. WARNING: a truck is broken down ahead
    D. A dignitary is coming through
    E. Nothing

2. You see a sign that says "Zebra Crossing Ahead." You should:
    A. Get out your camera to take pictures of the zebras
    B. Ignore the sign because it is only for tourists
    C. Slow down and watch for pedestrians in the crosswalk

D. Speed up and watch for pedestrians in the crosswalk

3. You see a sign that says, "Pouring Petroleum Products on the Road Strictly Prohibited." This means:
    A. You should not stop and change your oil in the middle of the road
    B. The government frowns on the black-market business of selling stolen diesel and petrol
    C. In an effort to modernize the distribution of diesel and petrol, the Ugandan government is outlawing the hand-pouring of petroleum products and requiring the use of automatic pumps.
    D. The government is trying to control the use of petrol in roadside cultic animal sacrifices.

4. Someone on the side of the road is waving their arm up and down as you approach. They are:
    A. Waving "Hello!"
    B. Asking you for a ride
    C. Trying to sell you a local newspaper
    D. Warning you that someone up ahead is changing his oil in the middle of the road

5. A taxi drives by with fish hanging from one of the side view mirrors. This means:
    A. He is advertising that he sells fish
    B. The driver is using the fish as a charm for safety on the journey
    C. One of the passengers has purchased fish, and it smells too bad to carry inside the taxi
    D. The bridge is out ahead

6. You see some men working on the road, filling potholes. This means:

    A. Over the last two years, the holes in the road have become so large that traffic has come to a standstill, so the department of transportation is finally taking care of it.

    B. After months of fundraising, the Mbale Beautification Committee has enough money to repair the potholes – with dirt.

    C. You are no longer in Uganda

    D. The President is coming to town

7. You see a 2-4 feet tall section of a banana plant with one stick on the top of it and one stick on the side pointing up a path. This is:

    A. A sign to direct you to a house where local beer is brewing

    B. A model spaceship built by some of the local children

    C. A sign advertising the sale of local bananas

    D. A scarecrow for the banana plantation

8. You see several banana plants freshly planted in a line on the side of the road. This means:

    A. Someone is planting a banana crop dangerously close to the road

    B. A dignitary will soon be passing by

    C. Someone has made natural-looking bus stops

    D. Mutant banana trees are trying to take over the road

9. You are driving behind a vehicle, and he puts on his right blinker. (Note - you are driving on the left side of the road.) This means:

    A. He will be making a right turn

B. He is telling you that it is unsafe to pass

C. He has a string of fish hanging on his turn signal lever

D. He is warning you that someone up ahead is changing oil in the middle of the road

10. An oncoming vehicle flashes its headlights. This means:

A. He pushed the wrong button on the dash

B. He is telling you to turn off your headlights since it is daytime

C. He is letting you know there are policemen ahead

D. He is asking if there are policemen ahead

E. Any of the above

11. A chicken runs across the road in front of you. You will most likely miss the chicken if you:

A. Swerve in the direction from where the chicken is coming

B. Swerve in the direction where the chicken is running

C. Slam on the brakes

D. Aim to hit the chicken

12. A pedestrian is walking across the road in front of you. You will most likely miss the pedestrian if you:

A. Swerve in the direction from where the pedestrian is coming

B. Swerve in the direction where the pedestrian is walking

C. Slam on the brakes

D. Aim to hit the pedestrian

13. Which side of the road do we drive on?

A. Left

B. Right

C. Middle

D. Whichever side has the smallest speed bumps
and the fewest potholes

14. You reach an intersection where all the vehicles are driving
around a circular median. This is called a "roundabout." At
a roundabout, who has the right-of-way?
   A. The vehicle already in the roundabout
   B. The vehicle trying to enter the roundabout
   C. The biggest vehicle
   D. The driver who is the most aggressive

15. You are approaching a crosswalk, and there are people in it.
What should you do?
   A. Honk, maintain your speed, and hope they stop
   B. Slow down and honk for them to get out of the
       way
   C. Stop and let them cross
   D. Try out the new cattle guard attached to the front
       of your vehicle

16. You are approaching a police check. You should:
   A. Speed through, knowing that the police have no
       means of transportation to catch you anyway
   B. Hand the policeman a 20,000/= note (about two
       dollars) and drive on through
   C. Stop and wait for the policeman to wave you
       through
   D. Hide your smuggled goods under the seats and
       hope that they don't check your vehicle

17. You are approaching the one working traffic light in Uganda,
and it is red. You should:
   A. Stop and wait for the light to turn green
   B. Use the shoulder or the turn lane to advance
       yourself as close to the intersection as possible

C. Cross over into the lane for oncoming traffic and proceed through the intersection

D. Stop and pick up paying passengers

18. If you have been stopped at the red light and it turns green, you should:

A. Start honking your horn before the red light fades away

B. Speed into the intersection even though other traffic has not cleared

C. Proceed with caution through the intersection

D. Do nothing to further annoy the taxi driver behind you, who has been honking his horn the whole time the light was red.

19. You start to go up a hill, and there is a new lane on the left. You should:

A. Only drive in that lane if you are going very slow

B. Only drive in that lane if you want to pass a vehicle in front of you

C. Drive in that lane because the oncoming traffic will use your regular lane for passing

D. Stay out of the lane because it is only for bicycles

20. You are traveling on a "highway" that is barely wide enough for two vehicles before the pavement starts eroding away from the sides. There is a large oil tanker truck approaching on the other side of the road and a bicycle on your side of the road carrying a double bed frame strapped onto the back. You should:

A. Try to pass the oil tanker on the shoulder on the other side

B. Tenaciously hold your ground and play chicken with the tanker

C. Maintain your speed and hit your vehicle's shrink button

D. Slow down, let the tanker pass, and then proceed past the bicycle

E. Take out the smaller vehicle - in this case, the bicycle

21. You are overtaking a vehicle. How much distance should be between you and the vehicle before you re-enter the lane?

A. One car length for every 15 kilometers per hour (Kph) that you are traveling

B. One car length

C. Three inches

D. When you are halfway past the vehicle, start moving over

22. There is a traffic jam ahead. What do you do?

A. Veer off to the side to form yet another line of traffic

B. Set up a jiko (small charcoal grill) and sell roasted corn

C. Assume it is the person directly in front of you who is causing the problem, so you lay on your horn in hopes of getting that person to move

D. Wait patiently until you can proceed

23. One lane is blocked off ahead. You see a man with a red flag. You should:

A. Charge the red flag like a bull

B. Wave at the man as you drive by without slowing down

C. Proceed slowly, trying to figure out how you can share the one open lane with the oncoming oil tanker

D. Stop and wait for the green flag

24. It is nighttime. Another vehicle is approaching you with its bright lights on. What do you do?

    A. Flash your lights to let them know their bright lights are on

    B. Turn your bright lights on and leave them on, knowing that the approaching vehicle will leave them on

    C. Aim between the two approaching lights

    D. Increase your speed and hope there is no pedestrian in your lane

25. It is the rainy season. You are approaching a pothole that is full of water. There is an oncoming vehicle on one side and pedestrians and bicycles on the other. You should:

    A. Stop and wait until you can go around the pothole

    B. Slow down and proceed carefully into the pothole

    C. Maintain your speed and hope for the best

    D. Time your entry into the pothole so as to splash the maximum number of people

26. You are trying to find a parking space in Kampala, but you have not been successful. You should:

    A. Angle park into a parallel parking space that is too small for your vehicle

    B. Drive your vehicle up onto the sidewalk

    C. Run down the "No Parking" sign and park

    D. Double park

    E. Keep circling until you find a space or until Jesus comes again, whichever comes first.

27. You come upon the scene of an accident. A beer truck has run off the road and hit a tree. You should:

    A. Stop to see if the driver needs help

    B. Steal some beer and speed off

C. Go get the police because they have no means of transportation

D. Cancel your plans for the rest of the day and join the crowd that is standing around watching the truck

E. Commandeer some beer and initiate a street party

28. Your vehicle breaks down in the middle of the road. You should:

A. Leave your vehicle in the middle of the road, and place boulders in the road to warn oncoming traffic

B. Pull your vehicle off the road so traffic can pass

C. Send someone for help, and then lay down and sleep underneath your vehicle

D. Stand on top of your vehicle to get good reception for your cell phone and call for help

Answer Key:

1. C; 2. C; 3. B; 4. B; 5. C; 6. A; 7. A; 8. B; 9. B; 10. D; 11. D; 12. C; 13. A; 14. A; 15. C; 16. C; 17. A; 18. C; 19. A; 20. D; 21. A; 22. D; 23. D; 24. A; 25. A; 26. E; 27. A; 28. B

** If you were successful in answering more than half of the questions correctly, you could be one of the better drivers in East Africa!

You Know the Pothole Is Big When…

Recently, Linda and I were driving from Nairobi to Kitale, Kenya, on what used to be a very good road. However, over the past five years or so, the section between Eldoret and Kitale has become so bad that we were reduced several times to literally crawling through potholes extending clear across the road. What made it worse was the rain shower that came up suddenly, filling the holes and hiding their real depth from us. It would have been a miserable 50-mile drive except for a change in attitude. Instead of fuming about our situation, we decided to begin a list of pothole jokes.

Since we were experiencing these craters in the rain, our first thoughts had to do with water. Then, as we thought about it, we decided to include descriptions of potholes during the dry season as well.

During the rainy season – You know the pothole is big when…

- You see local people fishing in it.
- You pass a sign that says. "Bridge Out."
- The locals start calling it Lake _______.
- The government starts a ferry service during the rainy season.
- A flock of flamingos takes up residence.
- Local people wash their clothes on the shore.
- Map makers decide to add it to the map.
- The wildlife starts using it as a watering hole.
- You can only cross at low tide.
- The nearest village is referred to as a harbor or port.
- Farmers tap it for irrigation.
- You pass a lighthouse.

• The government decides to build a dam on it to generate electricity.

During the dry season – You know the pothole is big when…

• Astronauts can see it from space.

• You can take up hang-gliding from the edge.

• The bottom gets direct sunlight only 30 minutes a day.

• It makes the list of the natural wonders of the world.

• Rock layers are easily identifiable back to the Cretaceous period.

• Signs warn motorists to take plenty of water during the crossing.

• You can graze your cattle in the bottom of it.

• Locals begin using camels.

• Shouting at the edge produces an echo.

Chapter 13
Electricity – Power On, Power Off

A few years ago, Nimule, Sudan, had no electricity. The closest electrical pole and power was more than 70 miles south in Gulu, Uganda. Any lights in Nimule were run by a generator for a few hours during the evening. Along the dusty main road, several signs announced cell phone charging via a solar panel for a few shillings. Non-government organizations (NGOs) used banks of solar panels that charged gel-pack batteries during the day to provide a little power for computers, lights, and small machinery.

I happened to be in Nimule, Sudan, on November 2, 2004, during the U.S. Presidential elections. The Sudanese believed, if re-elected, President Bush would continue to pressure Sudanese President Bashir's regime in Khartoum to participate in peace talks with the South Sudanese. So, in the bush and dark, my Sudanese friends cranked up a generator to power a satellite TV to watch U.S. Presidential election results because their future hope of peace, they believed, rested upon the results. Bush won re-election and South Sudan gained their independence in 2006.

In western countries, we take electricity and its availability as an absolute necessity. So much of our daily life is "connected" to and dependent upon the use of electricity. However, in East Africa, electricity can be unpredictable and erratic, especially during the dry season, because there is not enough water flowing through the Nile River to power the dams. How does one cope? How can we prepare for a powerless trip, project, or business activity?

Doing Without Electricity

The best way to describe the frustration of living without electricity is to share part of my journal during my stay in Mbale, Uganda. The following provides a detailed account of the difficulties we faced as well as ways we sought to cope with the continuous power outages. Electricity outages remain common and unpredictable in appearance and duration.

As I write this, the electricity is off - again. (I will transfer my writing from this pad of paper to the computer after the electricity returns.) It went off this morning at 6:30 AM, and now, at 5:00 PM, we are still without power. Repeated phone calls to the electric company do not help. They only know that the power supply was cut off at the dam in Jinja, Uganda and diverted to some other location. They told us this morning that electricity would return in four hours. At noon, we called again, receiving a promise that it would return at 2:00 PM. It still is not on, and the electric company no longer answers the phone.

A major frustration about a lack of electricity lies in our expectations. We live in Mbale, the 3rd largest city in Uganda. Our house is wired for electricity like all the houses around us. There are streetlights on several major roads in town. Shops sell all kinds of basic electrical appliances and parts. We paid a $150 deposit to hook up to the electric supply. There is a meter on the side of the house to record units of electricity used. Each month, a man comes by to read the meter. The society around us is set up to run on electricity. So, we expect electricity. Only electricity is not dependable.

Due to seasonal low water levels in Lake Victoria and the Nile, the dam in Jinja often cuts back production to a fraction of its capacity. This means the Ugandan electric company, Umeme, must shut down large sections of the country at a single time while keeping only strategic areas powered. It also sells a portion of its electricity to Kenya for foreign exchange. Sometimes, Umeme's power-sharing causes the electricity to be off for 12 hours at a time. Sometimes, it is less. Other times, it may be off for a day or two.

When the electricity goes off for several hours, we try but always fail to get an accurate answer as to how long it will be off. Sometimes, Umeme prints a power-sharing schedule in the newspaper. However, they never follow it. In effect, the electricity can go off at any time, for any length of time. Life and work just become much more complicated, slower, less efficient, and much more costly.

Consider the following situations:

- After preparing a casserole and placing it in the electric stove (or microwave) for the family's supper, the electricity goes off unexpectedly until after bedtime.
- The bread or cake in the oven gets only half-baked and must be thrown away.
- Friends are invited over for an evening visit, but the power goes off, and the meal and activities must be done by candlelight.
- After a long day out, the family sits down to watch a movie, and the electricity goes off after 20 minutes of viewing.
- Phones, computers, the Internet, iPads, and office equipment are rendered useless after a few hours without a charge.
- The refrigerator and freezer become warm enough that food spoils and must be thrown out.
- There is no hot water for a shower. The heater has not been on long enough during the day to heat water.
- Halfway through a shower, bath, or restroom stop, the power goes off suddenly, leaving everything to be finished in the dark.

• You try to read a book by lantern or candlelight, but it hurts your eyes.

• You struggle to stay awake until a reasonable time, so you sleep through the night while fighting off mosquitoes that you can't see.

• It is 10:00 PM, and the temperature is still high from a very hot day. You lay in bed sweating, thankful for a little relief from the fan - which suddenly stops because the power goes off.

All plans connected to electricity must be changed because of electrical blackouts. We become cut off from the outside world in a matter of a few battery hours.

The first way we responded to the electricity outages was to try and continue our regular routine and figure a way around the obstacles that having no power created. We raised money and purchased a generator and two jerry cans to store petrol. However, with petrol costing over four dollars a gallon, we ran the generator sparingly. We bought boxes of candles and matches and two pressure lanterns for dark evenings. We learned the most strategic places to put candles in a dark house.

However, as the outages continued, we learned to adapt. Because food spoils in prolonged droughts of electricity, our market purchases and diet changed to a simpler menu. When finances allowed, we bought a gas-powered stove so we could cook and heat water when the electricity was out. We learned how to take baths out of a basin in our regular shower stall. We washed clothes at odd hours of the night to take advantage of the power; then, we hung them outside on the clothesline, not expecting the power to be on.

At last, we were able to purchase a battery backup system that charged when the electricity was on and automatically switched to batteries when the power went off. It was wonderful. Often, the switchover was seamless and unnoticed. It greatly reduced the stress we bore and allowed us to resume some semblance of a regular family and work routine. The only drawback to the backup system was that it would not power the heating elements of the microwave, water heater, or dryer. We wired the house to exclude them from the battery backup. That was an easier adaptation than having no power at all. Still, there were times when the electricity was off for so long that the batteries would run out, and we would go back to living in the dark. But those times were much less frequent.

For visitors to East Africa, going without electricity during a brief visit may be an adventure even though it interrupts the schedule. However, it becomes a difficult hardship to bear for the long-term resident. Constant power outages become an unrelenting, irregular aggravation that has no end in sight. For example, during one four-year period of living in Uganda, the longest we had electricity without interruption was 12 days - one time. We had electricity twice for 10 days without interruption. A few times, we had power for five days. For many months, it went off every day.

However, let me switch from describing the drawbacks of this dark scenario and listing a few positives that can help adjust our attitudes when sitting in the dark and unable to "connect." Going without electricity forced us to slow down and sometimes do nothing but wait. Westerners especially pride themselves on being busy. The value of a trip is often measured in the number of activities accomplished rather than the relationships built. As a result, visitors to East Africa must learn to re-prioritize. The East African experience is not ruined by a lack of electricity. It is altered to include new adventures and experiences not available when the electricity is on. Rest. Slow down. Enjoy what and who is around you.

Power outages provide time for face-to-face family activities. Instead of everyone sitting and watching television, checking updates on social media, or binge-watching some TV series, power outages provide an opportunity for social interaction. No electricity means playing games, reading a book together, painting, drawing, completing household errands, working in the yard, or any number of other activities that would be lost to the Internet-connected Western visitor.

While sitting and waiting, there is an opportunity to drink some tea or coffee and watch the birds, take in a sunset, or listen to nature around you. It is a time to journal, reflect, and meditate on important life matters. It provides a chance to play a guitar or piano. If anything, think about how electricity has helped AND hindered modern society.

For East Africans and for the wiser long-term residents, having no electricity is a great time to visit with friends. It is a time to find out how they are doing, share ideas and news, and talk deeply. It is an opportunity to learn their stories, share their successes and heartaches, and dream together. Relationships developed during power outages will last much longer than any project or activity. Going without power may help one clearly see the faces and smiles of East Africa instead of an inanimate computer screen.

We realize that electricity has become a core need in our modern society. Yet, electricity is a fragile commodity that struggles to supply our ever-growing demands. East Africa is less connected, and many have already purchased solar panels and battery packs to power single-dwelling compounds. Their electrical needs are small, and they have learned to be self-sufficient in so many ways. In fact, someone said Africa will be the first continent to become self-sufficient in energy. It may be that the West's future will see each house powered separately and not dependent upon a central power grid. That would certainly be more strategic in case of outages or war or some other major problem. Perhaps by the time we get to that level of self-sufficiency, Africa may already be there to welcome us.

Cultural Insights/Principles

• East Africa uses a three square-pronged electrical outlet like much of Europe. A sturdy adapter that is capable of multiple prong configurations will be needed and can be purchased online or in airport shops.

• Not all international adapters have a place for three-pronged American plugs on computers. They only have two-pronged options. Purchase an American adapter that goes from three prongs to two prongs to utilize an international adapter for 220 volts.

• Remember, electricity in East Africa is 220 volts and not 110 volts. Be sure your chargers, computers, phones, and any other electrical appliances can handle the switch lest you burn something out quickly.

• Electrical outlets are not as numerous in hotels and houses as in Western countries. If electricity is really needed, it might be good to bring an extension cord.

• Purchase and carry a small flashlight in your bag wherever you go.

• A headlamp is very useful for keeping both hands free for nighttime activities.

• In much of East Africa, one can find D-size batteries and AA-size batteries. It is much harder to find C-size batteries and AAA or AAAA-size batteries. If you have something that uses these, bring extra batteries.

• If electricity for your phone or computer is important, consider purchasing external power sources that can be hooked up for charging them.

- Bring a book, binoculars, and a journal for your visit.
- Take advantage of downtime. Don't see it as an interruption but rather a gift for building friendships.
- Make a list of intentional questions that you would like to ask a friend.
- Carry a camera and take photos of everything. Remember not to take just nature photos. Take lots of photos of faces, smiles, and interactions (ask permission first before taking photos). Video some East African songs and children's laughter at play. Some may ask for copies of photos, but just tell them they are digital photos and that nothing will be printed. This avoids mailing expenses as well as any problems with jealousy from those who did not get a picture.
- Learn to be flexible. If a project is delayed, spend time visiting with your hosts. That may turn out to be much better than completing a house or clinic or finishing a business deal.

Proverbs

"It is better to light a candle than to curse the darkness" – African Proverb.
"If you are hiding, do not light a fire" – African Proverb.
"The light of a thousand stars does not equal the light of the moon" – African Proverb.

Chapter 14
Sleeping in Mud Huts
in Real Darkness

After my Kalenjin friend Enoch Sawe saw his first scorpion in the rocks in Lodwar, Kenya compound, he immediately determined it was a creature of the Devil. He was also determined not to sleep on the ground, as had been our plan. So, that night, we found ourselves sleeping on top of the lengthy luggage rack of my vehicle about seven feet off the ground. I remember Enoch peering over the railing one last time at the rocks before going off to sleep. I also remember thinking how beautiful the stars were that night, how the heat of the desert became cold by morning, and what a memorable night of camping it was. My Lodwar friends thought our behavior was odd, but perhaps they stared most at Enoch, their fellow Kenyan, more than me.

Visitors to East Africa will likely be guests and recipients of hospitality at some point in their stay. This may also include a visit to someone's house. Living styles are very different and do not always reflect economic status. Why are homes maintained the way they are? What is the significance of little furniture or the crowded conditions of seating in the guest room? What are the East African cultural values that guide the use and maintenance of houses? Are we truly seeing everything accurately when we visit a traditional home?

Observations from an Overnight Stay

My visit to Chemoi and Tande in Western Kenya provided me with an opportunity to spend the night in my friend's mud hut. It reminded me that there are several differences between the Holiday Inns in America and the average run-of-the-mill mud hut in East Africa.

First, nearly every mud hut that I have seen has the same basic design (round) and color (dirt). Most have the same style of roof (dried brown thatched grass). Most use the same substance to harden the floor and keep dust from being a problem (cow manure). Some provide an artistic flare by using different colors of mud to draw shapes or images on the outside walls. Most are just plain.

To enter a mud hut, you normally must bend down to avoid cracking your head open on the roof poles supporting the grass roof. For a long time, I thought East Africans just liked to build houses short and their doors painstakingly low. With a little more experience, I have come to understand that lower roofs protect the outside walls from being washed away during the rainy seasons. This means less work in rebuilding and more gymnastic exercise in entering and exiting the house.

Once inside, a five-second survey completes the tour of the house. There are no additional rooms. There are no narrow hallways to walk. There are no small closets to fuss about. There are no complaints about the carpet becoming worn or the walls needing paint. There is no need to worry about dusting. It was this kind of round mud hut that became a home for the night for me and my coworkers James Luchivya and Robert Nakola. I had stayed in mud huts many times before, but this night was memorable because of my friends with me, the hospitality of the family, and the evening rain that impressed upon me how close I was to nature.

Normally, a family builds a small cooking hut behind the main house to keep the fire away from all the family's possessions. If the family is poor, the woman cooks inside a single hut. You can tell when she habitually does this because the inside layer of grass and roofing poles will be soot-covered, and the air has a smoky scent. It is good to have a fire inside the house occasionally because the smoke gets rid of all sorts of creatures that like to live on the grass roof. Kenya has lots of geckos and bugs, and Uganda is especially blessed to have huge lizards 12 to 18 inches long in brilliant orange and glowing blue colors. All these creatures like to crawl about the top wall plate and scamper across the grass roof and poles. Termites also like to digest the wooden poles and can sometimes be heard moving along inside the walls. (I have frustratingly proclaimed on numerous occasions that all of Uganda sits upon a huge termite mound.) I don't have the space to mention all the flies, mosquitoes, ants, spiders, and various bugs that have been our unexpected dropdown guests in past mud hut visits.

This visit to Chemoi and Tande, provides an excellent opportunity for explaining sleeping arrangements. James, Robert, and I were to share one small mud hut about 15 feet in diameter. As I entered (at about 10:00 PM) for the first time, I discovered a small lantern on the one little wooden table that gave light to the room. The only one-foot square wooden window was already shuttered for the night. The floor to the right was covered with two thin mattresses and blankets for two people. Just to the left, a metal frame bed had the same kind of bedding. James and Robert looked at the metal bed and insisted I sleep on it. I laid down on it and sunk immediately into a fox-hole position with my knees scratching my chin. I then determined to share equal status with my friends. I insisted the metal bed be folded up and leaned against the wall. I took the mattress and blankets from the bed and laid them on the ground next to theirs. I had brought with me two items they did not possess but silently coveted. I pulled out of my bag a mosquito net, which I strung up, and I unrolled a sleeping bag, which I quickly snuggled down into.

I learned at a large meeting many years before that a mosquito net also provides a natural barrier to encroaching bedmates. Without the net at the large meeting, I woke up in the middle of the night to find two other men, one on each side of me, who had snuggled up close to me and put their heads on my large pillow. I struggled to get up because both had also laid down on the edges of my sleeping bag. I decided immediately to relocate to my car, where I slept in my sleeping bag sitting up. Somehow, that seemed like a better alternative than sharing my pillow and sleeping bag with strangers in the large dormitory room.

Another quick observation should be from the reverse side. While I write from the guest's perspective, the East African host is always curious to know how his guests are faring and what they think of the accommodations. Many know Western visitors have never slept in a mud hut before. So, hosts are anxious about providing sufficient for them. An example of this curiosity is illustrated by Larry Stephens, a friend and missionary from Kisumu, Kenya, who many years ago visited a village in South Nyanza, Western Kenya. Larry arrived to spend the night without the aid of a mosquito net. The hosts did not "smoke" the room like they do for themselves, fearing the smoke would overwhelm the visitors. Yet, in the morning, the host noticed that Larry had not been bitten and did not complain about the ever-present mosquito. The East African host and others traveling with Larry secretly believed he had some kind of magical powers that kept mosquitos away. At that point, the host had not been introduced to mosquito-repellent gel that was easily rubbed onto the skin.

Before sleep came to me in Tande, I observed two additional notes about mud huts. When the lantern was extinguished, there was absolutely no light at all inside. The closed wooden window did not allow any of the moon or starlight to enter. The door, which was made of large metal cans that had been cut, flattened, and shaped for a door, blocked out every beam of light as well. I felt the blackness of the night completely envelop me as I lay on the floor. There was no electrical hum and no green glow of a clock nearby. The second observation came from the grass roof. Since there were no ceiling boards, the outside sounds seemed especially close. As we settled down for the night, a rain shower passed by, causing the wind to stir the leaves of trees above us. My last thoughts before slumber were the sound of the rain that pelted the grass roof. Being so close to the rain and yet not getting wet made me think of sleeping outside under a big tree. The rain came down, and yet I miraculously stayed dry. I suppose I could imagine anything in the blackness of the night. The total effect was one of calmness as nature's music lulled me off to sleep. Such experiences escape the modern man who imprisons himself within his sturdy house, surrounded by technical gadgets that buzz and hum and whir. Nature is shut out, and the bond between man and his environment is severed. He sleeps within and is surrounded only by the things he has made.

There were times, in the beginning, that I did not carry a mosquito net with me for sleepovers. This made me much more vulnerable to nighttime visitors. One night, I had a rat run across my chest and wake me. At least, I think it was a rat. Since it was completely dark, I could only guess. I also estimated he must have been big because he was heavy. Several times during other sleepovers, I was awakened by geckos that dropped out of the grass roof onto me. As I woke, I could hear and feel them run off to one side or the other. On another occasion, I had not noticed the rooster who came in and bedded down near my backpack. The next morning, around 4:30 AM, I was rudely awakened by this extremely loud, raucous crowing inches from my head. I jumped at the sound with my heart racing. I started the day in a bad mood because of that rooster. I confess I also secretly wished for that rooster to be our lunch later in the day. He survived.

On a different village visit, my friend Arturo was excited about his first mud hut stay. He confessed, as we put up our foldable wire cots (cots are better than sleeping on the ground), that he had never gone camping in America. I gave him instructions on how to set up his cot, open his sleeping bag, and hang a mosquito net. Arturo was not necessarily a large or clumsy fellow, but he was unfamiliar with the routine. It took him 15 minutes to get undressed, find a place for his glasses, figure out how to get into his sleeping bag, which he zipped up to his chin, and position his pillow and netting around him before reaching over to turn his flashlight off. He placed his flashlight under his cot so he could reach it easily in the night. Not being used to a cot, Arturo flopped around a lot, causing his cot to come undone in the middle. One quick turn in the middle of the night, and suddenly Arturo was thrown out onto the floor, still wrapped up in his sleeping bag. His fall pulled the mosquito net down and wrapped his sleeping bag up in it. His flashlight was lost in the shuffle, as were his glasses. Of course, his surprised cry woke me, and I instantly knew what had happened. After I stopped laughing, I found my flashlight and helped Arturo get back into bed. I think he didn't move again all night.

I learned through the years that it is a good idea not to drink too much liquid before getting into a sleeping bag under a mosquito net in a jet-black room with no toilet within 50 yards. The idea of having to go to the bathroom in the middle of the night almost needs to be anticipated, or else you might not make it. It would also be a good idea to have a good flashlight handy for those midnight calls or for any strange sounds or unwanted visitors that might come your way. Another necessity of mud hut stays is a roll of toilet paper in your backpack.

Take, for instance, this mud hut scene in Tande and put it against any Holiday Inn in America. Since I arrived at night, I didn't get a chance to see if there was a swimming pool close by. It didn't matter, I never swim at a pool in America either. I knew that my hosts in Tande did not have cable, Wi-Fi services, or even local television.

My Tande "restaurant" offered lots of tea (watch those liquids), ugali, and a tasty piece of chicken, all by lantern light. The silverware wasn't spotty. There wasn't any silverware. My host laughed, lifted his curled hand up and said, "This is the original fork." There was not a dripping faucet all night. There wasn't a musty smell from the carpet. The air-conditioner wasn't broken, and the train tracks weren't right behind the room. Plus, they didn't have a 10,000-watt neon sign that illuminated the entire parking lot and everything in the room and doubled as an airport runway signal for landing jets. The highway was not nearby, so I did not have to ignore the drone of cars driving by.

Instead, I was treated as an honored guest, given the best house in the compound, overfed, waited upon meticulously, and allowed to sleep enveloped by the African night and its whispers. I think the mud hut and Holiday Inn both have their advantages and drawbacks. But I must admit, I feel very comfortable and peaceful in a mud hut. And I would rather get up in the middle of the night and go outside for the latrine in East Africa than go down in the middle of the night and get ice from the ice machine in any urban city motel.

Home Visits

Many rural houses are sparsely filled with furniture and almost no decorations. There may be no beds at all, and the entire family sleeps on mats which they roll out on the floor at night. Or maybe the parents have a twin bed they sleep on with children on the floor. A cupboard may be used for kitchen utensils and plates and cups, and a metal trunk or two holds all the family's clothes. The largest room or partitioned space will be to receive guests. Stools and foldup wooden chairs sit along the wall, or if possible, a couch covered with crocheted coverings with a small wooden table in front of it fills the room. The wealthier families may have the guest room filled with couches and chairs to the point of being difficult to walk among the furniture to sit.

The frugal number of possessions is partially due to poverty, but a second reason is the close-knit community. Community pressure constrains the acquisition of many things. Since homes are open to neighbors who visit frequently, anyone who appears to be prospering ahead of others will be overwhelmed with requests for help. It is never wise to turn away neighbors in their need. So, to avoid jealousy or excessive requests, families purchase a meager amount of furniture, household goods, and clothing, no greater than their neighbors, to cover necessities. They do not keep things that are not needed on a regular basis.

A third reason there are few things in the house has to do with the value of living life outdoors. East Africans highly value their friendships and relationships and often will visit with them outside instead of inside the house. Visitors, traditionally, will greet in the yard and sit under the shade of a special tree planted specifically for hosting guests. Work, bathing, cooking, eating, drinking, and socializing are all traditionally accomplished outside. Houses are seen as places to sleep and shelter from bad weather or thieves. So, it is not surprising that few resources are used to build huge houses or even to maintain a simple mud hut. More resources are used to support the active networking of communal lifestyles. Better is a meal with a friend than a decoration for the wall. More valued is the planting of a tree where neighbors can rest than purchasing a couch for a tiny room. After all, the couch will wear out, but the tree will be enjoyed for years. It is better to have nice clothes to wear in the community kept in a battered metal trunk than to have fewer clothes and a nice dresser.

Thus, a visitor may misjudge his host's economic status and abilities if he/she observes only a few possessions inside the house.

The visitor may think their hosts are suffering from poverty. What they may not realize is that wealth is utilized for building social connections more than acquiring personal properties. East African cultural values of friendships, community, sharing, and life outdoors trump personal or familial possessions. For East Africans, houses and kitchens may be utilitarian in appearance because real wealth, to them, will be measured in the respect and support given and received by the community. Do not be fooled by the grass or rusty tin roofs, small rooms, and meager furniture. East Africa and its people are wealthy in many unseen resources. Such communal values could be an important lesson in priorities for every visitor who comes to East Africa.

Cultural Insights/Principles

- In rural areas, the direction from which the rain usually comes is a factor in where the doors are placed on the houses and may not always be convenient for road or path access.
- If there are multiple houses in a compound, normally, all the doors open to the center of the group. This may be a sign of security issues more than an intended convenience for socializing.
- A lot of people use a grass roof to hold items. It is not uncommon to find a toothbrush, comb, mirror, or some other item stuck into the grass just above the wall for easy access.
- People who believe in traditional medicine and witchcraft may place a specific twig or flowered branch above the door to ward off evil spirits or to block sicknesses from entering.
- Among the Bagwere, there may be a grassy patch in the middle of the compound where a special clay pot has been buried with a sacrificed chicken in it to ward off evil spirits.
- Bagwere homes may also have a small hole in the wall to allow the Mukama Spirit an honored entry to protect the home.

• There may also be special trees or shrubs planted for specific spiritual purposes. Do not assume everything is random.

• Witchdoctors may live in houses without doors to allow free access for all spirits.

• A compound with numerous houses will reflect an older couple with adult male children who have constructed their own houses. If there is a kitchen behind one of these houses, it may indicate that the young man has married.

• East Africans routinely sit as guests and keenly inspect the compound of their host to determine much about the family's wealth, character, diet, and familial stability.

Proverbs

"Home is not where we live, but where we belong" – African Proverb

"A small house can lodge a hundred friends" – African Proverb

"A husband may be the head of a home, but the wife is the heart of a home" – African Proverb

"The wise traveler leaves his heart at home" – African Proverb

"A man does not go far from where his corn is roasting" – African Proverb

"Better a close neighbor than a brother far away" – African Proverb

"Before buying a house or piece of land, see who your neighbors will be" – African Proverb

"It is better to be kind to a neighbor than travel the world to offer incense to our ancestors" – African Proverb

"No matter how rich a man is, he cannot sleep on two beds at a time" – African Proverb

Chapter 15
Celebrating Weddings With Dances, Songs, Ululations, and Food

All visitors to East Africa may not realize how much weddings, though grounded in civil laws and shaped by religious ceremonies, provide a powerful insight into cultural values. The initiation of social marriage, extended family dynamics, forms of celebration, and support are on full display. Local traditions permeate the social and religious foundations of the marriage ceremony, and there is a big difference in urban and rural, rich and poor wedding practices. Weddings offer a wonderful opportunity to connect deeply with families and friends in East Africa through the celebration of a special event. If a visitor receives an invitation to a wedding through a friend, business relationship, family member or church, do not hesitate to accept. Attend and enjoy the rich cultural celebration on display.

A Teso Style Wedding

In more than 30 years of living in East Africa, I had the opportunity to conduct numerous wedding ceremonies. One of the more memorable ones was a village wedding held just west of Soroti, some 85 miles northwest of Mbale. The wedding was held on the drier, grassy plains of north central Uganda in the heart of the lovely Teso people. Their wedding customs, influenced slightly by Western culture, are lively, colorful, and festive. I thought it would be good to describe my experience chronologically as I observed everything.

First, I must describe the location of our wedding ceremony. We gathered in a church building central to the families of the bride and groom. It was a mud building with a thatched grass roof. The only lighting came from the openings for two doors and two windows. This made the inside dark for photography and for reading my prepared speech. Twisted wooden poles formed the roof structure to which the grass had been expertly tied. The floors were mud that had been smoothed with cow manure, giving it a hard and slightly greenish appearance but with no odor after drying. Several poles were placed in the middle of the building as support for the long roof. They were not straight but curved and trimmed where branches had been cut off. All these physical aspects gave the building a rough yet intriguing characteristic.

For decorations, balloons were hung above the pulpit area. A balloon each of blue, yellow, green, and red was tied to the crooked poles with pieces of plastic strand taken from a sugar sack. A larger purple balloon was tied higher up in the middle. Added to this splash of color, red bougainvillea flowers had been gathered and placed in small bouquets around the room. Rather than using vases, the stems were tied together and stuck into the cracks of the dry mud walls. These were the only decorations added for the wedding festivities.

A choir was formed to sing during the wedding ceremony and to do one of the most special tasks of this Teso wedding. They were assembled to escort the bride into the building. She had come early to a mud hut not far from the church building where, with the help of several friends, she dressed in her wedding attire. When the groom finally arrived and came in to stand with me, it was time for the choir to go and get the bride. The choir filed out of our building, singing and clapping and dancing. They moved slowly to the front of the small hut not far away. There, they sang and danced for several minutes before the bride appeared. She was dressed in brilliant white that seemed to stand out among the colorful dresses and dark faces of the singing group around her. As she walked, there was a pattern to her steps. The group, in amazing unison, took two steps forward, paused, and then took one step back. This made the whole procession move slowly. Around this procession, younger girls waved homemade flags, danced, and ululated in happiness. (Ululation is a loud, long, high-pitched, trilling yell that symbolizes joy at weddings and sadness at funerals. It is very common in Sub-Saharan Africa and the Middle East.) Two women were appointed to hold a cloth over the bride to shield her from the sun. It took several minutes for her to get to the building, but I had to admire the joy and happiness expressed by the entire crowd. I also knew the value of taking their time. To many cultures, the longer something takes, the more important it is. With this value undergirding our ceremony, nothing was going to be done quickly.

Just in front of the pulpit area, two chairs were placed for John and Gila (the groom and bride), where they sat instead of standing during the ceremony. Each had an attendant behind them. I began the expected 45-minute sermon on the importance of marriage, the bonding of families, and the commitments and responsibilities that were being made by both. All of this had to happen before we repeated the vows. All during my sermon, John and Gila's attendants continuously fussed over their charges. The woman attendant straightened the bride's scarf. Then she wiped the bride's face from any perspiration (it was almost 100 degrees with no air-conditioning). Sometimes, the attendant would physically turn the bride's head and use her discerning eyes to search for any defects in Gila's makeup. She would also periodically pat down the bride's neck, arms, and legs to keep them dry as well. Once, during the ceremony, I looked up from my notes and saw the attendant pushing a small towel down the back of the bride's dress to wipe her back.

The male attendant also had his ritual. He continuously wiped the face and forehead of the groom and straightened his tie and jacket.

Twice while wiping his face, the groom had to remove his glasses (which he borrowed from someone for the wedding ceremony to exhibit a higher style of dress) so the attendant could wipe his eyes. The male attendant also had a small aerosol can of something that smelled like perfume. The writing on the can had been rubbed off, so I could not tell what the spray was exactly. At least three times, he sprayed the perfume onto the head of the groom.

During this whole procedure, the bride and groom sat passively, accepting the attendants' attention. It appeared the attendants worked in unison except for one time when the male attendant reached over and sprayed perfume on the bride. The woman attendant stopped her work and gave the man a drop-dead look, which he ignored. The Western visitor may not understand that such extravagant attention to the bride and groom was to demonstrate how important they were and to display extraordinary honor to them on such an important day. The passive, solemn faces of both the groom and bride were to demonstrate their understanding of the gravity and importance of what they were committing themselves to. There would be time later for laughter and celebration. During the ceremony, they were expected to display the utmost respect and decorum.

No rings were exchanged during the wedding ceremony. Even though rings are a Western idea, cheap brass rings are often purchased for East African weddings and then sometimes worn afterwards. I see rings more often on the women than on the men. Rings are not a traditional practice and can be bent or broken in the hard work done both on the farm and in the community. John and Gila explained later that they did not want to spend money on rings.

After the vows were exchanged, John and Gila were escorted by their attendants to the very front of the building and seated behind a small table. As the choir sang several songs while dancing and ululating, people began coming forward from the audience (without instructions given) and placed gifts on the table. Several of the people brought money and placed it in a basket in the center of the table. The presenters would then shake the couple's hands and wish them well. I watched closely to see how much money, on average, was brought forward. Most offered currency equivalent to 5 or 10 cents. The amount was less important than the public display of offering a gift in solidarity with the wedding ceremony. At the end of the singing and donations, someone counted the money in front of everyone (for accountability and transparency) and announced the collection was about $5.30.

Most of the people in attendance brought plastic cups or dishes to the table. An older woman came up with one bright red plastic cup, set it on the table, and then shook the couple's hands. The next couple placed a green plastic plate on the table and shook hands. At the end, 43 plates and 20 cups were collected. Each cup or plate, at the time, cost about 25 cents in the market. One woman brought a small broom forward and placed it on the table. A man brought a small container of petroleum jelly and put it on the table. The jelly is often used as a facial cream to keep their skin from drying out in the heat. Another man came forward with a small plastic bag of dried fish. Each of the dozen or so fish was about the size of two fingers. I had purchased a dozen ceramic mugs from the market in Mbale and placed them on the table. They cost me about 10 dollars, which probably equaled everyone else's gifts combined. Strangely, I felt embarrassed by the extravagance of my gift.

During this whole gifting procession, the groom and bride sat stoically without smiles. Without a doubt, they were happy. I, on the other hand, grinned and smiled like a child in front of a candy counter. Whenever a solemn gift bearer would shake my hand, they would see my smile and smile back. All during the time people brought gifts forward, there was a cultural opportunity for certain representatives from both sides of the family to stand up, make comments about the groom or bride, and express their happiness for the wedding. While this may take a long time, it is important to demonstrate the support of both families for the marriage. In a culture where extended family is highly respected, their public approval is strongly desired during the wedding ceremony. It adds honor to the bride and groom.

Often, a large cake is made, presented, and literally cut into crumb fragments so that every one of the 200-300 people attending may have a chance to taste it. It is less a refreshment and more a participatory event where all the guests show their connection to and support of the couple's marriage. Since our ceremony was 20 miles from the nearest town where an oven was located, no cake was attempted or purchased and brought to the event, however.

Of course, I must mention the meal served to all the guests. I, being a guest from far away, was escorted to a small hut about 100 yards away. There I found some of the wooden fold-up chairs were placed around the same table that had been used for collecting gifts. Usually, the families of the bride and groom, the pastor and special guests are served food first. Children are served last if there is sufficient food left for them. On my table were huge bowls of ugali (cornmeal cooked into the consistency of playdough) and millet ugali (ground millet and cassava cooked the same as ugali). Then, each person around the table was given a small bowl of three meat chunks and soup. Being a connoisseur of African cuisine, I could tell right away that the meat was not beef. We learned that a goat had been slaughtered for the wedding. This wedding party was really feasting! Another bowl was given to each guest, showing how special the occasion was. The second bowl contained a small piece of goat liver or kidney, some intestines cut into inch-long sections resembling noodles, and a piece of the stomach. The stomach piece was easy to identify because it had a greenish terry-cloth appearance. Remember, our food was not served until 3:30 PM. I had not eaten anything since 7:00 AM. I attacked my bowl of goat meat, tore huge pieces of ugali off the mounds, and stuffed myself. I also ate the liver pieces but passed on the noodles and terrycloth. That was all right because it went out the door and was eaten by some other guest.

After such a satisfying meal, I discovered, not surprisingly, that my vehicle was needed to take the newly married couple over to their house. They wanted to ride in style, and since my Toyota four-wheel-drive double cab pickup was the only vehicle around, I was nominated. So, I drove the lovebirds (and about 20 girls in the back who were ululating) over to their house using an almost unmarked trail. For their use of the truck, I was rewarded with a warm soda. At the home of John and Gila, I received another meal while 45 adults and 42 children watched (I counted). By the time I returned to the church building, it was almost 7:00 PM. I had just enough light to put up a tent and prepare my camp. I spent almost nine hours at the wedding, and even though I retired early, groups of people stayed up and talked and laughed until the early morning hours. I felt as though I had successfully participated in a Teso wedding. I also felt, in a tiny way, a part of the community. I slept well, even though my sleeping bag was too thin for the hard ground.

Cultural Insights/Principles

- Weddings never follow a time schedule. They are always late, long, and full of celebration. So, don't make the mistake of being on time.
- Weddings may be held at a church or public building. It is not uncommon for weddings to be held in the compound of a family member.

- Ululation is a big part of women expressing their happiness about what is happening. The first time you hear it, you can be shocked and even jump because of the loudness of the shouts.

- Solemnity is traditionally expected of the groom and bride during the sermon and vows, but joy is exuberant during all other parts.

- As a guest, ask beforehand if you should take a monetary or physical gift. If it is a physical gift, ask for guidance on what, how much should be spent, and whether it should be wrapped.

- Importance is measured in the amount of time it takes to complete a wedding ceremony. The longer it is, the more important. Weddings can take all day, so be prepared.

- Weddings are often judged not by the vows made but by the amount of food prepared for the guests. If guests go home hungry, it is not a good wedding.

- As much as food is a climax for East African weddings, there is also great emphasis placed on entertainment consisting of music (live or prerecorded), singing, humor, and numerous speeches. The entertainment causes many weddings to go on for a long time.

- Since weddings can be an all-day affair, it is wise to eat well before traveling to a wedding as it may be a long time before you will have a chance to eat something (usually after 4:00 pm).

- Modern weddings in East Africa cost a huge amount of money. Bridal dresses, men's suits, and attendants' clothing can be more than stylish, almost lavish. If invited to a wedding, ask someone knowledgeable for guidelines on how to dress – casual, business, or formal. Dress may depend upon what role a person has, i.e., guest, participant, or distinguished guest who may sit in a place of honor.

- Modern weddings often have more than one photographer. They can be distracting and even pushy in getting pictures. Their behavior is parallel to the attendants. The more active and intrusive they are, the more they are showing honor and earning their pay.

• Weddings are not just the union of a man and woman. It is the union of two different families.

• Weddings are attended by a huge number of family members from both the groom's side and the bride's side. Neighbors and church friends are also expected to attend if possible.

• Various East African communities celebrate their weddings differently. Some may have an event that looks like a mock wedding before the actual wedding itself (a way of adding prestige to the real event). Others may hold a pre-wedding event intended to solicit funds from well-wishers. A Western visitor needs to know what kind of event he/she has been invited to avoid unpreparedness or a wrong expectation.

• If a visitor is visiting a friend's wedding in a rural area and they drive their own vehicle, they may be pressed into transporting some part of the bride's or groom's family. This is less likely in urban areas, but they should still consider the possibility and adjust how they wish to respond. Volunteering one's vehicle may encounter overloading, numerous trips, and HOURS of chauffeuring passengers. It is possible for a visitor to attend a wedding by hiring a private vehicle to take, drop off, and return to collect them.

• In a rural area, it is possible to see an older man and woman with children and grandchildren participate in a marriage ceremony to fulfill church obligations because they were married in a traditional manner where the groom's uncles negotiated a bride price with the bride's family, drank beer, exchanged gifts, and participated in ritual processions of dance and songs as the bride moved from her home to the groom's. Such traditional marriages, though recognized as legal by the government, are not recognized by churches or registered with the government.

Proverbs

"A man without a wife is like a vase without flowers" – African Proverb

"Marry the girl of a good family, though she be seated on a mat, very poor" – African Proverb

"One thread for the needle, one love for the heart" – Sudanese Proverb

"Do not correct with a strike that which can be taught with a kiss" – African Proverb

"Love, like rain, does not choose the grass on which it falls" – Zulu Proverb

"If you laugh at your mother-in-law, you'll get dirt in your eye" – Kenyan Proverb

(Symbolically, laughing at in-laws will only cause familial problems. Better to always show respect.)

"If you marry a monkey for his wealth, the money goes, and the monkey remains as is" – Egyptian Proverb.

Chapter 16
Funerals – A Time of Mourning and Communal Solidarity

Families grieving over the loss of a member do not have the services of a funeral home or hearse to help them, as in many Western countries. Often, families must do all the work themselves in attending to the dead, from preparation of the body all the way through the burial. During a time of death, internally held beliefs and values rise to the surface and are displayed in numerous activities incorporated into traditional burial practices. The cultural gap bertween Western visitors and East African hosts becomes very apparent at funerals. How is grief expressed, and is it gender specific? Are there cemeteries? Who handles the deceased? What are the spiritual beliefs surrounding the dead? It would be beneficial and instructive for visitors to be aware of some of the cultural dynamics that appear during funerals and to learn the appropriate behavior for attending should the need arise.

A Baby's Death

It was 8:45 PM, and the room was dark. The small lantern on the wooden table seemed to have all its light absorbed by the dark mud walls and grass roof. The dark faces of the six people in such a poorly lit room appeared to have no features at all. It was probably just as well. This way, I could not see their painful expressions.

About two and a half hours before, I was just sitting down to supper with my family and another family whom we had invited over. Linda had prepared a special meal that took several days to put together, and I was really looking forward to sharing it with friends.

Just as we sat down to eat, someone banged loudly on our gate by the road. Annoyed at the interruption, I got up slowly and walked to the gate, determining in my mind how to get rid of the intruders who were interrupting my delicious meal.

When I opened the gate, Herbert Wakamoli and his wife stood there with shocked expressions on their faces. Herbert explained, in short, stuttering sentences, that they had traveled to Mbale, Uganda, earlier in the day because their child was seriously ill. They had spent the whole day seeking treatment, and now, at 7:00 PM, Herbert asked me for help to return home. He stood there holding his child while his wife looked down at the ground.

I asked him how much money he needed to get a public taxi back out to his village of Toma Butta. He said the last taxis had already left for the night, and none were available. This frustrated me because any other answer now was going to cost more money. I asked how much it would cost for a private hire vehicle. Herbert sat down slowly on the grass, still holding his child, and said that no private hire would agree to take them. I became inwardly angry because it seemed to me that Herbert was trying to get me to agree to drive them home. I was reluctant to do that since it meant missing my special meal and time with my friends. I also didn't understand why any vehicle would refuse to take them. So, I argued with him that surely someone would agree to the right price. I even offered to call a private hire and see if they would help. Herbert was adamant that they would not agree.

I am not sure at what point it was, but during my discussion with Herbert, it dawned on me that his child had not moved at all since their arrival. It struck me also that normally, the wife holds the child. In this case, Herbert held the baby the entire time. Suddenly, the realization hit me hard in the pit of my stomach. Herbert was holding his dead child. The baby had succumbed to sickness during treatment in town. I realized, then, that no taxi or even private hire would allow Herbert and his wife into the vehicle with a dead baby in their arms. They feared the spirits of the dead, and therefore, they always refused to carry bodies to the village. Herbert was right. There were no transportation options available to them except me. He knew that I, as a Christian, did not fear the spirits and would be willing to help. I stopped arguing and, ashamed of my initial insensitivity, expressed my deepest sympathies to Herbert. I told him I would be right back.

Inside the house, my family and guests had already begun to eat. My wife Linda could tell something was wrong. I explained Herbert's situation and said I needed to skip the meal and plan to drive to the village. I called Phillip Shero, my co-worker who worked with Herbert, and Phillip said we could take his truck. James Luchivya, another coworker, also agreed to make the nighttime trip. While we waited for Phillip, I took out two bottles of soda and some bread for Herbert and his wife to share. I knew they had not eaten anything for hours as they watched their child's life slowly slip away. Though they claimed not to have an appetite, they seemed grateful for the cool drinks.

Phillip was recovering from a bout of sickness, so I agreed to drive. Phillip and I sat in the front seat while James, Herbert (still holding the baby), and his wife sat in the back seat. We talked some while driving out, but it was difficult to know how to comfort a family who had lost their only child after years of barrenness. Phillip was also moved by the child's death. Just two months before, he had held the child and prayed for it as Herbert proudly named the child Isaac Phillip (partially after him). The joy of that day seemed far away now.

We stopped briefly at Mayenze, a sister church to Toma Butta, to inform Stephen Namabako and others of the child's death. Stephen dropped what he was doing and climbed into the back of the pickup to go with us. He intended to help with funeral arrangements. We drove the remaining three miles in silence.

I turned the truck off the main road, onto a small feeder road, and finally up a trail as far as we could go toward the house, but the last 100 yards had to be walked in the dark among the banana and coffee trees. As soon as the truck door was opened, Herbert's wife literally fell out of the truck onto the ground and began to wail. This scared me because she had been silent the whole time. Herbert walked silently ahead of us, still holding the baby. As we spread out down the trail, I walked at the rear of our group and shined a big flashlight on the path. Neighbors, understanding the purpose of the wailing, came out of their houses to join us. People startled me as they stepped out of the bananas and coffee trees and started wailing together with Herbert's wife. The lamentations grew in volume and intensity the closer we came to the house. All of Herbert's neighbors were alerted by the wailing, and the news of the baby's death traveled quickly.

We stopped momentarily outside Herbert's house while a lantern was lit and chairs were arranged. Hebert stood silent among the weeping crowd, seemingly unmindful of what was happening around him. When we entered the house, Herbert's mother and father greeted us. A young teenage man took the child from Herbert and stood among us. Herbert went out to begin making funeral arrangements. Stephen Namabako took a reed mat and arranged it on the floor while a woman carried a single mattress into the room and laid it on top of the reed mat. I helped spread a clean sheet over the mattress. The child was gently laid on the mattress in the center of the room by the young man. Stephen arranged the child and his blanket as we sat down on wooden chairs at the head of the mattress only a few feet away and at the farthest point from the door.

Herbert's mother, grandmother to the baby, took the only lantern and fell to her knees beside the baby. She brought the lantern up close to examine the child. She reached out with old, wrinkled hands that looked tough even in the darkness and stroked the child with loving caresses. She massaged the baby's small hands and rubbed the tiny fingers. She touched the baby's legs and feet. She gently rested her hand on the child's chest for a moment as if trying to compel breath back inside. She knelt closer and turned the baby's head toward the light. She looked deeply into the face of the child and examined it closely. With a gentle and experienced touch, she closed the child's eyelids and pushed the mouth closed. Her gentleness and gracefulness in the whole process impressed me as symbolic of the entire country's experience with life and especially death. After closing the baby's mouth, the elderly woman bent down over the child and let her head touch the mattress, where she let flow a stream of tears. At that moment, my heart broke about how I had been frustrated with Hebert for interrupting my supper, and I cried together with the grandmother.

At one point, the grandmother rose up a little and used her shirt tail to wipe her face and nose, and then she bent back down again. After a few minutes, she looked up at us and, with a calm and loving voice, thanked us for our help.

I surveyed the situation and became fearful we would end up spending the entire night at Toma Butta. Normally, overnight vigils are customary when a family member dies. I did not know of any culturally appropriate way to leave those who were grieving, and I feared our departure would be interpreted as uncaring. However, around 10:00 PM, the family suggested we return home to get some sleep. Stephen Namabako agreed to stay the night, and he offered to help with the funeral the next day.

<hr>

It is customary in East Africa for infants to be buried quickly – often within 24 hours. For older people, the family may wait three or four days before conducting a funeral. This allows time to purchase a coffin, dig a grave, and alert the extended family members.

Funerals are a communal event attended by all neighbors who are able. They come to express their sympathy and solidarity with the grieving family. Young men are pressed into digging duties while female family members wash and clothe the deceased. Women neighbors help in preparing food for the family and visitors. Men visitors tend to sit quietly and may talk in whispered tones. Females tend to start ululating as they enter the family compound and will often throw themselves onto the ground before the deceased to show their sympathy to the family for their loss. To an outsider, the wailing may look fake or contrived. Traditionally, it is a powerful demonstration of unity during grief.

A long time ago, graves were dug down, and then a trench would be dug further into the bottom of the grave. Within the trench, the body would be placed. Then sticks and grass were laid across the trench so that dirt would not hit the body directly. Some tribes made a cut into one wall of the grave where the body would be laid. With the introduction of coffins, trenches and cutouts are no longer used. Some coffins have a glass window where family and visitors can see the deceased. An open-casket funeral is rare since embalming is not normally practiced. In more remote areas, I have seen coins laid upon the eyelids of the deceased to keep them from opening and a cloth tied under the chin to keep the mouth closed. Such traditional practices contrast starkly with the technical expertise of our modern, Western funeral services.

By the time I returned home, my visitors had already departed. The meal was removed from the table, and leftovers were placed in the refrigerator. I missed my special supper, but I did not feel like eating. Herbert's loss struck me deeply. My inward selfish heart and my outward benevolent actions convicted me of my hypocrisy. Yet, through this ordeal, I gained a valuable lesson on service and friendship. I also watched one of the most touching examples of a family wrestling with an unexpected death on life's journey. Even in loss, Herbert's family expressed patience, hospitality, and genuine appreciation for all those who came to mourn with them. It was a powerful example of community support. Neither will I soon forget the touching love of a grieving grandmother.

Cultural Insights/Principles

- Death is handled by the family and neighbors and completed on their property. Community graveyards are not normally used.
- The deceased may be laid on a bed or mattress or in the coffin once it arrives. Visitors normally come in to view the body and offer prayers or show their sorrow by crying.
- Gifts of money may be offered to help the family pay for funeral expenses, which often include a coffin, blanket, digging of the grave, sometimes cement for a headstone, and food for those who attend.
- Some relatives may come and stay with the family for several days before going home.
- Neighbors usually help with cooking, serving, and cleaning.
- Often, church leaders from different denominations band together to offer help in conducting funerals.
- In some cultural situations, the grave of a mother-in-law or father-in-law may be covered before a son-in-law or daughter-in-law can pass by. This is a cultural way of expressing respect for a close marital relationship that is guarded by strict sexual taboos.

- Graves are often dug in places of respect within the family compound.

- It is common to find a cement covering or headstone marking the grave.

- Some tribal groups may butcher (sacrifice) a small goat or cow to feed the visitors and to honor the deceased.

- Dirges or funeral songs exist in all East African funeral ceremonies. They are usually sung after the burial and after most guests have gone back to their homes.

- Burial dirges, traditionally, were meant to drive away the death spirit. These songs were sung by dancers who decorated themselves with twigs or other items. However, this practice is decreasing.

- Luo and Luhya tribal communities of old, and probably many other tribes, used professional mourners during funerals. These were only hired when a prominent person in the society died. Their death spirits were considered "heavy" and needed special professional exorcists who came mourning, praising, appeasing, and influencing the spirit of the deceased to be calm and to take their designated place among other honored spirits.

- Modern funerals may use recorded remembrance music. One famous Tanzanian musician called Remi Ongala composed a captivating death song called Kifo Hakina Huruma (Death has no compassion), which can be found on YouTube. All tribal communities have their well-known musicians for dirges.

- Some traditional beliefs hold that the spirit of the deceased may remain around for several days, observing the family, and can affect everyone with blessings or curses.

- Public vehicles, if pressed into service, may charge extravagant prices to carry a dead person.

- Traditionally, in some tribes, the driver of the "hearse" may be given a black chicken, which he must throw out the window on his way home so that no evil spirit will follow him home.

- If a person commits suicide, traditional belief holds that person was forced by evil spirits. Someone may be paid to hit the body numerous times to chase away the evil spirit before taking the deceased home for burial.

- If a person is hit by a vehicle and lying on the side of the road, some tribal traditions hold that people walking up and finding a dead person must tear off leaves from a nearby bush and throw them on the dead person to show the spirit they had nothing to do with that person's death.

- Should tragedy strike and a visitor die in East Africa, it is important to inform their embassy to ask for assistance in embalming and, if needed, for flight arrangements for returning the deceased to their homeland.

- It is important to get a police report and a death certificate from the government to aid in all necessary paperwork back home.

- An embassy often keeps a few coffins that may be utilized in emergency situations, or they may have information on the best place to purchase one.

- Burial options in East Africa are available if the cost of a return air flight is prohibitive.

- Indian cultural practices prefer cremation. This is an option, but potentially complicated.

Proverbs

"Death is like a robe everyone has to wear" – African Proverb

"If you're a good person even after death, your grave is loved" – African Proverb

"Death is blind" – Swahili Proverb

"Death is always news" – African Proverb

Chapter 17
Singing Loudly and Energetically: Which Song, Verse, and Language?

Whether it be a church service, a school choir competition, or a public holiday celebration, it becomes apparent to Western visitors that East African singing is stylistically different than other regions of the world. Whether dressed in modern clothes or in colorful traditional dress, cultural values shine through in singing styles, lyrics, dancing, and the whole-body experience of music and song. How does singing shed light on any culture? How can singing help us understand East African culture more deeply? How can we look beyond the differences and learn to appreciate the singing skills in a wide variety of languages and styles?

When East Africans Sing

When I moved to East Africa, I struggled with public gatherings where singing was included. The language barrier, exuberant clapping, dancing, jumping, and ululations were so unfamiliar to me that I had difficulty participating. For the visitor, it is easy to politely clap and sway a little and be only superficially engaged in the social event happening all around. Some visitors concentrate on the activities but not on the songs or their meanings. In effect, visitors lose a significant opportunity to experience and understand the powerful window of song in East African culture. Let me first share some obstacles that I initially encountered before I delve into the deeper cultural insights embedded within the lively East African traditions of singing.

Language – The most obvious difference is language, but it is more than that. Most visitors sing songs almost exclusively in a single language. Ugandans sing in more than one language. In fact, it is a common experience in a church service to hear songs sung in FOUR different languages. They will sing in English, Swahili, and Luganda, and if we are in a remote area, they will slip into their local tribal tongue. I struggle to keep up with the first two languages. Ugandans seem to float back and forth effortlessly through multiple languages. A choir will stand and present two songs - in two different languages. A song leader may continue the same song but switch to another language for a few verses. The crowd follows the song leader's changes without missing a beat. Coming from a mono-linguistic background, I marvel at the smooth transitions between languages while singing. East Africans, who are comprised of more than 300 different tribes spread across five countries, have learned not only to navigate but to thrive in their multi-lingual existence. They are accustomed to having one or more languages spoken at home, another in the market, many others by fellow citizens, and still another by the government and international tourists. What is a reality of home to them is disconcerting to most visitors who must learn to embrace such linguistic diversity and marvel at its beauty, complexity, and commonality.

Songbooks or Sheet Music – Another difference I noticed quickly is that choirs never use songbooks, sheet music, or overhead projections of lyrics. Traditionally, many people were non-literate. What good is a songbook to someone who never learned to read? Pair non-literacy with poverty, and it results in a strong tradition of learning culture, social skills, life lessons, local history, and other important communal guides orally through song and storytelling. Such songs are learned by practice and repetition. When the audience is mostly non-literate or barely literate, public gatherings consist of significant portions of singing. The more literate the audience becomes, the less singing is used to teach, guide, and shape.

On another note, if someone could print and sell songbooks, who would be able to purchase them? Which language would be used for the songbook? Or how many languages would one have to type, edit, and include to make a songbook truly functional? Songbooks also, surprisingly, become a hindrance to the traditional practices of clapping and dancing while singing.

Antiphonal Singing – Whether because of a lack of songbooks or despite them, East Africans sing antiphonally. The leader may sing a phrase that is either repeated or answered by the audience. This enables the song leader to add as many verses as he wants, switch languages, and even move into the next song without disruption. The audience responds to the leader's direction and glides through each transition without difficulty. The effect is marvelous. It is like watching a well-rehearsed dance couple weave around the dance floor - one leading, the other following. The result is a continuous session of songs that is uninterrupted by the calling out of numbers, the sound of pages turning, and the giving of instructions on which verses to sing.

Voice – One difference I have difficulty training my ears to accept is voice quality. I was taught in the choir to produce a singing voice from the abdomen. The choir director told us all to sit up straight and use our diaphragm. But East Africans develop and use a nasal or head voice. In fact, East African singers covet this loud head voice that carries over other voices and leads the group. Such a voice, traditionally without microphones or speakers, makes it easier for others to follow in antiphonal singing. While I can appreciate the energy and loudness of such singing (I believe 10 East Africans can outsing 100 Americans), I still find the diaphragm-controlled voice more pleasing to my ears. That is probably because of my cultural upbringing. I am sure East Africans find our Western voices odd to their ears. The visitor must realize that just as musical styles and voices have been nurtured and refined over generations by the Arabic, Indian, and Far Eastern peoples, the same is true of East Africa. Initially, their singing may sound discordant and unpleasing to Western ears, but with an effort to attune one's mind to be receptive to new voices, intonations, accents, rhythms, and styles, a visitor can grow in appreciation and enjoyment of East African music. Uninitiated Westerners may consider East African singing to be "incorrect" because it is different from their own culturally cultivated styles, but visitors must realize East African music and vocals have been developed over generations and have their own level of cultural functionality and sophistication just like European Opera, Japanese Kabuki, or the Hindustani music of India.

Women – For East Africans, women tend to be the traditional song leaders. It is common for women's groups to dress up in beautiful, colorful dresses for holidays and community celebrations and then to ululate, sing, and dance for the adoring crowd. Many school choirs are led by strong women voices who introduce the songs and lead the group through the verses. Even in churches, women may be called on to lead a chorus or song and often arrange special songs and dances for visitors. This is not to say that men do not lead songs. They do, but women seem to have a much more prominent role in public traditional singing than men.

Clapping – About 90% of the songs I hear are accompanied by clapping. With singing lasting 20-30 minutes, my hands become red and sore. But East Africans seem impervious to such ailments. Some of the loudest clappers I have ever heard are in East Africa, and I am not talking about straight clapping. Some clap double-time or in the off-beat. Others emphasize every other beat. Some clap once in two beats. The result is a neatly orchestrated symphony of rhythm. I remember once standing by a man who seemed to be clapping completely off the rhythm. I was shocked by this and thought that I had finally discovered the first East African man without rhythm. Then, as I listened more closely, I realized he was clapping in triplets. I was so awed by this that I stopped singing just to listen to him. I believe such rhythm reflects traditional festivities and practices. Circumcision ceremonies among the Bagisu of Eastern Uganda, for example, are rumored to include as many as eight different drummers, all beating a different rhythm, to produce a complex, tantalizing, sensual beat for their dances and songs.

Movement – East Africans cannot sing without moving. For an East African, singing IS moving. The whole body is used as an instrument to express the song. Some singers sway back and forth with their heads tilted back. Others take short steps sideways, back and forth, in a shuffling rhythm to the song. Some move only the heels of their feet, leaving their toes to stay in basically the same position. A few take steps slightly forward and back. Many spring up and down as they clap. A few of the energetic almost run in place. The result of this is a good physical workout for everyone singing - a kind of public aerobics session. This means very few songs are sung sitting down. Nearly all are sung standing up. In addition to the feet, some singers include gestures that accompany the words of the song. This is most often seen in school choirs, where nearly every song is accompanied by choreography.

Lest a visitor feel tempted to ridicule this excess of movement, let us remember that body language is a form of communication. Anthropologists have noted that non-literates communicate in more ways than the current three Western nations – seeing, hearing, and writing. East Africans incorporate spatial, tactile, olfactory, and kinetic, among several others. Movement is a fundamental form of communication, and East Africans are good at reading body language. They can tell a visitor from a long-term resident simply by the way they walk. They can tell the loud argument on the street is a fight or friendly banter by the way the participants move. Singing without moving their bodies is not fully communicating in song. East Africans must engage the whole body when they sing. It would be good if singers sweat a little (olfactory) while singing, and it's not bad to bump into each other either (spatial).

Harmony – Harmony may not have been utilized fully in traditional antiphonal singing, though there is room to argue for traditional chords of harmony. With the introduction of Western Christianity, harmony became more prominent in worship. British education systems introduced choral music in the school curriculum and developed local, regional, and country-wide competitions. Today, most East Africans still sing the melody, both in the lead and antiphonal parts. Harmony is most common in school or church choirs, which tend to sing four-part harmony, though tenor is usually the least present. Occasionally, I have observed some songs among the Kalenjin tend not to end on the tonic (first note of an eight-note scale). This is disconcerting to me because it makes me feel as though the song has not ended properly. They do not seem to think so. Listening to the traditional singing of the Kupsabiny of Eastern Uganda has made me wonder if they use a slightly different musical scale. While some of their songs seem "off" to me, the performance meets the approval of knowing local audiences. It is possible musicologists would identify a different musical scale or that Kalenjin uses quarter tones instead of half tones as in Western music.

Instruments – Consider also that traditional instruments consist mostly of drums (Ngoma), rattles (Njingiri), bells, and whistles, which generally do not set a "key" for the melody of each song. Drums essentially provide a rhythm. A lyre/harp-type instrument is used by the Luhya (called Litungu), Kisii (Obokano), Kalenjin (Bugandit), and Luo (Bul) tribes of Western Kenya. Tribes who keep cattle often fashion a wind instrument from the horns of their stock. The Teso of North Central Uganda may be the most musical of all, with its numerous drums, finger pianos, and lyres.

When piano keyboards were introduced in the 20th century, East African singers struggled to hear and adapt to the key of the piano. Later, pianists learned to alter the keys of their electric pianos to fit the choir. Over the last 40 years, choirs have become very refined in synchronizing their singing with "keyed" instruments or recorded music.

Why Is Music Important?

My personal observations about East Africans singing are rudimentary, but unfortunately, it may still be more observant than the average visitor. Even the long-term visitor may hear East African music and not give it much thought or attention because it is so different than music from home. It may sound odd, dissonant, or just attract attention because it is novel. However, all visitors will miss an important key to understanding East African culture.

Scholars define culture in many ways, but one of the simplest is "the learned and shared views, values, and behaviors of a specific people group." One may ask, "How are these values learned or shared?" Of the ethnic pillars of language, art, music, and religion, music is a significantly popular way of reflecting and shaping culture. A culture's views and values are almost always represented in the lyrics and styles of their music. For example, if a culture values the acquisition of wealth, then music will glorify such endeavors through its imagery in verse.

Pre-literate cultures used music to tell their stories, express emotions, shape identity, teach values, and celebrate victories or special occasions. Music formed the historic records of pre-literate cultural groups. Music expresses cultural pride and swells patriotism through national anthems. Music moves people emotionally. It builds bonds of unity and appreciation better than almost any other cultural activity.

While music can capture cultural events and values like a time capsule, it can also be rebellious in that songs may push boundaries of expression and free speech beyond cultural norms. Music may highlight cultural views and values that are overlooked or not being discussed. Thus, musical trends and content provide an insightful view into current cultural dialogue, values, social issues, and emotions of a particular people group.

If music is inextricably linked with the cultural context in which it is produced, consumed, and taught, then anyone who wishes to understand East Africa more deeply must engage in its music. Learning songs helps one connect and identify with local friends and associates. Music can also be utilized to express oneself more powerfully and emotionally than speeches or classroom instruction alone. Whether to entertain or to play a crucial role in shaping and reflecting culture, music cannot be separated from the environment in which it exists. The visitor to East Africa who gains a greater appreciation for, observes how all the senses are incorporated, and understands the multiple functions that music serves culturally will be able to participate more emotionally and bond more deeply than those who too quickly dismiss East African singing and music as a mere novelty.

Cultural Insights/Principles

- Ask about local instruments and singing
- If possible, listen to and record local singing

- When drummers perform, watch to see if they use different beats
- Notice who leads the singing for choirs, holiday celebrations, and church services
- During circumcision years (even years), and if you are invited to this private ceremony generally closed to outsiders, ask for an honest interpretation of the lyrics. You might discover the most erotic verses you have ever heard.
- With greater connectivity via the Internet, satellite TV, and radio, West African, South African, Western, and even Indian and Arabic music and lyrics can be found, especially in tourist venues.
- Purchase some East African music.
- Discover famous musical artists from East Africa and search for their music.
- Being able to recognize or sing local songs together with your hosts is a powerful way to bond and show respect.
- A group traveling to East Africa may consider researching a song they can learn to sing to their hosts.

Proverbs

"Music speaks louder than words" – African Proverb
"The best music and dance always come from home" – African Proverb
"Even without drumbeats, banana leaves dance" – African Proverb
"A child brought up where there is always singing cannot fail to sing" – African Proverb
"When the music changes, so does the dance" – Nigerian Proverb
"The song that has no leader goes wrong" – Kenyan Proverb
"Even the sharpest ear cannot hear an ant singing" – Sudanese Proverb

"If you can walk, you can dance. If you can talk, you can sing" –
Zimbabwean Proverb
"The mosquito is small — but when he sings, your ears are full of
him" – African Proverb

Chapter 18
The Aged and What We Do With Them

During a village visit, an old widow stood up and asked me for financial help in front of the entire audience. They all looked at me to see how I would answer her. Somehow, I knew this was a test, but I did not know the best way to respond. She sought money for food, but I could not be sure she would use the money judiciously, so I hit upon an idea. Since our meeting had ended, I took her by the hand and led her across the road to a small store. Many in the meeting followed us, curious about what I had in mind. At the store counter, I got the owner's attention, pulled out 300 shillings (at the time worth about $10 dollars), and told the widow to select any goods in the store up to that amount. The old woman clapped her hands, started jumping up and down, and pointed to sugar, tea leaves, salt, margarine, matches, and some kerosene for her lamp. The crowd behind us started laughing and clapping with her. She hugged me several times and blessed me. For months after that, whenever I taught in a village near her, she would walk the distance to see me and thank me again publicly.

A few years ago, government statistics noted that 50% of Uganda's population was under the age of 17. This reflected a staggering population growth rate, but it also reflected a poignant fact about the absence of the aged. Visitors may ask, "Where are the elderly in East Africa?" What are the cultural guidelines for interaction with and care for the aged? While East African social interaction shows great respect for older members of the community, how does that honor extend to the finances, family, and health issues of older people? This topic is especially difficult for me because when I speak in public gatherings, I mention former leaders of East Africa that my younger audience do not know, and they are amazed that I knew them.

Comparing the Aged in East Africa and America

Joyce is a tall Ugandan woman standing almost 6 feet in height. Her long, thin fingers reflect her general appearance. She is extremely slender, though Joyce does not look undernourished. In fact, her bright eyes, broad smile, and clear complexion exude energy and enthusiasm for life. Her arms and legs are long and spindly. Even her traditional dress (called a gomesi), with seven yards of flowing material, cannot hide her gaunt features. The colorful dress seems to hang on her narrow shoulders and fall to her ankles without touching much else.

Joyce is an attractive, well-dressed woman who lives on a half-acre farm that she bought herself. She makes a meager living, selling vegetables from her garden and running a small hair salon. Joyce only reached the fifth grade before money for school fees was diverted to other family needs. She speaks timidly in broken English, but she has a confident, poised voice when speaking Luganda. At 15, Joyce married and two years later had her first of three children. Joyce's husband eventually left her and moved to Masaka, Uganda, some 40 miles north. He took the children with him (a right he has since he paid the traditional bride price), and eventually, he married again.

With no more education than fifth grade, no theological training, and little Christian experience, Joyce became the pastor of Simba Church... and it grew. I doubt people were attracted to deep theological lessons each Sunday. Rather, I believe people were drawn to Joyce's humble but stately posture and her unassuming love that permeates her every mannerism. She speaks honestly and openly. She does not try to dominate. She gathers advice and leads by consensus. Her refreshing leadership is appealing to many in the area. While a dozen men attend Simba Church these days and an assistant pastor leads some ministries, Joyce still has a prominent role in the group. Joyce is one of those people who ages gracefully and increases in wisdom.

Joyce stands out because she is the exception to the rule for the elderly in East Africa. Her financial situation has remained meager but stable, and her social influence has increased with age rather than decreased.

Several years ago, Linda and I escorted a Kenyan couple, James and Noeli Luchivya, to America for a 17-day visit. It was fun to watch their almost childlike excitement in experiencing new things like an escalator, all-you-can-eat restaurants, clear roads without potholes, almost no pedestrians, Texas hospitality, shopping malls, Omni theaters, and surprisingly for us, the true wealth of the average American compared to global economics. What impressed James and Noeli the most was the elderly of America. To better understand their surprise, some background is needed.

The Luchivyas know retirement in Kenya is forced upon government and educational employees at the tender age of 55. Many older citizens, who have lived so close to the poverty level all their lives, are unable to save anything for their later years. They literally enter retirement with no savings and only a few possessions that would not even fill an American living room. To make matters more difficult, the sons of older Kenyan parents often press for their inheritance (dividing up the farm) as early as possible, leaving older men and women with meager financial, familial, and societal powers. In fact, once most older Kenyan citizens reach their sixties, their children and grandchildren begin caring for them. Such pressures to divide land and distribute wealth are not a lack of respect for the elderly. Rather, it is the culturally pragmatic utilization of family wealth for the benefit of the entire family. Such practices are more common in poverty-stricken countries. The parents want to bless their children, and the children will, in turn, provide care. Never will the elderly be sent away from the family.

Few old people in Kenya make it to their seventies or eighties. Medical issues of old parents become a "family" decision because there are generally no viable health insurance options, and financial responsibility for paying doctors and hospital bills falls upon the extended family. On one occasion, I observed a father passionately argue against his scheduled throat surgery for cancer because he did not want to impoverish his extended family for a risky procedure. The family argued for the surgery and expressed willingness to give up their wealth because of their love for their father. He argued that his individual suffering should not become the entire family's suffering. Poverty causes many difficult decisions to be made in caring for the elderly.

One of the first observations James and Noeli made about older Americans was that they lived alone in their own homes. Of course, American extended families are not as cohesive as Kenyans', but most older people in America still tend to have family living close by, just seldom next door or on the same compound. Independent living was a major difference the Luchivyas observed between Kenyan and American older citizens.

A second observation was the apparent mobility of older Americans. James and Noeli marveled how older people drove their own cars, boarded airplanes, and took long trips without anyone's help. In Kenya, it is rare to see older people driving a vehicle. Most public service vehicles, buses, and trucks are driven by young men. Only the wealthiest families have cars for older people. Almost no older people in the village drive. In America, everywhere James and

Noeli went, they saw white-headed people driving new cars and engaged in the daily errands of life.

A third observation was the financial independence of older Americans. James remarked several times that older people were shopping in stores, wearing the latest fashions, eating in restaurants, carrying large shopping bags, taking grandchildren to the movies, and doing numerous activities that, to them, reflected much more personal wealth than was possessed by their Kenyan counterparts.

Their fourth observation struck me as a larger gap than the previous ones. James and Noeli noticed that many older people in America were actively engaged on the Internet. Many American senior citizens worked on computers, followed family on Facebook, wrote emails, or shared birthday parties and other family events through Skype, Facetime, Zoom, or some other app. Many older people carried smartphones, took digital pictures, recorded movies on their cable TVs, and seemed to be at ease around many technical gadgets that older Kenyan citizens would not even know how to operate. James and Noeli thought older Americans, generally, were much more interested in continuing to learn and engage in modern technology than older Kenyans.

However, the most significant observation of the Luchivyas had to do with the amount of societal power retained by American seniors. Older Americans were still in charge of large corporations, ran for President of the United States or some other political office, continued to work, led churches, helped their children, sought another job after retirement, or even went back to school. Generally, America's senior citizens participated actively in every part of the social, political, economic, and spiritual life of America. Instead of being financially or physically sidelined, older Americans were very much the leaders of American society. This was markedly different from their Kenyan experience. Older citizens, while honored and acknowledged publicly with verbal terms of respect, generally struggle with health and financial issues that limit their engagement in social activities. The meager resources of most elderly in Kenya do not allow them to travel or financially help their children. Poverty reduces the elderly to being dependent upon their children. James and Noeli were stunned by the huge differences between the Kenyan and the American elderly.

I do not suggest there are no old people in America who must depend upon their children for help. There are very many. Nor am I saying there are no independent, active older citizens in Kenya. They also exist, but the difference in percentages is so great that it was a staggering reality for my friends.

As I reflected on these observations, comparing differences between Kenyan and American senior citizens made by my Kenyan friends on their visit to America, I was deeply shaken by it. Over the last 40 years, East Africans have made tremendous strides in economic, educational, and medical development, as well as business and employment opportunities. All of these have brought overall improvements for East Africans. Yet, the cultural, economic, and societal constructs still greatly limit the aged of East Africa, who may not even know their real age because they were not born in a hospital nor ever obtained a birth certificate.

The interaction of the young with the aged in East Africa is a complex social function. Publicly, there is great respect and honor shown to the aged regardless of wealth, education or physical abilities, and any visitor would be wise to identify and spend time greeting and acknowledging the elderly to gain their respect and support. If the elderly are rich and display good character and wisdom, their voice may be more influential than the community leaders, who, out of deference, may take cues from their wealthy elders. In such circumstances, the real power brokers for a business deal, community project, or church outreach may be contingent upon the approval and support of the older citizens who sit quietly in the audience. It would be wise for any visiting businessman or project leader to not overlook the elderly but discern as quickly as possible who the influential leaders are and to seek their counsel.

At the same time, even the poorest and weakest older people in a community should be respected and not overlooked. The visitor should not evaluate a person's importance by their clothing, posture, participation, ability to speak English, or their place among the crowd. While the aged may be financially dependent upon care from their children, they still have a voice in social and community affairs. Many projects have been undermined by elders who were marginalized by outsiders who were not sensitive to the cultural dynamics of the aged in East Africa. I cannot count the number of times visitors to East Africa have been called to the police station to answer for cultural mistakes made against the aged.

The visitor who wants to succeed in East Africa must be attentive to the aged. Greet them extensively. Acknowledge their presence in meetings. Seek their counsel in front of others. Listen to their stories and proverbs. Garner their support. Occasionally and judiciously, with the advice of others, help the aged with small gifts of appreciation. Doing this will increase your status and respect among the young and the old, rich and poor, strong and weak, government officials and common citizens. In the communal societies of East Africa, paying attention to the aged is always an excellent basic social courtesy as well as a wise professional strategy.

Cultural Insights/Principles

• Old parents are respected AND feared because traditionally, East Africans believe parents have the power to bless and curse their children and grandchildren.

• Often, when housework becomes too hard for the parents, a female grandchild is selected and sent to live with and care for her grandparents.

• If grandparents live within a family compound among several of their children, they may often move from house to house for their meals.

• If children work far from their parents, it is important for children to visit regularly and to carry a gift of food, money, or something small when they go. It is a way of showing respect.

• It is wise not to overlook the aged in any meeting, even if they do not lead or speak a lot. Show them respect by greeting them elaborately and including them in your public speaking.

• Traditionally, the aged told stories and taught the younger generations their history and important cultural points.

Proverbs

"A village without the elderly is like a well without water" – African Proverb.

"When an old man dies, a library burns to the ground" – African Proverb

"Those who respect the elderly pave their own road toward success" – African Proverb

"The strength of the elderly is in their ears and on their lips" – African Proverb

"The mouth of an elderly man is without teeth, but never without words of wisdom" – African Proverb

"The youth can walk faster, but the elder knows the road" – African Proverb

Chapter 19
Gender Roles – He Does, She Does, We All Do!

I watched the male tailor measure a rather large Ugandan woman for a new gomesi – the culturally colorful traditional dress that often contains up to seven yards of material. For years, tailoring was a man's world, and few women learned the craft, though that is changing now. The woman had selected the material she wanted; now, the tailor needed specific measurements to shape the dress. With his tape measure in hand, the smallish gentleman expertly whipped the tape around the large thighs of the woman and pulled it tight. His hand was pressed with the tape on her buttocks. He quickly moved around to the front and measured her belly before pushing the tape up under her very large bosom. Each measurement was written down before going to the next place. Then, without hesitation, the man threw his tape around her bosom in front and pulled tight enough to get an accurate measure. The woman stood still and seemed nonplussed by the personal touches of the tailor. She evidently had purchased such dresses before. The tailor's measuring tape flew around her neck, then from neck to coccyx, and tightly around each upper arm. I felt awkward watching the tailor's hands-on exercise for measuring. The woman was used to this procedure, for there were no female tailors as an option. It was just the way things worked. It had always been that way.

Visitors to East Africa are often impressed by the hospitality and gentle, open nature of their hosts. They do not always see the underlying gender roles and responsibilities that govern normal behavior. Gender roles culturally shape personal identity within the context of community values and expectations. Disregarding cultural gender roles may result in a loss of respect or cause ostracism and public criticism. Failure to conform can also affect all social interaction, employment, and even financial opportunities. Visitors do not always realize that they bring with them certain expectations and values that may be very different from their East African counterparts. What are the traditional gender roles and responsibilities of East Africa? How do these affect our interaction? How can the visitor avoid mistakes in pushing for actions and responses that are against local gender roles?

The Jobs of Men and Women

All cultures reflect characteristics that facilitate the distribution of duties according to gender. These "gender roles" are defined as socially shared expectations of normal behavior for men and women, especially in the division of labor and personal and communal responsibilities. Traditionally, within East Africa, women, more than men, occupied roles that involved domestic activities and communal behavior such as nurturing children, gathering firewood and water, food preparation, and providing service to others both within the family and community. Men generally occupied roles that involved economically productive activities such as hunting, tending livestock, farming, and employment outside the home. Men also tended to manage social, political, and economic organizations. Gender roles in East Africa tended to be pragmatically defined based on gender characteristics and the demands of the surrounding living conditions.

Gender roles have always been a dynamic that changes because of economic, medical, and educational development, technological advances, and international influence as the world grows more interconnected. Traditional gender roles, while very similar across tribal lines, vary somewhat between the numerous tribal cultures of

East Africa. This makes a singular, comprehensive list of gender roles in East Africa impossible.

Still, visitors to East Africa would do well to engage themselves in the learning and understanding of gender roles and normative behavior of individuals with whom they interact. Without realizing it, visitors may collide unexpectedly with cultural expectations on the division of labor and responsibilities. Or they may request action outside the normative behaviors of a male or female friend or co-worker.

Recognizing that some unstated gender roles and expectations exist, I spent time during my stay in East Africa interviewing groups of men and women from various tribes to compile a common list of gender roles and expectations. This list is illustrative and not comprehensive. However, it may be used as a starting point for understanding and digging deeper into gender roles. This will enable visitors to build an understanding of how to engage East African friends and co-workers for maximum success.

Since the 1960s, Western cultures have aggressively sought to break down the distinctive categorizations of gender roles and expectations between men and women. The rationale for this effort was based upon the declared liberation of women. Although the Western world has undergone cultural upheaval adjusting gender roles, East African rural culture still maintains a delineated structure of gender roles with clear divisions between men's and women's roles. This does not mean international influence has not had its impact on music, education, social media, movies, female advancement, and social justice, to name a few. Uganda has already celebrated its first female Vice President, as well as many female members of Parliament in East Africa. There are also new emphases throughout East Africa on women's rights, family planning, women's education, Aids awareness, and an ever-expanding opportunity for business and social enterprises open to women. However, village life has been less affected by these international movements and continues to hold to a more traditional structure for gender roles.

One village visit to Magale, Uganda, illustrates my general experience in gathering data on gender roles. In Magale, I interviewed a group of men and women from different tribal backgrounds coming from both Kenya and Uganda. To my surprise, both genders enthusiastically gave examples of gender roles. I compiled a short list of some of those separate responsibilities. It was interesting to me to observe the strong convictions held about the division of labor for men and women. Nearly everywhere I gathered information for this study, I found both men and women believed gender roles were natural, obvious, expected, and thought to be held in a similar fashion by other cultures as well. They often responded, "It is just the way it is. Isn't it this way in your country?" The following examples are loosely grouped by category.

House Construction

This group of men and women adamantly claimed men were responsible for building the house. Some cultures even prepare young men for this responsibility by demanding they build their own small house within their father's compound once they reach puberty and can no longer stay in the same house as their mother or sisters. Thus, when a young man marries and needs to build his own house, he already has some experience. Construction work for the man includes selecting the ideal site and orientation of the house, its size, and the floor plan of the structure. The man measures the walls, digs the holes, cuts the poles, muds the walls, builds the rafters, and roofs his home with either grass, papyrus reeds or iron sheets. If he has enough money, he will use clay tiles. The man will also construct and install all the windows and doors. One slight variation appeared in the discussion of house construction. Abigail, from the Kabras tribe of Western Kenya, said women were responsible for mudding the house. Kabras women gather their sisters and female relatives, and together, they dig the ground, carry water, make mud, and then apply it to the walls. This is a Kabras woman's cultural way of claiming the house as hers. In fact, Abigail said women are so resolute about this responsibility that if they don't mud the house, they will refuse to live in it.

House Compound

Maina said the man is responsible for digging a hole for the latrine and building a small structure for it. Gideon added the man also plants a hedge for a fence and boundary delineations (and keeps it trimmed). The man also selects the kinds of trees, fruit or shade, and plants them within his compound. He is also responsible for keeping the grass cut away from the house (this is to prevent fires and to reduce rodent infestation). Grace spoke up and said, "Women put the final decorative touches on the house," to which everyone nodded their heads in affirmation. Grace gave additional information about decorations when I looked puzzled. She said, "Women bring different colors of mud (black, red or gray) to decorate the house with lines, pictures, symbols, etc." Maina spoke up again, saying women are responsible for coating the dirt floor with cow manure. (Cow manure is used because it hardens and soaks up liquid. Without a manure coating, the dirt floor becomes dusty and muddy with a spill. Thus, the cow manure reduces dust and makes it easier to sweep.) Maina noted women also smear the latrine floors with cow manure - a job usually done by hand. Women also sweep the compound and keep it clean.

Farming and Gardens

Jacob added to our conversation, noting that men take responsibility for plowing (mostly by tractor in Kenya and by hand or oxen in Uganda) as well as purchasing seed and fertilizer. Among the Bagisu of Eastern Uganda (where Jacob is from), the man takes responsibility for planting the banana grove. This staple food of cooking bananas (Plantain bananas) may require a sizeable area of the farm. He will also plant sweet bananas for sale. Jacob continued, "Smaller garden plots, where digging is done with a hoe, may be shared by the man and woman." He looked at the women for agreement. They shook their heads yes. The women traditionally share in the digging of a vegetable garden and may take the lead in sowing seed for tomatoes, beans, potatoes, greens, onions, cassava, sweet potatoes, cabbage, and occasionally peppers and lemon grass (for flavoring tea). "Men," Abigail interjected, "plant and care for pineapples, avocados, passion fruit, peanuts (called ground nuts in East Africa), coffee and tea, all of which are regarded as income-generating crops." Women dig, plant, and weed their vegetable gardens without help from the men.

Household Chores and Cooking Food

Women carry the larger burden with the daily chores around the house. They are responsible for retrieving water (perhaps about 10-15 gallons a day) from a local source (usually a spring, stream, or well). If they have children large enough to carry water, the young boys or girls can be sent for water. Women also gather all the firewood for cooking. Women and young girls do all the cooking, washing, and serving.

Robert, a Kenyan, argued that he couldn't help his wife withdraw water. He said when his wife was sick one time, he went down to the stream to get water. By the third day of drawing water, the other women at the stream started complaining that he was trying to find another wife. His wife and other women laughed at this. Abigail raised a hand and said, "Among the Kabras people, it is considered a shame for the man to grind his maize meal or to carry his own water. If his wife is sick or on a journey, he will solicit the help of a sister or niece."

I spoke up in this lively conversation and told a story about getting water. In the Masai area of Kenya, a missionary friend noticed the women's plight of having to walk a long distance for water. To help, and without consulting the women, he bought a donkey and made a small cart to carry all the water containers to and from the village in one trip. Rather than being joyful, the women refused to use the missionary's donkey cart. He later discovered women looked forward to being away from the house for a while and enjoyed the conversations with other women as they walked. It was their only time for social life, which they wanted to protect. The missionary eventually sold the donkey and cart and left the women to carry their water. The women in our group laughed (Grace was the loudest) and said it was true. Women enjoy a break from household duties and enjoy talking with other women.

Sarah described her cooking responsibilities. She said, "Meals are prepared over an open fire with a pot sitting upon three huge stones positioned around the fire. Meals are boiled over the fire and consist mostly of a large staple food of maize meal, millet meal, rice, or plantain bananas." To accompany this main dish, Sarah noted women gather from the garden some greens, potatoes, or some other vegetables and cook them in a separate pot. I asked whether there were traditional ovens. Bakeries are in most large towns, and East Africans love bread. Abigail and Sarah both said there were no traditional ovens for baking bread or cakes. Grace added, "For generations, women ground the maize or millet meal on a stone or inside a hollowed-out log." Jacob interrupted Grace to say that with the introduction of grinding mills, men took over the job of carrying the maize on bicycles to the mills for grinding and paying for it. However, if the men do not go, they will give just the exact amount of money necessary for grinding to the wife.

Maina, with a serious tone in his voice, said, "Even though the woman cooks, she must ask her husband for permission to slaughter a chicken. Animals such as chickens, goats, ducks, pigs, and cattle are considered family property/wealth, and there must be agreement on the slaughtering of one. All the men and women agreed with Maina. Sarah said, "Bugwere women of Eastern Uganda traditionally do not eat chicken, eggs, or fish. They were taught such food was for men only and not women." I was shocked and asked that if some Bugwere women came to a public meeting in Mbale, Uganda and were offered chicken today, what would they do? Sarah said, "Even when given the chance today to eat chicken or fish, Bugwere women will refuse. They prefer beef." Then Sarah paused for a moment, looked at her husband and continued, "So, if the man wants to bring home some special food for his Bugwere wife, he will stop at the butchery and purchase a half kilo of beef." Then Sarah and the other women started laughing while exchanging some knowing glances.

Before I moved on to another topic, Abigail added that women wash all the clothes outside in a plastic basin and hang them on a line or over a bush for drying. If something needs to be ironed, then a large, heavy metal iron with a compartment inside for hot coals is used. Since most houses don't have electricity, a coal iron seems like a very practical option.

Business Opportunities

Emma spoke up for the first time, saying, "For most tribes, the butcher has traditionally been a man. This is because being a butcher has to do with carrying and cutting heavy pieces of cattle." When I asked if there were women butchers, everyone laughed. Then, Maina said thoughtfully and, looking down as though there was some shame in it, "I saw a female butcher in Nairobi once." The rest of the group was surprised by this revelation. They sat around in silence for a moment and thought about it.

Traditionally, a man handles all the money. He will make all the purchases for his house. Seldom does a wife know how much money the husband has. It is a closely guarded secret. If the wife needs food for the home, such as sugar, flour, cooking oil, salt, spices, etc., she informs her husband. Most of the time, he will go to the store and buy it. Or he may give her the exact amount for the items she wants.

Clothing

Robert spoke again, "If clothes need to be purchased, the man goes to the store. He will buy all his own clothes and his wife's." I interrupted him and asked how a man could buy clothes for his wife. (I was showing my gender role expectation here.) Robert said nonchalantly, "He will know her sizes, and he will purchase the dresses, shoes, undergarments, and belts without her input." If he wants to have a dress made for his wife instead of a store-bought dress, he will instruct her to find a tailor – who is a man. Female seamstresses are still rare, though they are growing in number. When I mentioned that my wife buys all our clothes, all the men laughed… a lot. When I told them my wife has equal access to all money, both the men and women marveled at that. At first, the women, especially, didn't believe it. When I insisted, they dismissed me as being a Mzungu (white man), whom they all knew had very strange customs.

A few years ago, Patrick Chebet, a Kupsabiny from Eastern Uganda, visited us in America. While there, he sought to purchase a new dress for his wife before returning. A friend took Patrick to the shopping mall and found the women's department. Patrick found a dress he thought would be perfect for his wife. So, knowing his wife's size, he began to put it on right in the middle of the store. Our friend panicked and quickly informed him it was not customary for men to try on women's clothing. Patrick paused, thought that was strange, and struggled with the American customs to purchase a dress for his wife. He had to "guess" whether it was the right size or not.

Children

Grace spoke up about women taking care of the children. Grace said, "Women will bathe them, feed them, clothe them, and tend to them during sickness. This constant care is one reason a child will often learn the mother's language first if the couple comes from different tribal groups. This is also the foundation for a proverb spoken often in East Africa, which says, "When you teach a man, you have taught only one. If you teach a woman, you teach a whole family." I was surprised that even the men agreed to this proverb. Grace said, "If there are older girls in the family, they may become guardians for the infants and toddlers. Jacob interjected, "At school age, the man will pay school fees and purchase the necessary school items."

Children may be a major factor in public seating as well. In churches or public meetings, men sit on wooden chairs or stools, while women lay out reed mats or cloth to sit on the ground or floor.

The reason women don't sit on chairs is more practical than a Western interpretation of submission. It is simply easier for women with infants to sit on the ground so that children can play around them or sleep next to them. Older women without infants find a bench or chair to sit on.

If a child needs to go to the clinic, the woman will go (perhaps with enough money to purchase medicine). If hospitalization is required, the husband becomes involved.

Jacob spoke up and said, "If the family owns larger animals, the man is responsible for their upkeep. He will watch after the cattle and lead them to places for grazing and watering." Eventually, he will give that job over to his son once he becomes old enough (12-14 years old). Goats, chickens, sheep, and pigs are all considered financial assets and part of the man's job. Grace spoke up with a point, "If there is only one goat, the woman may be the one looking after it." The men agreed with that. Robert said, "Among the Bugwere, men do the milking. They consider it shameful for a woman to milk a cow. If a man knows a woman has milked the cow, he will refuse to drink the milk."

Jacob added, "At harvest time, the man is responsible for gathering in the produce - though harvesting is shared for many crops. The man will decide how much he needs to keep and how much he needs to sell, though these days nearly everything is sold to avoid theft." Maina said, "Traditionally, the man planned and built granaries necessary to store his surplus. However, these have almost vanished in the last 30 years." The whole group thought about that for a moment, with some shaking their heads, bemoaning the decay of society to the point that theft from one's neighbor is now an all-too-common occurrence.

Transportation

I asked about transportation. Joseph, who had been quiet most of the time, spoke up, saying, "If the family owns a bicycle, then the man mostly travels with it. The woman may use it occasionally to carry maize meal back from the grinding mill or to purchase small items from the store. Older children may use it to carry water or some store items if the woman is too busy to go. Mostly, the man travels outside the compound, and he uses the bicycle." Over the past 40 years, I have noted a transformation in transportation. In the 80's, many people walked or rode a bicycle. By the 90's, most used bicycles and a few had motorcycles. By the 2000s, public motorcycles were everywhere, and a few families began to drive cars. In most cases, men drive motorcycles and cars. All buses and taxis are driven by men. A few women with government jobs or who are wealthy drive vehicles. The majority do not drive. Instead, they rely on public transportation.

There are many more delineations between gender-specified duties, but these will suffice to give a picture of how different life is in rural East Africa. Their system of dividing responsibilities reflects a simple, agrarian lifestyle with a strong patriarchal rule. Some of their practices may offend Western sensitivities, but no more than ours may offend them. Urban gender roles are changing, but everyone is only a generation or two away from the traditional gender roles and values still embraced by their parents or grandparents. There is great value and practicality in the traditional agrarian gender roles and responsibilities that have worked for generations. The face of modernity may have a slight foothold in East Africa, but how shallow it is may surprise you.

———————

Why Is Understanding Gender Roles Important?

East Africans are comfortable with specific roles and responsibilities assigned to the man and woman, and they may project those expectations upon a visitor. Additionally, responsibilities change as a person matures. From infant to child to adolescent and adult, East African culture has specific roles for each age. Gender roles encompass qualities that are generally regarded as typical or ideal for each sex. They help define a person's identity, status, and value within the community. Individuals are recognized and respected for the roles they carry out. Public support and praise are given to those who perform their duties well. They are also judged and criticized by the community for failing to fulfill their roles.

You may have heard of the 17th-century Latin philosophical proposition on individual identity by Rene Descartes, who said, "I think, therefore I am." East Africans instead emphasize the more communal view of the South African principle of Ubuntu, which states, "I am because we are." Gender roles play an important part in each person's identity and value within the community. Fulfilling gender roles allows one to gain respect and honor from others.

These gender expectations and understandings are so engrained by culture that cross-cultural encounters can be shocking or destabilizing to individuals who hold different role expectations. It can also be extremely disruptive to culture to have powerful or influential outside visitors who expect or even demand different gender roles than generally accepted by the community. Visitors to East Africa need to be sensitive to gender roles and not assume their own cultural values are equally shared by their East African friends and coworkers. It has been a frustration of East African governments for decades that Western countries offer financial aid with stipulations that they must embrace Western values and rights concerning women, homosexuals, and transgenders.

Cultural Insights/Principles

• Take note of who does what consistently. If there is an exception, ask about why that person is doing it.

• Notice where people sit. Are men and women separated? Or is it mostly women with children who are separated?

• Before assigning job tasks, ask for guidance about how they should be divided.

• Allow local customs to guide you on whether to hug and if hugging is permissible, pay attention to how it is done and where hands are placed.

• Avoid hiring a female to oversee work that is traditionally done by men and men to do traditionally female work. Seek guidance from local leaders and friends on how best to select the right person for a position or responsibility.

• Western gender roles are more easily found in urban areas of East Africa but less so in rural areas. In visits or work, be aware of where you are.

• Traditionally, women tend to wear more dresses in the village and more jeans or slacks in the urban areas. In fact, dress and hairstyles may be good indicators of a person's beliefs on gender roles.

Proverbs

For Women: "You are beautiful. But learn to work for you cannot eat your beauty" – African Proverb.

For Children: "The child who is not embraced by the village will burn it down to feel its warmth" – African Proverb.

"The best way to fight an alien and oppressive culture is to embrace your own" – African Proverb.

"If men swear that they want to harm you when you are asleep, you can go to sleep. If women say so, stay awake" – African Proverb.

"If you think you are too small to make a difference, you have not spent the night with a mosquito" – African Proverb.

"Once you have carried your own water, you will learn the value of every drop" – African Proverb.

For Men: "It is not work that kills, but worry" – African Proverb.

For Men and Women: "Teeth that are together help each other in chewing food" – African Proverb.

Chapter 20
What's It Like Being a Minority White in East Africa?

As the large meeting began, as is customary, visitors and neighbors began to introduce themselves to be recognized and appreciated for attending. The emcee of the meeting gracefully moved through all the neighbors and local village leaders, calling many by name and listing their titles and responsibilities. Finally, he paused and looked directly at me, saying, "Now, we will give any visitors an opportunity to stand and introduce themselves." All eyes in the building turned to me. Since I was the only white person in a crowd of over 200 Kenyans, it was obvious he wanted me to stand and say something. I thought for a moment about looking around as though searching for this visitor he was alluding to and seeing if I could pretend ignorance. However, I was sure they would not catch my sense of humor, so I stood and greeted everyone, introduced myself, and how I came to be present at their meeting. With that accomplished, our emcee moved on with the meeting. It was only a moment, but once again, I was reminded that I was different. I did not fit in, and everyone around me knew it. No matter how I tried to "blend in," I was not going to succeed.

Many who visit East Africa may feel like they have favored status since tourism is a significant part of the national budget. Local businesses and hotels cater to international visitors and their needs. Some tourist destinations may have locals who speak Italian, German, or even Chinese. Such conditions mask the tensions of being a minority visitor. Long-term visitors may discover the underbelly of being a minority in East Africa. How does it feel to be a minority? What are some of the drawbacks and advantages of being a privileged minority? How does a minority status affect relationships and work in East Africa?

Perspectives of a White Man in East Africa

For the first 22 years of my life, I grew up in America and enjoyed the personal rights and privileges afforded me by the Constitution of the United States. I always believed that our country was based upon the value of equality of all people regardless of race, religion, gender, sexual orientation, education, or economic status. From childhood, I was told that anybody could become President of the United States. I was exposed to some minimal opposition to this viewpoint (mostly by the media's coverage of social or racial tensions), so the idea of inequality was not new to me. I never considered myself to be insensitive. Rather, I would say that I had never been personally exposed to the difficulties, both obvious and hidden, of being a minority. However, after moving to East Africa, an extended stay opened my eyes somewhat to how a minority feels within a society.

Perhaps the most obvious and most immediate feeling of my minority experience is the realization that I am physically different than almost everyone else on the sidewalk. Within the town in which I walk, I see almost 100 percent black faces. (Today, I saw only two other whites during the entire time I was in town - walking the streets and shopping.) I can FEEL the stares of the majority of people walking past me or from across the street. I physically stand out. I am not the "norm." As I pass, sometimes conversations stop as everyone huddled together stops talking and watches me. Only occasionally do I sense hostility. Mostly, I sense curiosity. Sometimes, I know that I provide the sidewalk group with a new topic for discussion.

My language is different from the majority. I grew up in an English-speaking majority. I only learned English in school. I was mono-lingual when I moved to East Africa. Everyone around me speaks at least two languages; others speak three or more. They move from one language to another easily. Sometimes, they begin a sentence in one language and finish in another. Or they "sprinkle" one language with phrases or words from another. When I speak English, people don't always catch my American accent. I repeat myself often because people say I speak too quickly. I use a slightly different English vocabulary than is present in East Africa, so sometimes, people don't understand what I am talking about. Even when I speak their language, I have an American accent. I don't always know the local idioms and innuendos as well as they do.

Culturally, I have a different belief system. My values, being dissimilar, cause me to react differently. I misread their facial expressions, gestures, and actions. The majority seldom understand when I am frustrated and do not have patience with me whenever I question the "status quo." I see problems and solutions differently. Often, my solution is rejected by the majority because I miss other cultural subtexts that would render my suggestion useless. I have dissimilar hobbies and interests. I conduct myself differently socially than the majority. That means that local festivities and holidays do not hold the same fascination to me as for the majority. I almost never feel inclined to participate. I just do not fit in well.

These cultural differences spill over into the economic community. The foods I like are not often found in local restaurants. They cater to the majority. Instead of pizza or hamburgers prepared the way I like, boiled bananas and peanut sauce, ugali and greens, rice and beans, and goat and chapattis highlight the menu. I don't know any place that serves Italian lasagna, but many places offer chapattis and chai. So, I tend to eat at home a lot more. Stores stock the kinds of clothes, shoes, accessories, and supermarket goods that appeal to the majority. Since I am the minority, nearly everything sitting on the shelves for sale does not appeal to me. Also, customer service is geared to the majority. Most store prices are set up for some bartering. But since I don't know the system, the clerks are less flexible with me than they would be with someone of the majority. They don't seem to mind if I must pay more than the "average" person. I have not built relationships, and I must learn how to greet and visit before purchasing items. Clerks either think it is fitting for me to pay more or laugh at my paying the higher prices.

Together with the economic part of culture, I have really noticed the advertisements. All the billboards and TV commercials that I have seen have black people in them. They are usually involved in activities that seem fun to them but not to me. They display interest in products that I do not want to buy. None of the advertisements represent my interests or entice me to purchase their product.

Thinking of advertisements, I recall several deodorant ads. I have discovered I smell funny to the majority. I don't know if it is because my skin is a different color and reacts differently to the climate and sun or if my minority diet causes it. Whatever the reason, I know that I smell differently than the majority. I have had little children come into a village house in the morning and pick the room I slept in by the way it smelled. That gets personal.

Friendships are usually very difficult. I struggle to cross the language, cultural, and interest barriers. Even with a genuine effort, I often fail to establish a relationship that is free of tension. In America, friendships are sought horizontally in the sense that we become close to people with whom we work, go to church, or participate in some kind of social activity. Normally, these people are on the same economic level as us. We shop in the same stores, eat in the same restaurants, live in the same kind of housing, and hold similar political, social, and economic values. Friendships in

East Africa may have some similar aspects as mine, but tribal considerations also impact my relationships. If I befriend many from one tribe, other tribes may distance themselves from me. Some friendships are horizontal, but there is great value in establishing vertical relationships as well. Many East Africans seek friends who are wealthy or in a position of power or influence. There is a desire to tap into that and gain some benefit. My home culture values trust and common interests as a basis of friendship. The culture of the majority seeks to build a social network for mutual benefit, and trust does not necessarily need to be a factor. Thus, friendships for me as a minority become more laborious than fun. Isolation is a phantom I must fight, and with my minority status comes a distrust of the majority.

I like my cultural differences. I don't want to change who I am, where I came from, and what I believe. Yet, if I embrace these too tightly, I will always be different and distant. Society's majority, unconsciously and sometimes consciously, pressures minorities into conformity. If I resist, I am seen as out-of-step or even rebellious by the majority. If I try to conform, I discover I will never be like them 100 percent. I will always be slightly different. There will always be a gap that only I must bridge, for the majority feels no need to try and bridge the difference. In my frustration, it would be easy to turn to anger or cynicism.

Because of my own experience of being a minority in East Africa, I have gained a new lens and understanding of minorities in my own country of America. I realize now that products and ads, movies, media, banking, education, the justice system, and many other institutions are established for and cater to the majority. This creates a disadvantage for all minorities and especially hurts the poor in those minorities. It has also caused me to be more sympathetic to the frustrations and cries of inequality by minorities at home.

So, how does my minority status affect the objectives of my work in Africa? How much must I understand the majority to work effectively and successfully? How much does my lack of understanding hinder my business, project, or work? How much does my difference become a barrier for my East African friends and acquaintances? Would I be more effective if I was one of the majority? The curious aspect of my situation is that being a white person from the West affords me a sense of respect for the majority. Yet I know almost nothing about the hurts, fears, dreams, and needs of the majority in East Africa, much less how to effectively identify with my associates. Clearly, I need to know more about the majority to be successful. That is a daily, tiresome task of any minority visitor to East Africa.

Yet, I must confess to a great advantage of my minority status. I am a minority with wealth and resources at my disposal. I cringe to think how hard it is to be a poor minority in any culture around the world. Without a voice, political influence, economic power, or social status, minorities suffer at the hands of educational, financial, medical, judicial, and governmental institutions that are geared to serve the majority. The laws, businesses, entertainment, and social interaction cater to and protect the rights and interests of the majority. Some of this cultural prejudice is purposeful, but most of it is constructed and maintained by a majority simply unaware of how it adversely affects the minority. The minority is simply expected to adapt to the majority culture.

However, I enter East Africa as a wealthy American. I come with economic power many times that of the average person I meet. I have access to and can wield sizeable resources to accomplish my goals. I can live in a home better than the average house of the majority. I can purchase, drive, and maintain a vehicle that a vast majority of East Africans cannot afford. Thus, even though I am a minority, I am privileged.

Having a privileged minority status means that I can get into offices that regular majority people could not enter. I can make appointments with village chiefs, district commissioners, and the chief of police without difficulty. I can hire legal counsel, get permits, register projects, purchase land, and initiate projects that many local majority people are simply unable to accomplish. Such resources and abilities attract the attention of many people who seek to become the friends of someone with such means. Strangers know my name and where I live. They also know what I am doing, and they offer to help.

Having a privileged minority status also means I attract a lot of the wrong kind of people. Troublemakers who have been kicked out of other institutions or organizations seek employment with the unknowing newcomer. Opportunists who are attracted to the wealth and resources look for ways to benefit. If I trust too quickly or unadvisedly, I find myself surrounded by thieves who undermine my work/project and who give the entire operation a bad name. I find myself paying too much for cheap materials; I am inundated with false receipts. I am overwhelmed by fees for phantom permits and licenses. So, I must spend a lot of time testing, sifting, and learning from my mistakes. I lose money. I am deceived. I must overcome mistakes the local majority does not have to face.

While being a minority does not result in any real sense of belonging or acceptance, being a privileged minority gives me a sort of celebrity status that provides more access to the powerful and influential. Financial means allow me to accomplish so much more than I could if I were a poor minority. As I learn to live in a majority East African culture, I gather a group of good majority culture friends and counselors who help me in my objectives. Our project and work gain traction and a solid reputation. With just a little money, I can change the lives of orphans or a sick person needing surgery. I can educate vulnerable children, feed the poor during times of famine, put glasses on the nearly blind, teach, encourage, and literally save the lives of some who would have no resources. Someone once asked me why I liked living in East Africa. I thought about it for a minute and realized the answer. I am addicted to helping others. I gain great satisfaction in touching the lives of others – and doing so to a much greater degree than I have in my own majority culture. The minority cultural gap that I must constantly bridge seems so small to the great good that can be accomplished for those who persevere as a minority in East Africa.

Cultural Insights/Principles

- Locals can tell if a minority is a tourist or resident by the way they are dressed and how they walk. Also, by how they order food, purchase goods, drive, and greet.

Proverbs

"Strangers cannot know the secret paths of the village" – African Proverb
"The stranger sees only what he knows" – African Proverb
"The stranger has big eyes, but he does not see everything" – African Proverb
"Travel makes one a stranger" – African Proverb
"When brothers fight to death, a stranger inherits their property" – African Proverb.

Chapter 21
Culture Shock – Does It Ever Go Away?

A few years ago, someone was talking to my wife Linda about her 25 plus years of living in East Africa. The guest asked, "Since you have been here so long, do you ever struggle with culture shock or wish you could just pack up and go home?" Linda thought for a just a second and responded, "About once a week." The visitor was surprised by Linda's response, but his question exposed his assumption that we had overcome culture shock and no longer struggled with it. This may have been based upon his observation that we knew the language and lived and functioned so well within the culture. However, Linda's answer made him realize culture shock is not a one-time event or brief period early on in cross-cultural living. For visitors to East Africa who will experience a very different culture, several important questions come to mind. What is culture shock? When will it hit? How long will it last? Does it ever go away?

Expanding the Definition of Culture Shock

I have never been satisfied with the term "culture shock" or its various definitions. Wikipedia suggests a definition that aligns with most textbooks. It basically defines culture shock as the anxiety, confusion, disorientation, and uncertainty felt when people must live and function within a different culture such as one may encounter in a foreign country. Most literature also states "culture shock" normally peaks between 6-18 months.

There are two points to these statements that I disagree with. First, that culture shock restricts itself to an unknown culture or foreign country. Second, that there is a window in which culture shock is experienced. The second assumes culture shock is generally overcome and not experienced again. One becomes acculturated!

After living more than 30 years in East Africa, I find that I am continually experiencing aspects of culture shock and that it does not go away. This leads me to believe that the term and definition are deficient and need adjustments.

To address the first point above, I submit that no individual American is an expert on all of America's culture or the whole country. No one can understand, explain, or move smoothly in and out of the different ethnic groups, languages, social and economic strata, be conversant with all legal technicalities concerning traffic, land, banking, contracts, courts, etc. While we grow up in our home culture and learn to navigate it our entire life, no one can understand all the different cultural stresses concerning gender, or problems of the homeless, widows, or orphans. Neither can anyone grasp entirely the many cultural pressures that go with the different stages of life such as the peer pressure of the youth, career pressures of the middle aged, or retirement and shrinking lifestyles of the aged. In fact, I believe as an individual grows, he/she is continually confronted and often surprised by the cultural experiences of youth, education, marriage, work, parenthood, old age, and death.

In truth, no one living in a foreign country is ever a "cultural expert" for that foreign country. Obviously, the person who has lived on the field for a year will know and understand the culture much better than one who makes 40 short term trips. The woman who has lived in a foreign field for 10 years will understand culture better than the one-year resident. However, length of time in a foreign culture is not always a consistent factor in expertise. It will also depend upon how much of the culture a visitor engages. One who never buys a piece of land, conducts a funeral or wedding, tries to register an organization, deal with government officials, or many other things will ever truly understand all the facets of the culture in which he/she lives. In fact, some visitors can become quite good at shielding themselves from culture to the point of being extremely naïve about what is going on around them or even within their own business or project.

My own understanding of witchcraft took a huge jump forward once we began to engage it seriously with a series of seminars in the late 80's. My understanding of the plight of orphans continues to grow as I now enter my 30th year of working with a children's home in Kitale, Kenya. After losing our primary school headmaster and two key teachers to the competition a few years ago, I have learned the hard way how to effectively compete with the other primary schools in the municipality at gaining higher marks in school performance. As we worked to establish LivingStone International University in Mbale, Uganda, I learned so much about land purchases, higher education, registration and accreditation needs, and an even deeper level of wisdom about how to navigate the Ugandan government offices involved from the local chief to the Minister of Education. The shocks were many. Did I know everything about setting up a university before? No. Did I understand Uganda's education system in the previous 25 years? No. Do I understand it completely now? No, but I continue to learn. I expect there to be even more "culture shock" experiences as we continue to build the university and oversee the children's home and primary school. I haven't even mentioned a continuously growing understanding of the people and customs of the various tribal groups in East Africa.

Vince Vigil, a friend, and former coworker in Uganda, and I once discussed "culture shock" and he suggested an alternative term. He thought "culture struggle" more accurately reflected our ongoing experience. Culture struggle could be defined as "a condition of *continual* stress, anxiety, and disorientation affecting someone who engages (either briefly or for an extended period of time) an unfamiliar culture or new aspects of their own culture, a new way of life, a new set of attitudes, new physical, legal, or psychological orientations, or a new system of organization." I believe culture struggle is not a one-time experience lasting a few months at the beginning of any foreign cultural experience or stay. Instead, it may be a large initial "quake" followed by numerous aftershocks as one continues to engage the culture in new and deeper ways. The more one engages the culture in various ways, the more aftershocks they will experience.

Some suggest that "culture stress" is the right term. I disagree. I think "stress" minimizes the cross-cultural experience. "Struggle" more accurately describes the personal battles with anger, frustration, and gut-wrenching emotions that come with the continuously disorienting battle of cross-cultural living and working. To paraphrase Louise Koonce, a former missionary who served in Rwanda, stress could be a 1, 2, or 3 on a scale of 1 to 10. She believes cross-cultural workers wake up every morning closer to 5 and go up from there.

A friend from Mbale once explained my "culture struggle" better than anyone else. He said, "You may learn to talk like a Mugisu, walk like a Mugisu, wear clothes like a Mugisu, tell stories and proverbs like a Mugisu, think like a Mugisu, and understand deeply the Bagisu mindset, but you will **NEVER** be a Mugisu. The only way to be a Mugisu, is to have been born to a Mugisu mother." His point was clear. No matter how well acculturated into the Bagisu culture I became, I would ALWAYS be seen as an outsider. For the Ugandans who know me well, they would appreciate how much I have learned, but they will never accept me as a Mugisu. For any

Ugandans who meet me for the first time, they will always assume I know nothing and treat me as an outsider. There is no path or program I can complete to make me exactly like one of them in heart, mind, thought, life experience, and action. There will always be a gap. I can minimize the differences, but I can never completely overcome it.

My good friend Dennis Okoth, a Luo from Western Kenya, reminded me that there is a culture struggle even among tribes in East Africa. He related a time when he and a group of men from Western Kenya traveled to the coastal town of Malindi, Kenya. They had heard a rumor that the Giriama people ate rats as part of their traditional diet. This was alarming and repulsive to the men from Western Kenya, and they feared such a meal would be offered to them. What would they do? How could they decline gracefully? Rats became the major topic on the journey to the coast. On the third day of their stay, the host mentioned they would cook a traditional field animal that they found very tasty. Dennis and his Luo friends fearfully asked if they were referring to rats. The host assured them he was not talking about rats. A couple of hours later the host proudly came in displaying the largest field rats they had ever seen. The Western men impulsively let out such a loud cry that it startled their host. They prevailed upon the man holding the fields rats by their tails not to prepare them. Their host ashamedly agreed. It was during the fourth night of the visit that the rains came down hard and long in Giriama. The Western men rushed outside to see if termites, a delicacy among Luo people, would swarm after the rains. Not far from their house they found a termite mound with termites flying about. The Western men danced and gleefully started filling their mouths with the flying termites. Part way into their feast, their Giriama host came upon them with wide eyes. He pointed to their faces smattered with wings and exclaimed in horror, "You eat bugs!" At that moment both the Giriama and Luo discovered a significant cultural struggle about diet within the same country. Other cultural shocks about diet would include the Luo's trying to drink the clabbered cows' milk of the Kalenjin, or the Kalenjin trying to eat the fish heads served by the Luos.

Some who visit, work, or live in East Africa try to avoid "culture struggle" by insulating themselves from the surrounding culture. They bring lots of food items from their home culture. They decorate their houses, purchase clothes, watch media from home, follow home news, talk, and chat with friends, and essentially remain connected to "home." They may even make numerous trips back and forth from home to East Africa. They minimize contact with East Africans, and the most dangerous of all practices, they unconsciously select local leaders who are most like them, so they do not have to expend a lot of time and energy learning local language and culture. Unfortunately, many locals who seek these positions are not always the most reliable, respected, or trustworthy. The unscrupulous local strives to shelter the visitor from other East Africans to make themselves indispensable to the visitor. They filter news and information from outside to the liking of the visitor, shield him/her from criticism, and chases away anyone who would expose the self-serving activities of the East African confidant. It takes a great deal of resolve and wisdom to avoid reliance upon a single individual and to seek guidance from a group.

Some common examples of this cultural insulation involve tourist packages that collect foreigners in tour vans at the airport, drive them to expensive hotels, provide international cuisine, and then escort them through well-rehearsed tours. Often the tour guide has learned some of the language of his charges whether it be English, German, Italian or even Chinese. Essentially tourists do not get a real understanding of what East Africa is like. They experience a carefully constructed tour that avoids the richer, deeper realities of local culture. Or consider the foreign diplomats who move to East Africa for a two or three-year stint. They are politically appointed and usually have little cultural or linguistic knowledge of the country they seek to serve. They engage their political counterparts who have learned from numerous appointees how to engage the newest representative. They know what to say, how to talk, and where to take the new diplomat. East African politicians know how to insulate the new appointee from political rivals, hide corrupt money management, and mouth the political issues of the visiting diplomat. Consider the independent missionary who moves to East Africa but does not belong to a particular denomination already registered in the country. He relies heavily upon nationals who cater to his Western cultural needs, lavishes him with praise, and insulates him from the realities of what is really going on in his ministry.

Western visitors improve their chances of success by struggling with culture, and seeking counsel and guidance from many people who are not connected by tribe, family, finances, or job. Too many times Western visitors, who rely heavily upon a single local leader and have failed to grasp the deeper meanings of East African culture, portray themselves as "experts" to those back home. Unknowingly, they proliferate prejudices and misconceptions of the real context, wisdom, and abilities of the East African people.

Let me reject any mantle of being an "expert" in East African culture. With this new term and definition, I find understanding in my continuing "culture struggle" in East Africa. This change in terms and definitions is significant because it helps to remove the guilt long-term visitors feel when they continue to struggle with many aspects of culture. Such visitors are NOT deficient. They do not have to pretend to be an expert. They can admit ignorance in many areas and confess that culture struggle continues to exist. They are NORMAL!!!

Cultural Insights/Principles

A family can be a microcosm of a larger culture. When 2 families become entwined, culture struggle exists. Even families and married couples that are "almost the same" will still experience the realization that they have differences in attitudes and habits that they must learn to navigate.

Proverbs

"Culture is coded wisdom" – Wangari Maathai (Kenya)
"A man without culture is like a zebra without stripes" – African Proverb
"Until the lion has his own storyteller, the hunter will always have the best stories" – African Proverb
"Show me your friend, and I will show you your character" – African Proverb
"The one who truly loves you, warns you" – African Proverb
"When you point to deep tribal truths, the visitor only sees your finger" – African Proverb

Chapter 21A Chart

CULTURE SHOCK/STRUGGLE/STRESS

Assessment Chart

While there is no easy way of measuring culture struggle, the late Dr. Dan Hardin, former missionary to South Korea, attempted to create a chart of categories reflecting important cultural differences that visitors must engage. With the family's permission, I have added a few categories.

To evaluate how great the culture struggle might be, Dr. Hardin suggested a dissonance scale of 1 to 5 with 5 being the greatest. If the category is very similar to the visitor's home culture, it should be rated 1. If it is very different, it should be rated a 5, with variations in between. ***The greater the numerical total, the greater the cultural struggle a visitor may experience.*** The chart is intended to be make the visitor aware of potential cultural dissonance they may encounter and is not offered as a scientifically accurate gauge.

Category	D-1	D-2	D-3	D-4	D-5
Language – Official/Trade/Tribal					
Government – Democratic/Socialist/Communist/Monarchy					
Economics/Banking – Wealth & Wage Gaps					
Education – Literacy/Education Quality/Family Options					
Climate – Artic/Seasonal/Tropical					
Geography/Rainfall – Mountainous/ Jungle/Plains/Agricultural/ Desert					
Household – Utilities/Appliances/Food Selection/Internet					
Urban/Rural – Lifestyle/Work and Family Schedules					
Medical – Hospitals/Emergency Care/Medicines					
Security – Family/Personal/Work					
Transportation – Public/Private/Road Conditions/Safety					
Religious Beliefs – Christian/Muslim/Hindu/Animism					
Work/Project/Ministry – Open/Regulated/Persecuted					
Corruption – Prevalent/Minimal/Non-existent					

Additional Resources:

Mission: A Practical Approach to Church Sponsored Mission Work by Daniel C. Hardin

Chapter 22
The Police – Friend or Foe?

I was new to East Africa, and I was late for a meeting south of Kitale, Kenya. As I left my gate, two men who knew where I was going for the day met me and asked for a lift to a funeral along my route. I could not decline. Since I was already full inside the cab of my pickup, they climbed into the back and settled down for the ride. Just two miles down the road, a policeman waved me to the side of the road. He spotted the men in the back and said I was breaking the law by carrying passengers outside the cab of my truck. I became angry since every vehicle that passed us was carrying someone in the back of their truck. I claimed I was only helping the men to a funeral, and I pointed out the policeman's duplicity in that he stopped me for an offense that other drivers were doing as well but passing by without being stopped. The policeman's eyes flared, and he demanded my driver's license. I got a ticket. That was not the best way to handle the traffic stop. Yet, I was new to East Africa, and I had not yet learned how to manage encounters with the police.

Any visitor to East Africa will likely meet policemen in some capacity. Police will be on the roads checking traffic or providing security at hotels or events. It is extremely important to know that the police are guided by well-written laws empowered by the constitution of the country. However, whatever the letter of the law may say, the spirit of the law is heavily influenced by East African cultural boundaries, expectations, and communal identity. So how are visitors best advised to act when engaging with police/law enforcement personnel? How does one behave during a traffic stop? What should the visitor do in the event a policeman is needed?

How to Survive a Police Traffic Stop

It was a late March day, in the middle of the week, when I scheduled an area meeting among five different churches in a village just a few miles south of Tororo, Uganda. My truck was in the shop, so I borrowed fellow missionary Phillip Shero's dark green Nissan pickup with the matching camper cover. James Luchivya and I left Mbale at 9:30 AM and made the 30-mile journey south to arrive just at 10:00 AM. To my surprise the other church members had already arrived and our small building was packed to the point of being stuffy inside.

Because it was a larger-than-usual meeting and more formalities observed, our gathering went long and didn't finish until after 3:00PM. This is an important note because it changed my situation for driving back. Since two of the groups came from the very road that I would be traveling and the lateness of the meeting meant they would be delayed reaching home, there was a mad scramble for space in the back of my truck upon dismissal.

I had been in East Africa long enough not to step into the trap of becoming angry. I also knew better than to lecture a bunch of pedestrians about how the truck was not built to carry such a mass of bodies. Any attempt on my part to cull the group or even select someone to get out would be disastrous for me concerning relationships. For several years, I had already accepted the heavy-laden vehicle as part of my responsibility in community relationships. After all, it was not my truck. In a collectivistic society, it is "our" truck. That means if there is space available and I am traveling in the right direction, then any friend has a free ride. Much wiser than my earlier days, I surveyed the crammed mass of people in the back of the truck silently, calculated my clearance and tire pressure, and figured I could make it safely to the first of two new stops on my way back home. The only time my Western culture flared up was during a moment of frustration that I had not been asked by anyone for the ride. They just assumed it was all right. However, I pushed that ugly, non-African thought back down and looked again at how far they had to walk to attend a meeting I called and allowed my appreciation and compassion to swell up for them.

I drove slowly the five miles along dirt paths and trails to reach the main tarmac road leading into Tororo. It was right past the junction that my traffic problem began. Between 9:30 AM and 3:00 PM, the traffic police had come to the Tororo junction and set up a roadblock. They placed their small police check signs in the middle of the road in both directions, and then they proudly positioned their eight-foot-long metal spike obstacles in such a way that every vehicle had to maneuver slowly around them.

I believe Ugandan law states that police should not stop a vehicle unless they have "probable cause." What that phrase means in Western culture and what it means in East African culture is totally different. The police in East Africa understand that phrase to mean they can stop all traffic, ask for insurance, driver's license, check for cracks in the windshield, inspect a travel medical kit of public taxis, sift through baggage or cargo, and make general comments about the maintenance of your vehicle. It primarily means they are looking for a defect of some kind. The purpose of finding fault is not for greater safety, but for providing a reason for the police to "squeeze" the driver for some financial assistance to let him go free. So, every police check has the potential of becoming a cat and mouse contest between the police and driver.

I must admit that according to the law, my truck was not licensed to carry passengers in the back camper section. I knew this and silently hoped the police would be so busy with the numerous big trucks that they would let the American drive on by. That was not the case. My passengers in the back made no effort to hide. In fact, they had all the windows open with arms and heads sticking out.

The policeman with the biggest stomach (culturally big people are perceived as wealthy, important and in this case the senior official present) spied my vehicle packed like sardines and stepped into the road. With a swift wave of his arm, he instructed me to pull the truck to the side of the road and stop. I knew our cat and mouse competition was going to be serious when he did not greet me pleasantly, but instead came close to my window and commanded me to get out of the truck. His serious face suggested I was in terrible trouble, but then again that is the way every policeman on the hunt looks. He walked like a prowling feline to the back of the truck while all the faces in the camper watched him silently. I slowly made my way back to the tailgate. He pointed at the camper and said, "Open it." I opened the camper door so that he could see a jumble of bodies all smashed into the tiny space. He looked at me as though I had twenty-thousand-shilling notes hanging off my shirt. He was hungry, and my future donation was going to provide his feast.

"What is this?" he asked as he jabbed his finger toward the people inside who were now silently, expectantly watching the cat and mouse begin their match. I began to explain that we had come from a village about five miles away and the passengers were riding back to their homes. Up went the policeman's hand stopping me in mid-sentence. With squinting eyes and a slight smile, he cocked his head sideways and asked, "You know it is against the law to carry passengers in the back of this truck?"

At that moment, while the policeman was mentally counting my money in his head, I had an ingenious idea. I knew he was not really concerned with me carrying people in the back. There were large dump trucks passing us as we spoke with people standing in the back. Other trucks full of charcoal had three or four young men hanging precariously on top. All of these passed us on the side of the road as my big-stomached policeman stared down at me as though I was his prey. He thought I would give an apology and beg for leniency. He assumed I wanted to carry these people. His whole ploy for getting something from me was based upon my desire to protect my passengers.

What he did not know was my slight, American irritation that they had filled my truck without asking. So, in an instant, I turned the situation upside down. I looked at him with the best frustrated face and voice that I could muster as a mouse. I said, "Yes, I know it is against the law to carry people back here. I don't like carrying people in the back of this truck. When we were leaving the village, these people climbed into my truck without even asking me. They showed me no respect at all. Yet, I knew that if I told them to get out, they would all see me as a bad person because I refused to share my truck space with them. So, thank you for stopping me and informing me right in front of them how they have caused me to break the law. In fact, I would be very happy if you told all of them to get out and walk the rest of the way home. I would like for you to order them out. Then they will see YOU as the bad person and not me. While you do that, I will stand right here and protest on their behalf and tell them that I wanted to help and carry them all the way home, but this bad policeman prevented me from doing so. Please tell them because I want YOU to be the bad man."

As I began to complain about the people in the back of the truck, they realized what I was doing, how I had turned the table on the policeman, and they started snickering. Even the policeman began to smile. When I finished, he looked at me with a smile on his face and asked, "So, you want ME to be the BAD man?" I said, "YES, please, YOU be the BAD man. Help me obey the law! Help release my truck from such a heavy weight! Please save me a lot of time from having to carry all these people to their homes. Then I can be the good man and we all will know you were the bad one who prevented them from getting a free ride."

At that point, the big-stomached policeman broke into laughter. He looked at me and then at the people inside the camper who were beginning to laugh. Then he looked at me again, gained his composure, pointed a finger at me and said, "You just go, AND take these people home." At that, the back of the truck erupted into applause for the policeman. I guess the big-stomached policeman wanted to be the good man, the hero, and not the bad man. Score one point for the mouse.

It is important to emphasize that most police men and women are good, polite, and very helpful. Traffic police often greet visitors and thank them for coming to their country. They may chat and smile and sometimes even salute as visitors drive off. There are a few, at the end of the month or right before Christmas when money runs out, who will set up speed traps to capture motorists and shake them down on the side of the road for fines that really should be paid at the bank with proper forms. However, it is better to not mention such forms during your police encounter lest you find yourself a temporary resident of a local jail cell, and your now larger fine will also include something for the court.

Like in most countries, police should be respected and obeyed. Their purpose along the main roads in East Africa is to ensure traffic safety, catch speeders, spot vehicles overloaded with cargo or passengers, respond to accidents, and direct traffic to ease traffic jams. Their presence and work are overwhelmingly positive. Visitors who are polite, humble, friendly, and responsive to police directives will be able to establish a good rapport with local traffic police.

In the event the vehicle you are riding in is stopped by the police, let the driver do the talking. As a visitor, do not enter the conversation lest you complicate and extend the encounter longer than the driver wants. The more time the police are with your vehicle, the greater the possibility of finding fault. Keep quiet! Answer any questions politely that the police may ask, but do not over-share. The police are expert fishermen, so don't be a wide-mouth fish in the vehicle.

For the occasional times when traffic police ask for something, the driver and visitor may carry bottles of water, fruit, or local snacks to give as a gift to the police who work in the sun all day. The gift will be a sign of "appreciation." If the visitor's organization has printed materials or brochures to hand out, give them as well. A small gift, any gift, is better than empty hands, and such generosity demonstrates a communal spirit of solidarity with those who are charged to keep the roads safe.

Cultural Insights/Principles

• Police use fear tactics as a way of controlling citizens in a fear/power culture. They will put on harsh faces, scowl at drivers or misbehaving people, and even resort to physical altercations to gain control of the situation.
• Police are not allowed to leave their posts on the side of the road. This means they cannot legally pressure a driver for a lift to the nearest village or center.
• Police are not supposed to accept rides in vehicles or commandeer a vehicle for personal or work matters. They can instruct a motorist to pull their car off the road and turn it off.
• Traffic police are not supposed to ask for passports or handle immigration matters. Many embassies advise foreigners not to hand

over important documents to local police. For the resident, it is best to leave passports at home in a secure place. For the visitor, rent a hotel safe rather than carry your important documents all the time.

- If a visitor plans on driving in East Africa, it is important to obtain an International Driver's License. Use it to present to traffic police and not the driver's license from home.

- If police are called to investigate a matter, they may request financial assistance to "push the case forward." In some instances, police stations may have limited fuel for vehicles, or they may request airtime for their phones (since all calls made cost money). However, excessive requests without official progress may need to be politely declined.

- Police investigators have been known to "squeeze" both sides of a conflict before settling the matter.

Proverbs

"Organization is impossible unless those who know the laws of harmony lay its foundation" – Egyptian Proverb
"Honorable is the person who is aware of their power, yet refrains from inflicting harm onto others" – Egyptian Proverb
"The law is a spider's web, only the little insects get caught in it" – African Proverb

Chapter 23
Poverty – Wrestling With the Economic Oppression of the Majority

Because Ellmore Johnson, an elder of our sponsoring American church, was visiting us in Kitale, Kenya, he was able to travel with me for a village visit in Misikhu some 20 miles south of Kitale. While at the meeting, an old man of almost 80 years of age entered and found seating near the door. He was about five feet six inches tall, gaunt of frame, and bare-footed. In fact, the soles of his feet suggested he had not put on a pair of regular shoes in many years. Yet, as he entered our room, he carried himself well for his age. His full head of white hair immediately made him stand out in the crowd. Another noticeable feature was his coat. At one time the coat had been a tan men's suit coat, but it had been patched numerous times with various colors of cloth. The stitching was poorly done and left a tattered edge around each large patch. In fact, the old man's coat looked more like a patch quilt than a suit coat. Ellmore noticed the man immediately. He was fascinated by the multi-colored coat. Ellmore was a sharp dresser who always wore a suit and tie even into his 90s. So, Ellmore felt a bond with the old Kenyan man. Our meeting went long and ended with a meal. The old man with the patched coat sat next to Ellmore. Through an interpreter, they had a great visit, but Ellmore was troubled. He just felt his new friend needed a better coat to wear. In a moment of generosity, Ellmore pulled off his coat, and gave it to the old man just before we left the village. The old man took the coat, clutched it to his chest, and then danced around in a circle showing the crowd what he had been given. The group laughed and clapped for him. For more than 25 years after that, Ellmore retold that story to me every time we met.

Sometimes an act of generosity can have just as much of an impact on the giver as on the recipient.

Every visitor to East Africa may meet poverty on a scale that they have never seen before. The gap between the rich and poor is huge, and the visitor may struggle mightily with guilt for being so rich, or with an overwhelming desire to jump in and help without truly understanding the complexity of East Africa's multi-faceted poverty. Simply giving resources is hardly ever the right action. Is there a good way and a bad way to help? How can visitors face poverty wisely, humbly, and with discretional generosity?

The Many Faces of Poverty

It was morning in Milanji, Mozambique. At 6:30 AM, the sun and people had been up for some time due to the positioning of the time zone. A polite knock on my door signaled breakfast was ready. My first morning in Mozambique found me sitting sleepy-eyed behind a small wooden table in what was probably built to be a small village store. Currently, it was empty and had been turned into my hotel room for the week. In front of me, a hot steaming strong tea was poured into a red plastic cup, and then a small can of sweet and condensed milk was offered. There was also a small wooden bowl full of sugar with a single spoon sitting by my cup. My host continued talking to me as he poured two large spoons full of condensed milk into his tea, and then he reached for the sugar bowl. He added four small spoons of sugar to his morning drink. I watched this amazing display of sugar intake with my sleepy eyes widening. I almost choked at the thought of that much sugar in my cup of tea. However, his actions caused me to stop and think about the differences in our diets.

For the rest of the day, my host will not see or taste anything sweet. He will drink water with his lunch and supper and for anytime he is thirsty. His meals will consist of large quantities of corn meal or rice, a few vegetables and occasionally a piece of meat. Often, his food will be boiled, salty, and contain very few spices. I cannot think of a time I ate out in the villages when I was served a dessert. There has never been a time when a pie, cake, cookies, candy, or ice cream was offered. Dessert is just not a part of the rural village dining experience.

Most East Africans say they drink a Coca Cola or some other soda maybe 2-3 times in a month – more if they have a little money. Chocolate is purchased as a special treat for Christmas. Cakes are made mostly for weddings, and ice cream bars are equal to a day's wage and seldom purchased (if they can even be found for sale). So, the only affordable sweet available to most East Africans is granulated sugar poured generously into the daily tea. As I mentally weigh the amount of sugar I consume in desserts, sodas, candy, and processed foods, I calculated my host could probably drink several cups of sugared tea each day without catching up to me. I stayed with my Mozambican host for seven days. During that time, I ate only local village cuisine. I had no American snacks or processed food. I didn't go out for any fast food. My body began to let me know I was missing my sugar intake. My perspective changed over seven days. I began to really appreciate and look forward to my only sugar dosage/dessert in the form of strong, hot morning tea. On the last day, my host was making tea for me one last time, and just before he finished putting in that fourth spoon of sugar, I looked at him rather sheepishly and asked if he would mind adding one more. Sugar time!

____

Peter Ochieno was a happy, smiling man who had a loving wife, Rose, and four small children on his three-acre farm in Soy, just 15 miles northwest of Eldoret, Kenya. Peter and his neighbors had migrated from Kakamega, Kenya, some 70 miles south, to establish a new farming community on land that the government had subdivided for small homes. Peter sought a new life for his burgeoning family.

Paul Mbili was a brother-in-law to Peter Ochieno. Peter's wife, Rose, had a sister who married Paul. So, Paul Mbili and his Elizabeth also made the journey to Soy and settled on a neighboring farm just east of Peter. The families were close. They visited frequently, traveled to Eldoret for goods together, and even worshipped in the same church. It was the latter connection that eventually caused family problems to befall Peter.

Missionaries, new to the area, accepted Peter's invitation to start a church on his land in Soy. The mission built a large church building before Peter cleverly revealed that he had not given the land freely but expected to be paid for it. Peter announced the price of the church plot to the missionaries, who did not know the amount was equal to what Peter had paid for all three acres of his farm. The missionaries felt betrayed by Peter but did not want to lose the building. So, in a special meeting at the church building with all church members present, they agreed to pay Peter.

On the day of the meeting, all the church members came. They had heard Peter was selling the church plot, but they had not heard how much money he was going to receive. Peter kept that secret. He did not want his neighbors to know. Not even Paul Mbili knew. Peter requested the missionaries give him the money sealed in an envelope and not state the amount of the sale. The missionaries did not follow Peter's instructions. At the appointed time of the meeting, the older missionary stood up and, to Peter's shock, tore open the envelope and counted out the money in full in front of all of Peter's family and neighbors. Everyone knew exactly how much money he had received. A gasp went up within the crowd. The amount was more than the plot was truly worth. Peter's heart and motive were exposed to the community.

The meeting ended abruptly, and the missionaries left, but they were not the only ones that left. As soon as everything was concluded, Paul Mbili, ran down to the main road and hopped upon a public taxi for Kakamega. Within three hours, Paul was sitting in his father-in-law's house, who also happened to be Peter's father-in-law. Paul dutifully reported that Peter had obtained a large sum of money that very day and that if they hurried, the father-in-law could claim some of the money for the outstanding debt on his daughter Rose's bride price.

The next morning, before Peter had even finished eating breakfast, his father-in-law and two uncles arrived at Peter's door. With serious faces, Peter's father-in-law spoke of a great need at home that required immediate financial resources. The three men sat looking at Peter as a person where financial help could come from in the form of a bride price payment. During the meeting, Paul Mbili also just happened to come by to visit Peter. The four men put such pressure upon Peter Ochieno that he ended up giving all the money to his father-in-law. Peter's secret plans were lost, the money gone, and his farm was one corner plot smaller, but his extended family was satisfied.

When I first met Gabriel Wanyama in the early 1980's he was already in his late sixties. He may have been five feet four inches tall and extremely thin. Yet, he was animated when he talked and still full of energy. Without the benefit of an income from National Social Security Fund (slowly being utilized among the professional working class) or his family, Gabriel rented a small mud hut in a slum area of Kitale, Kenya, for a meager amount of money. The hut was less than 6 feet across. A dirty reed mat stood against the wall as an indication of what Gabriel slept on at night. (When I visited him once, I realized I would not be able to sleep in his hut without bending in some way to lay on the floor.) All his possessions, besides a blanket with holes in it and a charcoal stove, two cooking pots and a few utensils, could be kept in a single small suitcase. To me, Gabriel was the embodiment of true poverty. Gabriel lived on handouts and assistance from his neighbors.

In such dire circumstances, Gabriel ingeniously found a way to support himself. Whenever his neighbors tired of his constant begging, Gabriel became a professional mourner. When he heard of a funeral nearby, Gabriel miraculously discovered a convoluted way in which he was related to the family, and then off he would run. Gabriel would sit by the fire and somberly engage those who came to the funeral. He would cry huge tears and wail profusely. Then Gabriel would stay and wait for his food. Unwilling to leave the family even for the night, Gabriel would insist on staying close to the fire to offer his heartfelt condolences. He would remain through the funeral and even comfort the family for several days afterward. All the time, he would be fed by the grieving family who politely refused to speak harshly to a distant relative and aged man of the community. Finally, when the family could no longer feed him, they would ask about his home and why he had not returned to it. Gabriel would sadly gaze into the fire and say he had spent his last shillings to come and console his extended family. He had nothing to pay the return fare home. At this point, the family gladly gave him enough money to return home and even a little extra for being such a good friend and relative of the deceased. Gabriel would sadly pocket the money and then reluctantly leave, waving goodbye to his dearly lost, distant relative.

However, instead of going home, Gabriel would hop on public transport and travel to another nearby funeral he had heard about in his fireside chats. There, he would repeat his routine. Gabriel would be gone for weeks at a time, and his neighbors back home would begin to worry about him. Then, he would return and beg and borrow from them until he heard of the sudden loss of a distant third cousin on his mother's side of the family. He would be off again to work his ministry of condolences. It was an awkward way to make a living, but without the social services of wealthier countries, Gabriel, a poor man without means, found a culturally honorable way of obtaining his food and shelter.

———————

Eliud, a farmer from Teso in Northern Uganda was excited when he obtained employment at Messiah Theological Institute as a guard. Even though he would have to leave his wife and family on the farm to care for their crops, Eliud could use the additional income to supplement his many household needs. Eliud and his wife calculated the cost of renting a small, one-room apartment in Mbale and the expenses of food and personal items, and they believed they could still make enough profit off the guard income to significantly help their home. So, Eliud moved from Soroti to Mbale and found a small room to rent within walking distance of his job.

Eliud brought a smile and a positive attitude to his work. He arrived on time and was flexible in his schedule, even helping his associates by covering shifts for them when sickness or home matters called. The money came in regularly, and for the first time in Eliud's young marriage, there was money to spare. Over time, he excitedly purchased a bed, a kerosene stove, a few cooking pots, and some pieces of furniture for his small apartment. It was evident to his numerous, nosey neighbors that Eliud was doing well. In fact, his accumulation of so many new things so quickly attracted the attention of all the occupants of the 10 apartments bundled so tightly together.

Eliud, who was used to living in the peaceful security of his farming community where he knew all his neighbors, many of whom were related to him, had not understood the very different dynamics of living in an urban setting among neighbors whom he did not know. Eliud naively assumed the best from all of them. His security work meant Eliud was away from home all night as he carefully guarded the Institute. Thus, Eliud was shocked to come home one morning to find his door had been smashed in and his small one-room apartment completely empty of everything. Eliud turned to his neighbors for help and information. Did they see or hear anything during the night? Had they fought with but were overcome by the robbers? To his amazement, ALL his neighbors had not seen or heard anything during the night. They were absolutely no help. Eliud could not believe that robbers had carried off his bed and all his kitchen utensils and clothing without being seen. He became suspicious of and alarmed by the lack of communal support and protection from his neighbors. Within two days, Eliud moved to a new rental room. After that, Eliud kept only a few things in his room during his employment. To his neighbors, he looked as though he was much poorer than them.

The lack of support for Eliud illustrates the jealousy his neighbors possess. In East Africa, everyone is fearful of getting too far ahead of their neighbors in wealth and possessions. Since the community is so valued, tight-knit, and reciprocal, if someone grows too prosperous, the neighbors begin requesting assistance. A mother is sick and needs medicine, or a student is short on school fees. An old man is hungry and needs some food. Or if a car is present, someone will need a ride to town on urgent matters. If help is not given, then jealousy begins to form in the hearts and minds of neighbors. There is a powerful reason all the houses look the same, and everyone is equal in possessions and wealth. On the odd occasion a very nice house sits in the village, it is because a rich person works and lives in the capital and has a poor relative attending to the farm (at all hours) on a small allowance. Visits by the rich owner to the nice farm home are unscheduled, unannounced, and short. Symbolic assistance to neighbors is made to keep the house and property safe. Such balances are key to communal harmony, but they can also be huge obstacles to personal financial progress.

Many visitors are struck deeply by the obvious "poverty" of many of their hosts in East Africa. It is important to note that "poverty" may be defined very differently in rich Western countries than in poorer developing countries. Occasionally, Western cultures use their own standards of poverty for measuring and responding to developing countries. Such a gap in wealth between the Western visitor and their East African host often creates a strong sense of guilt for the visitor. The visitor feels "obligated" to do something, to "help" in some way. Often the sense of guilt overrides common sense and wisdom in how to respond in a way that doesn't do more harm than good. Throwing money at something is hardly ever the solution since it may create major problems between the host and his neighbors and extended family. Many East Africans say pumping money into a person robs him of his self-esteem and causes his family to see him as a beggar rather than a provider. Importing an impressive number of financial resources, medical equipment, educational materials and computers, or other physical project needs is usually not a good idea either. It takes tremendous wisdom, lots of patient research, and a strong will to resist the temptation to rush in and help whenever personal guilt pushes a guest to do something. The best approach is to build a partnership, equal in responsibility, input, and contribution (It may mean one side gives money and the other side their strength, skills, and time). It means asking for a lot of advice and counsel within and outside the target audience, as well as legal assistance. Go slow. Don't assume that the reason "poverty" exists is because of a lack of resources. Poverty has many faces. It is complex, and there are many reasons and conditions that affect and sustain it. Simple, quick Western answers may destroy more than they seek to help. Incomplete answers, without cultural guidance, may rob the intended recipients of their dignity and create social problems unseen by the visiting temporary aid worker. If poverty has many faces, then there must be a multifaceted response that is carefully, patiently, culturally, and wisely developed by both sides of the cultural and financial divide.

Cultural Insights/Principles

- East Africans do not display their wealth in possessions as Westerners do. Rather, they hide it lest friends, neighbors, and family request financial assistance.
- Practical use is more important than decorations.
- The possibility of theft while away from home keeps many from purchasing numerous possessions.
- As a Western visitor, do not allow your feelings of guilt over the gap in wealth to cause you to interfere in a family's or project's financial budget or operations. You may cause a greater problem rather than help.
- Seek ways to help a group rather than an individual to avoid jealousy or a show of favoritism.
- Seek ways to help that have lasting effects over short term relief. For example, iron sheets for a building will last at least 15 years and be a gift to many people instead of an equal amount of funds to purchase food that is consumed in a week's time.
- Help projects or individuals that have been publicly supported by others.

- Do not be the first to give, but it is all right giving a larger contribution than others.
- Avoid any requests for secretive assistance. Instead, seek counsel from a group to determine the best way to respond.

Proverbs

"Laziness and Poverty are cousins" – African Proverb

"Both the rich and the poor are buried in the same size of grave" – Kenyan Proverb

"Poverty is slavery" – Somalian Proverb

"Make some money but don't let money make you" – Tanzanian Proverb

"The wealth which enslaves the owner isn't wealth" – African Proverb (Nigerian)

"The poor man and the rich man do not play together" – African Proverb (Ghanaian)

"With wealth, one wins a woman (able to pay his bride price)" Ugandan Proverb

"Dogs do not prefer bones to meat; it is just that no one ever gives them meat" – African Proverb

"A real family eats the same cornmeal" – African Proverb

"Poverty without debt is real wealth" – African Proverb

East African Poverty Means:

1. Using scraps of newspaper or magazines for toilet paper because money must buy food.
2. Using your legs and feet as your primary source of transportation. A bicycle is a luxury.
3. Wearing the same trousers and shirt all week.

4.   Shopping for "replacement" clothes, not accessories, at the secondhand store.

5.   Wearing shoes that are too small because they were the only ones available in your price range.

6.   Using a pit latrine away from the house.

7.   Bathing in a cubicle with only a basin of water and a piece of soap.

8.   All cooking is done over a fire between three rocks. You can't afford to purchase oil for frying, and there is no oven for baking.

9.   A complete set of kitchen utensils includes 2 aluminum cooking pans, 1 knife, 3 spoons, 4 enamel plates, 3 ceramic cups, a tea pot, a plastic basin, a box of matches, and small plastic bags of salt and sugar. You borrow a thermos (for serving hot tea) or extra plates if visitors come.

10.   Furniture includes bedding (probably a straw mat with a sheet or blanket because a mattress would be a luxury), 2-3 stools, a lantern, a small crude wooden table, 3-6 local advertisements nailed to the wall for decoration, and a sheet hung up to separate the sleeping area from the sitting area.

11.   Getting news from your neighbor because you do not own a TV, VCR, DVD, radio, or any kind of music player.

12.   The only book you possess may be a tattered Bible without the cover and missing several sections.

13.   A woman's task is to gather enough firewood and water for the day and prepare any food available.

14.   The man's task is to find enough money to buy the day's food and hope that no one becomes sick.

15.   Older children help mom care for smaller children. If money is available, they may attend the local, poorly-run, overcrowded school and have no schoolbooks.

16.   Not having life insurance, medical insurance, a pension, a Social Security system, a bank account, or any kind of savings.

17.   Not dreaming of the future, but thinking only of how to live through today.

Chapter 24
The Unseen Potholes of Intervening In Medical Emergencies

Noeli, a dear friend and Kenyan coworker, was traveling into town one day on the back of a motorcycle. Like so many women in East Africa, she rode side-saddle because of her skirt. Though she had done this many times, this day was going to be different. Someone walked out in front of the motorcycle driver causing him to swerve abruptly to miss him. Noeli lost her balance and fell backwards hitting her head on the concrete curb. She lay unconscious for some time while others attended to her. Her sister Nancy found her in a local clinic as she was regaining consciousness. The only problem, besides a massive headache, was that Noeli did not know her name, where she was, or who Nancy was. She was frightened and could not understand why nothing was familiar. I rushed to the clinic and, with doctor's orders, took Noeli to the hospital for x-rays and a CAT scan. As we waited for the technician, Noeli eyed me suspiciously. I had known her for more than 20 years and had even conducted her wedding. Yet, at that moment I was a stranger. I was scared and ready to do whatever was needed to help Noeli regain her memory. Fortunately for us, her memory returned within 48 hours, but it was a very long two days.

It is possible that during a stay in East Africa, a visitor may find themselves involved in a local citizen's medical situation. Medical institutions and care may seem familiar, but family decisions and responses to medical needs may be surprising. How should a visitor respond when their host or friend has serious medical needs? Should an offer to help financially be extended? What extenuating circumstances does the visitor need to be aware of concerning a local citizen's medical problems?

What to Do with David Kanja?

David Kanja was born in 1970 and grew up in Uganda's tumultuous times of Idi Amin and Milton Obote II, so he was only 25 when Linda and I moved to Mbale in January of 1995. I remember meeting him for the first time. David stood five foot six inches tall, and his feet seemed too wide and too small for his legs. As I shook hands with him, I noticed that his fingers were short and stubby and rough as though they had done a lot of work in the fields. He dressed nicely and spoke English very well and politely. Overall, David was an average Mugwere in appearance who lived in Kamonkoli just five miles out of Mbale.

David's home life was difficult. His father died before David reached his teens. I never could ascertain what had happened to him. David's mother was alive when I moved to Mbale, but she also died shortly afterward and was buried on a small plot of ground not far from David's mud hut. A pawpaw tree grew at the foot of her grave. At an early age, David became the keeper of a younger brother. His only other family was an aunt (a sister to his mother) and her family. They owned land next door, so often David would spend his free time at their house.

When we first came to Mbale, David began attending a study group I arranged in Kamonkoli near his home. Nearly every week on Tuesday office day, David would either walk or ride a bicycle into town and bring some news to us. Sometimes he didn't have any real business issues we needed to address, he just wanted to visit. At first, we didn't have an office building, so we would sit under trees in my yard and talk. Later we built a small verandah where we could sit sheltered from the rain. I cannot count the number of times that David came to my house to visit, drink tea, and talk about our study group in Kamonkoli.

His greatest passion was a vision for a church that would powerfully impact his own community. He felt we should be working to quickly establish the same kind of church in Mbale. When we first arrived, our mission work immediately pulled us to the villages, so we neglected starting a church in Mbale for several years. David became our conscience to remind us of the need for a town church. On many occasions, David brought someone to my house and introduced them as a person interested in a town church.

When his mother died, David moved into Mbale and began working for Pepsi. He loaded trucks with crates of sodas and did numerous other odd jobs. During this time, he rented a small room in Namatala, a poor part of Mbale close to his home in Kamonkoli. Surrounded by drinking parties, drunkards, prostitutes, and other unsavory characters, David started a small Bible study group in Namatala. He gathered a few friends (no more than 10) and started teaching them in his one room home. On several occasions, I went to his home to lead a study. David's group just never seemed to gain traction and grow. Eventually, it fell apart. David lost his job at the Pepsi factory, and he returned to Kamonkoli. Somewhere in the back of my mind I can't help but believe that David felt we should have done more to help his study group in town. Perhaps we should have. Our organizational plans were to find a piece of land in a prominent place and target the middle class of Mbale. Our earlier experiences with the poorest people in Kitale, Kenya resulted in four small churches on the outskirts of town – often unknown to local government and town officials and the better part of the population. We desired, in Mbale, to try a different approach this time around, and David was frustrated by it. Yet, he was always kind and insistent that we should not neglect Mbale town.

In 1997, things went horribly wrong for David. For some reason he became mentally unstable. He went to a local market area and did something to incur the wrath of the local villagers. He was beaten severely. When we heard of it, he was already in the district hospital in Mbale – Ward 12, the mental ward. As I walked into ward 12, I met Simon Rwasizeki, David's uncle, who was sitting outside waiting for me. I can still remember how my skin crawled as I walked into ward 12. It wasn't really a ward. It was a dilapidated, old building without a front door (literally off its hinges). The concrete floor was broken in many places. The wiring was pulled out and the darkness was compounded by the dull paint on the walls. I couldn't tell what color it was because the dirt so thickly covered everything. The whole building stank of urine because there were no working toilets. Each room was more like a jail cell than a hospital room. The doors to each room were reinforced (at least the two that were still hanging on their frames) to literally imprison their patients. I found David in one of these rooms lying on a reed mat and covered with a blanket. He had bruises all over him and he was unable to talk. Simon informed me that the hospital staff had put him on some kind of mind-altering medicine and heavily sedated him. David had that far-off look in his eyes, and he just lay passively on the ground – unable to communicate with me.

David stayed in the "hospital" for about a week before being released. He returned to Simon's house in Kamonkoli where he continued his medicine. A few days later, I went to Kamonkoli to visit David and check on his progress. He would sit on a chair with glazed eyes and not talk. When I asked him questions, he would just look at me. It appeared to me that the medicine he was taking made him lifeless and dull. I couldn't tell if he knew who I was or not. Neighbors came by to visit David and observe his current condition. Rumors sprang up that David had been bewitched at some time by his mother who had a reputation for dabbling in witchcraft. She reportedly disliked some of the things David did. The neighbors pointed to David's lethargic nature to prove their conclusions.

Over the next few years, David's health improved some. He was able to walk about. He had enough mental capabilities to come to town or to take long walks in different directions from Simon's house in Kamonkoli. However, he did not completely recover. One time he even came to our new church building in Mbale, but I am not sure he understood what he was seeing – that it was the fulfillment of his dream for a church in town. He never mentioned it as such, and I never tried to explain.

In February of 2002, David was out on one of his walks when he encountered a person burning off his field in preparation for plowing. For some unexplained reason, David walked into the fire. Neighbors ran into the field and grabbed him, tearing off his burning clothes and rushing him to the local clinic. Simon brought him home and tried looking after him for weeks, but he did not tell us about it until much later. A friend of David's came to the office to report that David had been burned and was really suffering. His friend asked for our help, so I agreed to go out with an America medical acquaintance and visit him.

On a Thursday morning, we drove out to Kamonkoli where we found Simon and his wife, David's aunt, working in the fields near their home. After greetings, they escorted us to the small mud hut where David was resting. I was unprepared for what I saw. There on a reed mat lay a living skeleton of a man covered with a blanket. I could hardly recognize him. David was lying on his side with his legs uncovered. Most of his lower legs were burned. They had not been treated well and the sores were filled with pus. Flesh was falling off around the huge sores, and the stench of rotten flesh filled the room. I gagged several times as David's aunt pulled back the blanket to expose numerous burns all over David's emaciated body.

My friend estimated that over 40 percent of David's body had second- and third-degree burns. He said David needed to be in a hospital immediately or he would die. David needed extensive medical treatment, regular changes of bandages, an IV drip, and a sterile environment. We talked a minute about costs, because if we suggested he be moved, the family might hold us financially responsible. I decided to take the risk. When we mentioned the hospital, Simon and his wife looked at us and said, "We have no one to sit with him." (Many East African hospitals do not provide meals, bathing services, or even a pharmacy. Normally the family provides someone to bring food, purchase drugs, and care for the patient while recovering.) Simon's response stunned me because he evidently had numerous family members who could go to the hospital and care for David. He was gently and culturally informing me that they had decided to withdraw their support and care for David. This put what we were seeing into sharp, painful focus. They did not want David to recover. They had purposefully chosen not to take him to the hospital, because they were ready for him to die. As I thought about it, I understood the hard financial drain that David had become on a family that made so little money. They had lived with the physical and financial strain of David's mental condition for five years. They no longer had the money or resolve to take him for treatment. And even if he recovered, Simon and his wife would still be the only source of food, clothes, and care for David. They were tired and their resources exhausted. David's burns only proved to them that his time had come.

Additionally, David's mental condition created tremendous community strain on Simon's family. David had made enemies by his crazy antics. He scared people. They thought he was possessed, and they distanced themselves not only from David but also Simon's family. Simon suffered strained relations with his neighbors who would find David walking around their compounds at all hours of the day and night. David would pick fruit from his neighbors' trees without asking for it. Neighbors would chase David away from their homes and children fearing for everyone's safety. Simon's family was ostracized by the community because of David's condition.

Medical insurance is a bane to modern America in many ways, but it does provide us with the opportunity to seek medical treatment that would often be beyond our own financial abilities. In a developing country where there is no such thing as medical insurance, families often make very difficult decisions concerning a family member's expensive health care. Sometimes the entire family will sit to decide whether to impoverish everyone for the sake of an operation on a loved one, or if it would be better for one to die to keep the others financially protected. Many times, I have stood on the sidelines unable to interfere and not asked to help while a family made these difficult medical decisions. I have helplessly watched an infant with a cleft lip and pallet die as the family starved it to death because they could not afford the surgeries needed to repair the deformities. I have listened to an elderly father passionately persuade his sons and daughters not to sell their cattle to pay for his throat operation, because there was no guarantee the operation would save his life. The elderly father refused to allow the family to impoverish themselves on his risky medical procedure. I have seen young men lame in a leg or foot use a walking stick because the family would not pay the hospital to set a broken bone. As I examined an emaciated and dying David, I knew that Simon's family had decided against spending any more money on him. They needed financial and social rest from David's mental condition.

Being culturally sensitive yet deeply grieved by the family's decision, we altered our approach a bit. My medical friend and I took Simon into town and purchased some burn crème and pain relief medicine. My friend gave detailed instructions on how to care for David at home. He told me privately that David would probably not last more than a couple of weeks.

Seven days later, I found a young man sitting under a tree in my yard waiting for me to return from my breakfast meeting. He was sent by Simon's family. David had died that morning at 2:00 AM. He lasted only a week. I gathered a few friends who knew David and we drove out to Simon's home. We prayed with the family, spoke kind words, and told stories about David. We gave a little money to help with funeral expenses. We sat with the family and nearby neighbors as a grave was dug next to David's mother and the pawpaw tree. Since we had a trip out of town scheduled for that same day, we could not stay for the funeral which they were going to conduct without waiting for the traditional two or three days. Yet, our coming to express our grief over David's death and the family's loss was more important than staying for the funeral.

David is gone, but his memory lives on with me. He was one of the few people in Mbale that remained consistently and passionately focused on our mission's goals. His call for a town church pushed us to establish one prominently on the main road going north out of town. In some ways, the work we see today is partly because of David's insistence. I don't know if he ever understood how he helped bring about such an impressive work, but if he can see it now I know he is smiling about it.

Western visitors step into East Africa with many cultural bags from their home country. One of those bags is filled with values, expectations, and assumptions about sickness, mental health, and medical emergencies. They assume everyone wants to aggressively tackle an illness or mental problem. Every medical emergency must be treated no matter the cost. In their zealous compassion, Western visitors may accidentally intrude into family and social matters that are much more complicated than they are aware of. They may not know all the financial, social, and familial ramifications of seeking or not seeking treatment. It is a must that Western visitors take a sideline seat whenever a local medical problem arises. They should allow the family and those concerned to take the lead and make decisions based upon their abilities, resources, and personal knowledge of the situation. A Western visitor should only help when asked and not before, no matter how hard that may be.

Let me give three cultural complications that Western visitors may cause by their presence and intrusion into a family's medical issue:

As soon as a doctor or hospital staff sees a Western visitor come into the hospital with a local patient, the price of that patient's treatment goes up astronomically. Their presence may secure better care for the patient, but it will be very costly during that visit and possibly for any subsequent visits. Western visitors would do the family a huge favor by staying out of sight, and if asked, help from a distance.

If a Western visitor pushes to take the patient for treatment or surgery to the best hospital in the nation's capital, the visitor is culturally assuming the cost of transportation, treatment, and extended care. If the visitor overrides the family's decision or persuades the family to do something they were not going to do, then the Western visitor becomes the sole financial source of the patient's treatment. Not realizing this and expecting the family to continue assisting with finances they did not agree to spend, can seriously damage budding friendships.

If a Western visitor helps one family with their medical issue, other families will come forward and seek financial help as well. An ever-increasing number of people will come forward with medical needs. Whenever the visitor refuses to help one family or starts turning families away, they create a communal rift in relationships. Why did the visitor help that family but not ours? This creates tremendous problems for the visitor as well as for the family the visitor helped.

So how can a visitor respond positively to a medical emergency?

David's story is a hard one to write. "Majority" world experiences are filled with tragedy, injustice, corruption, suffering, and hard personal and family decisions forced upon them by poverty. Wealthy Westerners who enter these difficult situations can be overwhelmed quickly. We might try to ignore the suffering around us, but it never goes away. We could try to shield ourselves from suffering with our resources, but our financial capabilities are never sufficient to confront all the problems that besiege us. We could be overcome to the point that we grow despondent and quit trying, and we could resign ourselves to an inactive hopelessness. None of these are positive or healthy responses to our suffering context.

So how do we survive and thrive in such difficult conditions? The harder question for some is, "Why does a loving God allow such suffering in an unjust world?" There is no easy answer to why bad things happen, and there is little benefit in demanding an answer. My own personal loss and years of witnessing the suffering, injustice, and poverty of others has forced me to stop asking "why the bad happens" and pushed me to start asking "how can I help?" There is little value in futilely tracking the multitudinous reasons for suffering. There is great value in doing something about it. I can focus on my personal response and choose to help alleviate the suffering of others, if only a few. In my many years in East Africa, I have discovered that by not becoming despondent, I can wisely utilize my time, energy, and resources, and maximize my impact. David Kanja reminds me I cannot solve every medical problem that comes to me, but I can sympathize with the family, stand in solidarity with them during their loss, and strengthen my relationships with those left behind. It was a hard loss but let me share with you just three examples of personal success in alleviating the pain of others.

Several years ago, my wife Linda intervened in Leah Ibale's looming medical disaster. Leah had miscarried five times previously and looked like she was on her way to number six. Linda strongly encouraged Leah to see a good doctor in Mbale, follow his instructions, and come to the hospital for delivery instead of giving birth at home. Linda's counsel and financial support helped Leah give birth to a big, healthy baby boy later named Emmanuel. There was great rejoicing in the family and neighborhood over Emmanuel's birth.

Kirk Hayes, a coworker of mine, once visited a village just after a young boy named Jacob had broken his leg playing soccer on an un-level field. Jacob's parents were financially unable to do anything and were going to leave the boy's broken leg unset. The boy would become a cripple using a stick as a crutch. Kirk couldn't bear the disastrous future of his young boy, so he paid for corrective surgery and rehab to the point that the boy recovered completely.

In a village in South Bugisu, I met an elderly woman named Esther who had a huge goiter on the side of her neck that caused her pain, immobilized her neck, and made it almost impossible for her to sleep at night. For less than a hundred dollars, I was able to pay for a surgery that removed the lump and allowed Esther to look and feel like her old self. Her family brought me a stalk of bananas and a chicken and celebrated loudly in my yard to say thank you.

Even with the admonitions for sensitivity and examples of potential fallout listed above, there are times when helping with a medical emergency is requested by the family and appreciated by friends and neighbors. The *key principles* on whether to help or not with medical needs is: (1) to be sensitive to the family's direction; (2) learn as much as possible about the hidden factors surrounding the problem; (3) discern the level of help that can be given without creating dependency; and (4) do not force foreign cultural values, expectations, and wealth in such a way as to destroy relationships.

So much good can be done when we respond in sensitive collaboration with our East African friends. So much harm can result when we push our way into a medical problem and run ahead quickly without seeing, hearing, or absorbing the signs and counsel around us. Visitors to East Africa may encounter and help someone like Leah, Jacob, or Esther. They may also grapple with a David Kanja. Be wise enough to discern the difference and respond compassionately and with constraint as needed to avoid personal, relationship, and cultural blunders that can cause more harm than good.

Cultural Insights/Principles

- In many places in East Africa, patients are required to purchase their own notebook and keep their own medical records. Doctors will write in diagnoses and medicines prescribed so that during the next visit, they can refer to the patient's personal history.
- While district hospitals exist and medical care is supposed to be free or very subsidized, the existence of private clinics and dispensaries reflects the generally poor care received in public institutions.
- Most hospitals do not have food service for patients. Families of the patient are expected to attend to their personal needs. This often means that a family member needs to stay at the hospital with the sick or injured.

- Often family members must go to a nearby pharmacy and purchase the medicines prescribed by the doctor. They must bring the medicine back to the hospital where the doctor and nurses administer them as needed.

- In some cases, hospitals will refuse to release a patient until their medical bill is paid. Delay in paying adds to the family's expenses.

- When death looks imminent for a patient, the family may insist on removing the patient from the hospital to avoid the additional costs of a mortuary. They will instead take the person home and let them die at home.

- Check with numerous sources for the best hospitals and clinics within the area of your stay in case of an emergency.

- If a lengthy stay is planned, it would be good to connect with a doctor and clinic ahead of time so that when a health issue arises, a visitor will already be registered/connected.

- When possible, avoid getting involved with medical issues of local friends and neighbors.

- If asked for help, make sure the request is not in private, but requested in the presence of many witnesses. Private requests for medical help may not be legitimate or money can be used for something else rather than medical problems. Without accountability, there is no way to know how much money may have been raised privately.

- Be careful of setting a precedent. If a visitor helps generously with one person, many others will expect the same level of help. If the visitor is unable to maintain such a level, they inadvertently create jealousy and social conflict.

- Normally, when a person has a medical need, they will seek to pay as much of it as possible; if the medical bill is still unpaid, they will reach out to the nuclear and extended family for additional support. If the financial burden remains, a family may seek help from their place of employment or local church. A visitor should be aware of what these other groups have done first before offering anything. If none of these extended groups have been contacted or have given anything, a visitor should be wary of offering financial assistance. A Western visitor should never be the first line of defense for an East African seeking medical assistance.

• Do not give money to the family. If medicine is needed, go to the pharmacy and purchase the medicine for them. If there is a bill at the hospital, check the bill and pay the hospital.

Proverbs

"Your food is supposed to be your medicine, and your medicine is supposed to be your food'" – African Proverb

"You have to heal the wound before it ignores the medicine" – African Proverb

"The forest not only hides man's enemies but it's full of man's medicine, healing power and food" – African Proverb

"A bad wound deserves strong medicine" – African Proverb

"There is no physician who can cure the disease of love" – African Proverb

"Before healing others, heal yourself' – Gambian Proverb

"A man with a cough cannot conceal himself' – Nigerian Proverb

Additional Resources:

Where There Is No Doctor: A Village Health Care Handbook *by David Werner, Carol Thuman, et al.*

African Friends and Money Matters *by David Maranz*

Chapter 25
What Happened to the Money?

A Kikuyu friend of mine set me straight years ago. He closed one eye, pointed a finger at me and said, "You Americans have it all wrong. You say, 'Time is money.' You are confused. In Kenya it is clear that time is time, and MONEY is MONEY." In his declaration, he succinctly explained the strong bond between money and relationships. There must always be time for friends and money is **extremely** important for everyone, but how East Africans manage the two together operates very differently than Western visitors assume or expect. Nothing can cause more broken relationships, sink more projects, and ruin well-intentioned business deals than misunderstanding East African concepts of money and how it is interconnected to relationships. So, what are those values? Why is my personal and "private" money management connected to friendships? What are the consequences of saying no to a financial request?

What Happened to the Money?

Peter Simotwo was one of the first people my wife Linda and I met when we moved to Kitale, Kenya in 1981. Recommended to us by missionaries in the Kericho area of Western Kenya, Peter came to us as a guard and potential project coworker. He was young and still unmarried. Peter had spent a lot of time with the Kericho missionaries and understood American culture better than the average Kenyan. He had a good command of English, so Peter often translated for us in our meetings. In fact, Peter became a trusted companion and cultural teacher concerning the ways and thinking of the people living around Kitale.

Peter was about five feet eight inches tall. He was thin, but strong in stature, He had sharp eyes that reflected a very thoughtful introspection. He was slow to speak. Peter was never first to answer a question posed to a public audience. He was content to let others speak their ideas, and eventually Peter would provide an answer that summarized and incorporated the general thinking of everyone including himself. He was wise and careful.

Peter was also a very strong Christian. He enrolled in and completed a lengthy Bible program, and he graduated with honors. Peter began to preach in his local church. He assumed the responsibility of youth leadership and never failed to attend church. He was considered by all to be a solid Christian young man.

Linda and I watched Peter meet and marry Judith. They provided a good example to their church and community because they followed the advice of their elders, shunned traditional marriage practices, and instead married in their church. They started a family and had several children. We were present at the birth celebrations for all those children.

At one point in Kenya's history, our team of American coworkers were not allowed to travel or work in Marakwet, an adjoining district encompassing the Cherengani Hills. We felt our program was blocked by political motivations that had nothing to do with our government-sanctioned goals. We were depressed. Then during a meeting, Linda asked why we thought only Americans could accomplish our work. "Why not send," she asked, "capable Kenyans to establish and lead the work?" Her question was both simple and brilliant. It didn't take long for our team to identify a leading candidate for this work. It was Peter Simotwo.

With guidelines and resources, Peter Simotwo and Felix Sanduku were sent to Marakwet. Both could travel and work there since the restrictions were directed at foreigners and not nationals. Peter and

Felix found and rented a place in Kapcherop and used their meager funding to travel and teach. Within three months they had accomplished more than we imagined possible. That successful work reinforced in our minds Peter's good character. He was someone we could trust to get the job done. This was true for almost 20 years of walking and working side by side.

When the children's home we managed suddenly needed a set of parents to care for the girls it was almost a given to consider the Simotwos. We approached Peter and Judith, and asked if they would leave their current places of employment and become the new parents for the children's home. Without hesitation, they both enthusiastically agreed. They felt a strong desire to nurture orphans and believed they had spent all their lives preparing for just that kind of work. In short order, they left their previous employment and moved into the home.

Judith settled in immediately, caring for the girls. She was a disciplinarian for all, but not too strict on the teenage girls. Quickly she gained the approval and trust of her girls and the staff of the home. We insisted Peter take over the financial responsibilities of the entire home, specifically in paying the monthly bills for electricity, water, and grocery accounts the home had at several stores. Peter seemed more than capable of handling the confusing bills of the municipality. The bills tended to run behind in accounting, so the balances always showed bigger balances than we owed. Credits would not show up immediately. Sometimes it would take a month or two for the municipality to show a payment had been made. However, Peter was able to gain entrance to the right offices, explain our situation, confirm past payments, and current balances, and pay the right amount. In addition to the home duties, Peter and Judith led the children in Bible studies and made sure all were present for Sunday services. It looked like a perfect parental match for the home.

However, this perfect picture surprisingly cracked. About eight months into their work, we discovered the electricity had been cut off for the children's home. The parents and entire group of almost 50 children were in the dark. By the time we arrived at the children's home, not only was the electricity off, but also the water. One of the other parents reported to us that the stores were also refusing to give us any more credit until we paid our balances.

Digging into the problem, we discovered our bills for all utilities and food had not been paid for four months. Shocked by this revelation, we looked at Peter Simotwo for an explanation. He sat for a moment, eyeing us with thoughtful eyes, fingers on his chin, as if he were gathering his thoughts. Then in a calm and unapologetic voice, Peter informed us that his father had become gravely ill and needed emergency surgery. His father was poor and without resources, so he depended upon Peter to find the funds needed for medical assistance. Peter and Judith did not have sufficient personal funds for the surgery, so Peter took the money for the home's bills and paid a deposit at the hospital. He agreed with the hospital administration to continue making a monthly payment until the debt was completed. It took him four months to clear his father's debt. At the end of his explanation, Peter sat back confidently and without a trace of remorse.

We were speechless, not just because Peter misused the home's money, but because he didn't seem to think he had done anything wrong. So, we pressed him about his use of the money. Wasn't it the children's home money he used and not his own? Peter readily agreed it was. Wasn't the money supposed to pay the bills of the home? Peter answered yes without hesitation. "Then why did you take the home's money?" we asked. Peter looked confused at us and answered, "Because my father was very sick. He would have died without the surgery." We pressed further, "Yes, your father was very sick and needed surgery, but why did you take money from the home?" Peter sat forward as if to explain a simple thing to someone not understanding, "Because I did not have enough money of my own. So, I had to use the home's money to save my father." Still amazed at Peter's apparent brazenness in taking the money and readily admitting it, we pressed further, "Taking the money from the home endangered the well-being of all the parents and over 50 orphans. They have had to suffer without electricity and water and now no food. Did you not think about how taking the money would create a bigger problem for you and the orphans later?" Peter bowed his head as though frustrated by our lack of understanding and repeated his most important point, "If I had not done so, my father would have died."

We were absolutely stunned by what we interpreted as a complete lack of remorse from Peter and Judith. Peter did not apologize for his actions. Instead, he tried to explain and defend them. Even more amazing to us was that he was surprised we expected him and Judith to pay back the amount he had taken from the home. We were unable to construct a satisfactory solution to this loss of home funds. Our trust in Peter and Judith collapsed. While seemingly perfect in every area, Peter and Judith exhibited a shockingly brazen attitude and use of the children's home finances that could not be allowed, easily dismissed, or ever repeated. After several days of discussion, we released Peter and Judith from the children's home. This painful action on our part drew shock and dismay from the Simotwos. Peter and Judith could not believe we had let them go. They cried loudly. Why? They kept asking us why? They simply did not see their actions as being grievous enough to push them away from a work they were very good at. Their release also caused a financial strain upon them. Suddenly both were without employment, and they blamed us for that burden. In hurt and anger, they withdrew from us. Our friendship was broken. We felt betrayed. They felt betrayed, and the home struggled for many months because of the debts it had incurred.

Western visitors engage East Africans with an unconscious assumption that money is valued and utilized the same in both cultures. Nothing could be farther from the truth. While there may be an International Monetary Fund (IMF), an international banking system for exchanging currencies and moving money around, only a cursory investigation proves that nations are far from united on how to handle money. Currency manipulation, trade imbalances, tariffs, taxes, and embargoes all point to very different values in money as a resource, how it is utilized, and how it affects relationships.

More projects than I can count have collapsed in East Africa due to money problems. Financial tensions have strained relationships, broken partnerships, ceased projects, and caused much hurt, suspicion, and even cynicism. The foundational cause of such turmoil is not necessarily Westerners engaging bad people in East Africa. Rather, turmoil comes from a misunderstanding of how each culture views, values, and handles money. Both groups must bridge the cultural money gap to successfully partner in any endeavor.

We could have handled the financial crisis with Peter and Judith Simotwo in a much better way had we recognized our own Western cultural assumptions about money that we were pressing upon the Simotwos. If we had known some of the basic values and uses of money in East African cultures, we could have bridged that cultural money gap and saved years of heartache. With a better understanding of how East Africans culturally use their resources, the following groupings and usage of finances demonstrate the unique understanding and use of money in East Africa. Hopefully, these insights will solve money mysteries and avoid many financial mistakes that harm friendships.

Money as a Resource

In East Africa, money is a much sought after resource. Rich people are very honored, and at the same time, the subject of much jealousy. The rich have a difficult path to navigate. On the one hand, people who have a lot of money and possessions and who keep everything to themselves are judged to be selfish and uncaring about the needs of others. Yet, those who are rich and wisely use their resources for the community's wellbeing are elevated to positions of honor and admiration for they are perceived as benefactors. As a way of helping others, rich people are expected to pay higher prices for commodities or make larger donations toward a problem than their poorer associates. So, the financial goal in East Africa is not just to gain wealth and possessions, but to wisely utilize it within the community to enhance relationships and respect.

Money and Friendships

Since East Africa is a communal culture, being rich has significant relationship dynamics that are not as robust in Western cultures. For example, money and resources in East Africa are important elements in building and sustaining friendships. **Without the mutual exchange of resources, friendships can be severely damaged, and an East African will question the validity of such relationships.** East Africans believe in cultivating and actively visiting their network of carefully selected friends, because they represent a network of resources.

What Westerners see and interpret as hospitality expressed by East Africans, is an investment of resources to foster new friendships and sustain old ones. Assisting friends and family in times of need is an important form of investment for future times when the lender may need help from them. In a sense, this effectively reflects an ancient cultural form of a modern banking system. Traditionally, among the Turkana of Northwestern Kenya, men beg for a goat from one family and turn around and lend a goat to another to build a network of security and partnership within an area. A man's wealth is essentially spread out and cared for by a group of partners who in turn entrust their wealth to him. In case of a raid, no one is completely wiped out. It also means neighbors are partners rather than competitors in the care and protection of livestock. This practice effectively creates a community banking system of holding and managing tribal wealth. This historical tradition of financial interconnectedness provides a strong motivation for why East Africans want to both lend and to be owed money by their friends, for such interaction reflects a healthy network of resources. They are each indebted to the other and recognize their bond.

If possible, East Africans will seek to build friendships vertically with people who are rich and have many resources. They will avoid friendships with those who are socially or economically poorer. Success in life is measured, not by a person's individual wealth, but by the magnitude of their friendship connections to rich people in positions of power or authority, for this greatly strengthens a poor man's resource network.

However, one must be clever to use personal resources effectively and not hoard, for unused resources are considered available to be borrowed by others. If money or resources are not being utilized, then family, neighbors or friends seeking to build a network, feel free to request to borrow something. People with resources must actively use their resources or tie them up in things that can't be borrowed. This is one reason so many buildings sit incomplete in East Africa. Any spare funds are immediately turned into bricks, sand, cement, or some other item that can't be borrowed because it has been "utilized."

Money Management

The management of money may present the biggest area of potential conflict in cross-cultural partnerships, especially if it is money utilized by someone other than the original owner. Many Westerners do not realize an important money principle at work in East Africa. Essentially, a person to whom money is entrusted, culturally, has a major say in how that money will be managed. This means an accountant or person who pays bills for a project, company, or organization, may pull idle money out to use for something else because they have the power to "utilize those resources." My Luo friend says, "Africans only have one pocket. Money from all sources gets mixed into one pocket and can be pulled out for any problem according to the owner of that pocket." Though budgets and designating funds is emphasized by the government and International partners in East Africa, such practices are not the "traditional" way of handling finances. In fact, it is a common belief and practice that any serious financial need that arises has first claim on any funds available to the one in need – personal or not. The same is true in making money. It is a common practice to over-charge to make a better profit, especially when the customer is not a friend or relative. It is also common to use funds "purposed" for something else if a quick profit can be obtained. Such practices are considered clever rather than unethical. There are laws in the books that address the misappropriation of funds, but in my almost 40 years of experience, these laws have rarely been enforced or acknowledged, and are usually wielded only against political opponents.

Money Accountability

Building upon the traditional Turkana example of network building, relationships greatly affect financial accountability. In the case of loans, anyone who releases his resources to another to help or build a relationship acknowledges that he does not need that money at that moment. Thus, the risk of a loan not being paid back is often assumed by the lender. Giving money demonstrates that the need of the borrower is greater than that of the lender. This fact causes the borrower to feel no need to urgently pay back any loan and, in a sense, reflects the clever selection of wealthy and powerful friends. If the lender never needs his money, then the loan becomes a gift after a period of time and is not mentioned again by either. If the lender needs his money back, then the lender must take the initiative and pursue it. He must also explain why his need is now greater than that of the borrower. If he fails to convince, he will not gain his money. If he forces repayment, he undermines the friendship. Because of this elaborate relationship/financial structure, many people live with outstanding loans that they never expect to pay back, especially if their lender is a very rich person, a powerful institution, International organization, or in Peter Simotwo's case an orphanage funded by Americans who could replace the money.

This attitude also affects the accounting profession. Those who can project a high cost for something and then obtain it for less may pocket the difference and cover their actions with altered receipts. Again, this is considered clever, not necessarily unethical. False receipts, or the lack of receipts, is a major problem for International organizations seeking accountability. Additionally, Westerners seeking to follow every shilling spent unknowingly portray a stingy, greedy spirit and that damages relationships. In the event an accountant is caught misappropriating funds, he may be released from his work, but he does not expect to pay back what he took. In fact, he is willing to tie up financial disputes in court for years to avoid paying back any funds he took. Often large corporations and projects eventually drop their court cases, cut their losses, and learn from their mistakes.

Employers and Employees

I learned quickly that I did not hire a person and his talents, I also hired his problems and those of his extended family. Westerners in their workplace are expected to leave their problems at home and show up for work and demonstrate their skills. In East Africa, employees come to work with their personal problems that often spill over into work and sometimes take precedent over work. At such times, employers are expected to provide salary advances and time off for family matters and for certain holidays. Funerals, because of their social networking, surpasses in importance just about any work obligation. Employees with a traditional African understanding of money, don't mind owing money to their employer. In fact, they consider debts as job security, because they will need to continue working to pay it back. Thus, loans and advances are extremely important for good employer/employee relationships. However, it becomes imperative for employers to set limits and guidelines on such expectations, in writing, at the beginning of any employment, before any requests are made, to keep loans and debts manageable. It is extremely important for projects, organizations, and even personal assistants to sign legally binding contracts for a year at a time that include qualifications expected; job description; salary; benefits; loan and salary advance policies; causes for termination; and guidelines for severance and settlements clearly stipulated. Legal counsel is strongly recommended.

Money and Businesses

Many East African private businesses and contractors promise big production but deliver less than stellar results. It is not uncommon to have a business promise to supply a certain item or goods that you want to get your money. Then they may encounter problems trying to carry through. They promise to have it by the end of the week, then next week, and then another time. Once money is exchanged, there is very little recourse in obtaining satisfaction, especially if there is a mistake in the order, or it arrives damaged, or if all the items do not arrive. The same is true of contracts being partially fulfilled. Small businessmen, like a cabinet maker, may need enough money up front to purchase all the wood, and then get paid for his labor at the end. Whether or not you are happy with the cabinet produced becomes immaterial. You either take the product or forfeit the pre-payment. For any Western visitor, it is extremely important to research reputable businesses in advance and develop friendship status with them. This does not guarantee universal success, but it can significantly reduce the number of failures the visiting customer may encounter.

Bargaining

Many stores in East Africa have fixed prices that are labeled and bar-coded for checkout and inventory. This practice has become more common over the last 40 years. However, many smaller shops and local markets have no prices listed. In such local or traditional situations, there may be different prices for wholesale; friends; regular customers; and the tourist and foreigner. The relationship between the seller and buyer will alter the price of goods sold. Bartering is the common way of purchasing goods in such shops and markets. Bartering is not just an effort to get the better prices, it is primarily to develop a friendship with the seller which in turn changes the prices of their goods. Visitors will get better prices if they spend time first to greet and develop a friendship, before purchasing anything.

Cultural Insights/Principles

• Avoid carrying lots of cash on you when traveling or visiting events. This is good for safety, but also for unexpected requests for help.

• When employing someone, get their Tax Identification Number (TIN) for the purpose of withholding taxes and National Social Security Fund payments.

• Pay all employees through their bank account and not in person to keep a legal record of payments. If the person does not have a bank account, work with them to open an account (provide counsel and direction). It will be better for them and you.

• Seek legal counsel on drafting contracts for ALL workers.

• Learn local prices through friends before making major purchases or enlisting private contractors.

• When using an accountant, check balances and receipts weekly. If possible, confirm major receipts for legitimacy.

• Avoid purchasing anything without receipts.

• Check with the labor office for employer/employee guidelines for salary, holidays, sick leave, severance, benefits, taxes, National Social Security Fund (NSSF), and how to handle disputes.

Proverbs

"If you get rich, be in a dark corner when you jump for joy" – African Proverb

"One cannot count on riches" – Somalian Proverb

"Money is sharper than the sword" – Nigerian Proverb

"Lack of money is lack of friends; if you have money at your disposal, every dog and goat will claim to be related to you" – African Proverb

"Much wealth brings many enemies" – Swahili Proverb

"Greed loses what it has gained" – African Proverb

Chapter 26
Corruption: Is It a Gift Or a Bribe?

While seeking a plot of land in Kitale's municipality for the construction of a children's home, we had meticulously prepared paperwork for the District Development Committee (DDC) Secretary. Every official we met praised our efforts and told us how much Trans Nzoia District needed a home for the abandoned children. There was no place to house or care for the orphans. So, we assumed our project proposal would be granted quickly. Surprisingly, the DDC Secretary delayed submitting our paperwork. Numerous trips to his office produced only promises of quick action and long explanations about his personal problems. When we went over his head to complain to the District Commissioner, our paperwork was mysteriously lost. So, we had to start all over again. In my naivety, I did not realize the Secretary was culturally requesting a "gift of appreciation" for his work on getting our paperwork ready for submission. Since we were not giving anything, our paperwork disappeared. We went all the way to the Provincial Commissioner who started an investigation. The Secretary was transferred to another district, and we obtained a plot of land. If we had been more culturally sensitive, we could have navigated that problem more wisely.

Western visitors naively think local officials will help them accomplish a project or effort that benefits the community. Yet, once paperwork must be signed, officials become vague, less cooperative, and unavailable. Why? What is the official trying to communicate? How can the visitor obtain the proper signatures for the project to succeed? How should visitors navigate the complicated system of corruption?

A customer steps forward and explains to the smiling repairman. She says, "My pressure lantern is broken and needs to be repaired." The repairman smiles and says, "Just leave me the lantern and 10,000 Ugandan shillings (about $10 at that time) for spare parts and come back tomorrow." The customer leaves the lantern and the money because she needs light in her home in the evenings. After the customer leaves, the repairman puts the broken lantern on the counter beside him and laughs cunningly to himself. He will use that lantern all day as spare parts for other lanterns that come to him. Then tomorrow, he will show the woman all the broken parts that need to be replaced. He will increase his profits and get an unsuspecting customer to purchase all the spare parts he needs for today's business. "I am very clever," he thinks to himself.

On the days the repairman needs to purchase spare parts, he goes to his friend in the industrial area of Mbale, Uganda. The repairman has purchased spare parts from his friend for a very long time. As the repairman enters, the shop owner smiles to himself. He thinks, "Today I will make a good profit from my long-time customer." The store owner's practice for years has been to secretly increase by 10% the prices on all his spares to this repairman. "I am very clever," he thinks to himself.

After his repairman customer leaves, the shop owner receives a visit by the Mbale municipal official in charge of shop permits. The official enters with a grim look on his face. He slowly inspects the room and gloomily announces his intention to close the premises due to health regulations. The shop owner is shocked and responds pleading that some kind of delay must be possible so that he can correct the unspecified faults. The official pulls out a notebook in which he begins to write up a report for his superiors. The shop owner explains the problems he will have if he is forced to close his store. It will bring financial hardships for him and his family. The official acts as though he must reluctantly shut the owner down while gently leading the owner to the official's true desire. The official thinks about this as he silently laughs to himself. There is no health regulation that he could use to close this shop, but by acting harshly, he can frighten the owner into responding with a gift of money. It will be a "pre-tip" for the official's supposed work to help the owner keep his shop open. After a long pleading process by the shop owner, the official leaves with a little extra sum in his pocket and the shop remains open. "I am very clever," the official thinks as he leaves the spare parts shop.

The municipal official reaches his office only to find another letter from his boss in Kampala. It seems the computer is still down and his monthly salary will be delayed another month. He regrets the computer difficulty, but everyone knows how problematic computers are. The Mbale official cries out as he thinks of all the expenses that are mounting up in his home. He has school fees due and a bill at the local store for food supplies he bought on credit. He begins to think of other shops he can threaten to close. Perhaps he can raise enough money to pay his bills.

The boss in Kampala smiles as he posts the letter to the Mbale official. He knows there is nothing wrong with the computer and that his officials in Mbale have received their allotted salaries into his office every month. By holding all the salaries for months at a time, the boss can bank them and keep all the interest accrued. Sometimes he can even claim that a month's salary was never paid without action being taken by the officials in Mbale. He smiles at how clever he is.

The minister for local affairs visits the boss in his office in Kampala. He enters, dressed in an expensive suit and tie, and is followed by two assistants looking nervous and hurried behind him.

He is a busy man. You can tell by the way he keeps looking at his expensive gold watch. The minister informs the boss that the President will be hosted at a government banquet in a month's time, but his office does not have enough money to pay for it. So the minister is informing each of his people that they will give a "voluntary donation" of a half of a month's salary to help pay for it. The boss quickly agrees with this suggestion knowing that if he refuses, his own job may be lost. The minister smiles to himself as he leaves, because he knows there is no banquet for the President. He simply needs a little extra cash to pay for his secret mistress. He and his aids exchange knowing glances as they leave the office. "I am really clever," he thinks.

At home, the minister is relaxing with his wife of 25 years when the phone rings. It is the President. Without thinking he stands up in respect as he talks on the phone. The president says he has been receiving complaints about the minister's work. He is thinking of shifting him out of the cabinet and returning him to his regular position as a member of parliament. The minister lets out an uncontrolled gasp as he thinks of the lost prestige, and the revenue he can squeeze from his people. He pleads with the President to give him another chance. Perhaps if he made a large donation to the President's campaign fund, the President would be patient long enough to let him prove himself. At length the President is persuaded to give the minister more time, but only if he makes that contribution quickly and for twice as much as he had suggested. Ouch! But it is worth it to stay in his position of power.

At home the President sits in his chair and laughs to himself. No one has complained about the minister, but he knows that all of his ministers desperately want to keep their positions and will do almost anything, including large donations to his "fund," in order to stay. He smiles about how easy it is to squeeze these men who pretend to be so important. As he thinks of these things, his maid comes in and brings him tea. He hardly notices her entrance.

Back in the kitchen, the maid prepares to go home for the evening. She hides a half kilo of sugar from the President's cupboard in her basket. She laughs to herself as she thinks of how regularly she steals food and small items from the most powerful man in the country. She thinks of herself as very clever indeed. She is about to leave when she sees the note hanging by the door. The President is reminding her of one more thing to do before leaving. She can even do it on the way home. So, she takes the President's broken pressure lantern and goes to a small shop on the way home. There, the smiling repairman says, "Just leave me the lantern and 10,000 shillings for parts and come back tomorrow."

Corruption vs. Relationships

How can an East African culture that emphasizes the importance of a friendship network allow corruption to flourish? If money is used to cultivate relationships, and the increase in the number of friends means a larger resource network, then why would anyone "squeeze" potential friends to gain a personal financial profit? With such a publicly stated ideal, corruption should not exist in the East African communal society. Yet corruption does exist, and this contradiction seems confusing and even hypocritical to Western visitors.

Proverbs 29:4 says, "By justice a ruler gives a country stability, but those who are greedy for bribes tear it down." This proverb underscores the effect corruption has on a society. Instead of promoting significant development and progress, corruption tears down the community. Since 1995, Transparency International has supported the use of the Corruption Perceptions Index (CPI), an assessment tool that utilizes 16 different surveys and assessments from 12 different institutions including the World Bank and World Economic Forum et. al. Annually, East African countries perform poorly in these surveys with Kenya and Uganda ranking around 137th out of 180 nations. Rwanda and Tanzania fair better at 51st and 96th respectively. Burundi at 165th and South Sudan at 178th are ranked the lowest on the index, meaning they have the highest corruption rate of all the East African countries. However, this is not just an East African problem. Across Africa, statistics suggest one in four Africans must pay a bribe to access services.

Proverbs 29:12 says, "If a ruler listens to lies, all his officials become corrupt." The proverb's corollary teaching demonstrates that corruption if allowed at the highest levels of government, will spread to every level of society. I have heard many citizens complain about corruption within the government. They admit that corruption is prevalent, but it is only a problem instigated by those higher up. They see themselves as victims of the system not the perpetrators. Yet, these same citizens, when faced with obstacles in accomplishing something, quickly resort to offering a bribe to make things easier.

My coworker Ian Shelburne explained this obvious societal contradiction of corruption existing within a relationship-oriented society most succinctly. He said, "We hear publicly the value and emphasis of relationships and friends, but what is practiced is every-man-for-himself. In truth, what is communally embraced is the 'appearance of relationship.'" Thus, the high ideal of community and friendship networking is, at best, superficial, and underneath lies a selfish agenda of "me first." This level of all-encompassing corruption may not be apparent to the tourist, but it will become experientially obvious to a long-term visitor.

This should not be shocking to any Westerner who has observed their own politicians who speak publicly of and urge policies for the common good, but who secretly fill their own bank accounts with kick-backs, bribes, illegal donations, and do the bidding of special interest groups. In fact, many nations and International organizations have found ways to institutionalize a system of bribery that functions within the current system of International laws. Yet, the different perspectives of bribes between Westerners and East Africans, and how to respond to the pressure to give them, creates unexpected social dissonance and work complications for the visitor in East Africa.

The Western view of bribes is fairly black and white. An online dictionary defines a bribe (describing the action of the one who gives) as "money or any other valuable consideration given with a view to corrupting the behavior of a person, especially in that person's performance as an athlete, public official, etc." Extortion (the action of the one who receives it) is defined as "the crime of obtaining money or some other thing of value by the abuse of one's office or authority". Whether you are the one giving or receiving, Westerners see the pre-exchange of resources for a favor or service as criminal. In essence, bribes undermine justice and allow criminals to gain an advantage over the innocent. Laws have been codified to punish both bribes and extortion.

The East African view of bribes is not as black and white. Because East African relationships are demonstrated by the exchange of resources, bribes become more of a gray area. What a Westerner would consider a bribe, the East African would call a pre-tip or a demonstration of appreciation for something that is about to happen. Oddly enough, Westerners don't mind giving money as a tip for good services rendered, but they become indignant if the person providing the service requests the tip in advance. What is the difference, anyway, between an African giving a bribe to rush something and a Westerner paying a fee for "express service"? To many East Africans, this Western delineation can be very confusing. To them, Westerners can, on some occasions, be very generous, but on other occasions, they can become extremely incensed at the thought of giving a financial gift. East Africans often struggle to understand why the timing, before or after the service, is so important in the giving. The East African practical mind sees both pre-giving and post-giving as an expression of appreciation and an opportunity for relationship building. This is an important fact to remember when living and working in East Africa.

Guidelines on Bribes

For the Westerner who visits, works, or lives in East Africa, here are three guidelines concerning bribes:

1. If possible, avoid *paying* any kind of bribe. Seek every possible avenue to accomplish your goal or objective without resorting to paying for something that should be rendered freely by social, educational, medical, business, or governmental services.
2. Avoid *offering* bribes to shorten the process, to make things easier, or to elevate your paperwork to priority status simply to gain an advantage over others for you or your project/organization.

Before I give step three, let me interject two important points.

The Practical Point

It is not uncommon to find an official, municipal, land, legal, or government matter absolutely tangled up in red tape (on purpose by bureaucrats) in order to extract a fee to untangle it. There will be no recourse (this has already been setup and tested before you arrived) except to pay the fee unless the goal is abandoned. This entanglement is usually demonstrated in that officials never provide clear and comprehensive steps to accomplish anything. They will purposefully be vague and leave out steps in order to get you back to their office for more "help."

The Ethical Point

Let me make a significant insight about bribes from a biblical point of view. All condemnation in Scripture concerning bribes is focused upon the person with power and authority who demands or accepts the bribe. There is no condemnation on the one who is forced to give it. It is the abuse of power, or the perversion of justice by the one accepting the bribe that is condemned, because its corruptive influence damages all of society. The Bible understands that the poor may be helpless before the powerful and therefore forced to give money in order to accomplish something. Only at that point, when all other options have failed or been blocked, should guideline number three be utilized. However, step three should never be used to simply make things easier or to gain an advantage over someone else.

1. If your efforts are blocked by someone in authority and it has become clear that all other avenues have been exhausted, you are left with no recourse, but to pay a bribe. However, I would suggest you use an African associate, legal representative, or organizational leader to address the problem. Western presence in any negotiation causes the "fee" or "pre-tip" to be higher. Local representatives can build relationships while bargaining for the final price.

Cultural Insights/Principles

• Bribes are not normally requested openly. They are vaguely referred to as help for "tea," "air time," or "appreciation" for the service about to be rendered. Thus, be careful about interpreting the request literally.

• Sometimes, officials may request to talk to National coworkers without the Western visitor present in order to speak more directly about a "pre-tip" fee.

• It is wise for Westerners to avoid being present or to have any part in negotiations for a bribe.

• Immigration and customs officials often require an agent to run the paperwork for clearing everything. Within the payment of the agent are certain "fees" for "handling," "processing," and "office expenses." Westerners should be advised not to insist on clearing or completing paperwork by themselves. Hire a good local agent and let them do everything in less time and money.

• Obfuscation and obstruction are key signs of corruption. When officials resist providing detailed reports about fees, payments, receipts, and costs, it is an indication that corruption is present. Insisting on accountability and transparency of that official or office can cause serious complications in completing a documentation process.

• East African laws on customs are amazingly detailed in listing items for which customs are charged. There is also a percentage of the value listed for each item. HOWEVER, at the end of this exhaustive list of items and percentages is the tiny paragraph that gives the customs official the power to determine the value of any item. Thus, the ability to determine the final amount to be charged lies in the hands of the customs official.

Proverbs

"Whoever tells the truth is chased out of nine villages" – African Proverb (Truth is something to be spoken carefully and never without consideration of another's feelings.)
"A lion doesn't turn around when a small dog barks" – African Proverb
"Choose your company before you sit down" – African Proverb
"Those who want rain must also accept the mud" – Ghanaian Proverb
"When the mouse laughs at the cat, there is a hole nearby" – African Proverb

Chapter 27
Indirect Communication: What Are We Talking About?

White-haired Gabriel stood up and, with a smile on his face, introduced himself and his lovely wife, whom he called "my sweet," much to the laughter of everyone in the room. After his introduction, Gabriel's face turned somber as he looked straight at me and began his analogy. He pointed out the window to a grove of banana plants surrounding our building. He said, many farmers say that when the plant is doing poorly, that there is a problem at the root level. I want you to understand that the problem we have here is not with the roots but with the leaves. He nodded his head quickly in an affirmative motion and then sat down. Even though I was not a farmer, I had a pretty good idea that banana leaves would not be the real reason a banana plant is suffering. I thought about the wrong kind of soil, not enough water, or perhaps the climate. At that time, I was not tuned in to indirect communication. After me failing to understand, a friend leaned over to tell me their group was struggling because the top people, not the bottom people, were fighting among themselves. Gabriel was indirectly telling me that the problem they had was with the leadership. He wanted me to address it and help save their small group.

Visitors to East Africa will initially think that everyone they meet is so friendly and hospitable. What they don't realize is the common cultural practice in conversational exchanges of avoiding direct confrontation or endangering relationships. Instead, indirect communication is universally practiced. How, then, do East Africans view Westerners who speak directly and forcefully? How can visitors navigate the indirect approach to communication? How can visitors ensure they are understanding everything clearly when metaphors, stories, and partial responses are the norm?

The "Art" of Communication

Bosco Mukholi knocked on the back door late in the afternoon. He was our gardener and he had finished for the day. His head was down and as I approached from the inside, he deferentially stepped back a couple of steps. This was his third time to come to me within a week to inform me of a family problem. Earlier, he told me a cousin of his had come from the village to stay with him temporarily as he sought employment in town. Bosco had readily welcomed his cousin to stay, thinking his help would be seen favorably by the extended family. The week of assistance turned into a month and then two without his cousin being able to find work. Then his cousin became sick and needed treatment at the local hospital. Medical bills piled up on Bosco and he sought assistance from me to cover the cost of treatment and medicine. I was able to help only partially, so Bosco worked out an agreement with local stores for a line of credit. He could continue to get food items for his family and pay later. But the debt had become so large that his creditors were threatening to call the police. Bosco's cousin seemed deaf and blind to the problems Bosco was having. He neither looked for employment, helped with household chores, or offered to return home and reduce the number of people Bosco had to feed. He simply sat around home all day and waited for each meal.

In the process of this mounting struggle with finances and family, I gently scolded Bosco for not telling his cousin to go home or to move somewhere else. As an American, I would have told my mooching relative to find work or go home. I would have given him a time limit on how long he could stay at my house. After that, I would insist on his departure. I would even forcefully remove him if he did not respond positively. I was incensed, on Bosco's behalf, that his cousin was taking advantage of him. Bosco would listen intently, thank me for my solidarity with him in this struggle, but he would not implement my suggestions.

After the hospital trip and mounting medical bills fell on Bosco, I offered to talk to his cousin myself. I offered to sit face-to-face with his cousin and tell him how he was shaming himself for being a burden to Bosco. I offered to tell him clearly and forcefully to go home. Bosco declined my offer to help in this way. Another time, I offered to forego the harsh words and just give the cousin some money to go home. Bosco politely declined my offer to extend transport money for his cousin.

I was becoming frustrated with Bosco. He seemed to complain to me about his cousin, but seemed incapable of solving the problem in a clear, direct, and efficient way. Finally, Bosco was at my door once again with his head hanging down.

As I stepped close, Bosco, with a sad look on his face, said he wanted to quit his job. I was stunned. He was a good worker. I knew he enjoyed working with me. We had no problems between us. I was shocked that he wanted to leave. I knew work and salary would be hard to replace. With all of the bills Bosco was facing, I could not believe quitting was going to make things better. I stammered when I asked him why he wanted to quit.

Bosco took hold of the porch pole beside him and, still looking down, scratched at a crack in the concrete floor with his shoe before answering. He said, he figured the only satisfactory way out of his family problem with his cousin was to inform him that he had lost his job and that he and Nancy were going to move back to the village to live. Bosco reckoned that moving would force his cousin to find another place to live in Mbale or to return home himself. Either way, Bosco would not have to directly force his cousin out of his house.

Bosco was willing to lose his job and suffer severe financial difficulties in order to avoid causing a family problem with his cousin whom he admitted was taking advantage of him. In fact, Bosco considered his solution as very wise in that he would rid his immediate family of his cousin without suffering a strained relationship with the cousin or any extended family. At that point, I realized how important family relationships were to Bosco. They were more important than a secure job and good salary.

When I realized Bosco was not quitting because he had a problem with me or the work, I relaxed and began to rethink how I could help Bosco. Rather than my American solution, we developed Bosco's solution with a slight twist. I "officially" fired Bosco on the spot. I told him to go home and announce this unemployment to his wife and cousin. Bosco would tell them that without a job they would need to return to the village. Then Bosco was instructed by me to sit at home and not come to work for up to a week if necessary. If he was able, I suggested Bosco reduce the amount of food he offered at each meal and begin to pack some boxes for moving. We agreed that on the third day of his home stay, Bosco would come to my house, and I would pay him a week's salary with which he could pay some on his store debt and keep his family fed through the week. Bosco's eyes brightened at our indirect, but cunning plan. He rubbed his chin, and with the first smile in weeks, declared it just might work.

On the third day when Bosco came by for his money, he had a big smile on his face. He said that morning his cousin inexplicably decided to move to an uncle's home about 30 miles away. He was gone before lunch. Bosco told me he invited his cousin to stay and help them pack up, but the cousin seemed more interested in a job opportunity where his uncle lived. He did not stay to help pack.

I gave Bosco some money and asked him to stay home and rest, take care of his wife, and pay some debts. Then, if he was interested in a job to come by Monday morning for an interview, we both laughed and he agreed. By Monday morning, Bosco was a happy man who whistled while he worked.

Visitors to East Africa are unaware to what lengths their hosts will go to avoid a confrontation that might harm a relationship. Since friendships are so important, people like Bosco are willing to suffer great financial loss to preserve even a bad friendship, because they know that one friendship is also connected to a whole host of other friendships that would also be affected by a single problem. Better to calm the waters than to create a disturbance.

For Western visitors, Bosco's response and solution to his cousin's burdensome stay appears dishonest, deceitful, and unscrupulous. Bosco essentially lied to his cousin in order to trick him into leaving. All of these descriptors would, to Western visitors, be much more round-about than just telling his cousin to get out of the house and go home. To my East African friends, it is much more damaging to harm the relationship than to be dishonest and deceitful about the circumstances, especially if the deception resulted in his cousin leaving on his own initiative rather than Bosco's insistence.

With this big gap in understanding, communications between East Africans and their Western visitors may be confusing and the cause of much frustration. And there is the real possibility that a Western visitor may feel like they have been lied to. If this happens, then I would say it is the Western visitor's fault. Let me illustrate.

If my gardener was outside raking leaves and accidentally hit a window pane and broke it, how I responded to him would dictate what and how he communicated the broken window pane to me. If

I went outside angry and shouted at him saying he broke the window, he would deny it stringently. He would claim a child running down the street threw a rock over the fence and hit the window. He would say a branch fell from the tree and cracked the glass pane. He would say anything, no matter how wild or obviously false, in order to shift my anger off of him and onto something else in order to preserve our friendship. If I didn't understand his values and communication style, I would think he was lying and would fire him for not being trustworthy.

However, if I went outside calmly and with a smile on my face and engaged the gardener. If I greeted him at length and asked about his wife and family and extended family. If I talked about a beautiful day and how good it was to stop and visit a moment, the gardener would be assured that our friendship was in good standing. Then if I happened to notice the broken pane of glass and mention how small of a problem it was and that it could be replaced easily. He would feel free and able to inform me that while he was raking leaves the RAKE hit the window (even here the trouble is on the rake not him). In this way, I would find out the truth of the matter, indirectly, while protecting our friendship.

I believe Western visitors, with their direct, aggressive style of communication, damage relationships and actually force East Africans to lie to them. While Western visitors highly value truth, East African highly value the preservation of relationships. This difference in values often creates tremendous strain on cross-cultural friendships.

Two Perspectives on Communication

Many Western visitors step into East Africa and see billboards and signs in English, and many officials and taxis and bus drivers and tour guides speak English. Visitors erringly think that a common language also means a common communication system and values. This is not the case, and visitors should be wary. Though Westerners and East Africans use the same English words, the connotations associated with certain words can be significantly different. Combined with the indirect communication style of the East Africans, communication can be a virtual minefield of misunderstanding.

The most difficult of the two for Western visitors and residents is the indirect style of communication. To illustrate the difference in thinking and value of the direct/indirect communication, I have constructed a thought process for both the Westerner and East African to help clarify the often imperceptible gap of communication even when we are using the same language.

American Visitors: Freedom of speech is a foundational American value that we fought for. Specifically, we value the ability to speak our mind. We value the freedom to express our views, criticize wrong-doing, applaud our causes, and argue our beliefs. We admire a person with convictions who can confidently articulate his point of view. Debate is healthy! Opposing arguments help clarify the truth, because it helps us remain objective and balanced. But when we sit with East Africans they tend to "beat around the bush." They fumble around and never speak plainly. Their indirect communication wastes time, prolongs meetings interminably, and keeps problems hidden in a fog of stories and metaphors. Such communication is confusing, frustrating, hinders efficient dialogue, and obstructs comprehensive solutions. Indirect communication comes across to us as clumsy, deceptive, deceitful, inefficient, and fearful of true and open communication. We rush to judgment that our East African brothers and sisters need to learn how to stand up and speak up. They need to understand that even if the truth hurts, we want to hear it.

East Africans: One of the core values of our community is the cultivation and preservation of relationships. While we may feel freedom to speak our minds, we will politely curb our freedoms in order to protect our friendships. In fact, we will take our time in every meeting to build relationships. To show respect and not hurt others we will mention difficulty indirectly, gently leading our listeners up to the problem but not touching upon it openly, to show esteem for our friends. We may stop short of exposing a problem so that our listener is not embarrassed by it. By describing without specifically speaking the problem, we allow the listener to fill in the gap and recognize it without our having to say something difficult to hear. If we are unable to meet our friend and personally mention the problem indirectly with him, we will send someone to inform them. Our communication may be indirect and time-consuming, but it is also sensitive, tactful, honorable, and can even be considered by us as a true art form of expression. Our American friends handle the truth recklessly and often unknowingly hurt others right and left. Their bold and aggressive, almost angry speech undermines relationships and isolates them from the community they are trying to reach. Their direct communication hinders everything they attempt to do. Americans think we waste time by our indirect communication, but it is the Americans who have a real problem with time. They cut their meetings short, seek the bottom line, speak directly, doggedly follow schedules, and have invented all kinds of time-saving devices. Yet we have never seen an American visitor with plenty of time saved up to do anything slowly together with us.

Violent Responses?

I must include one other aspect. Some suggest that indirect communication in East African culture is like an abusive family. Everyone learns to avoid saying things for fear of retribution by the angered. While there is some truth that individuals will hold their tongue rather than confront for fear of violence, I would argue this is true for most people in all cultures. Many people simply don't like conflict whether it is abusive or not. In some instances, East African culture sees physical abuse as an acceptable response. However, it is also countered with a proverb that says, "The medicine of fire, is fire." This means the best way to control an angry person is with an equally angry response, or a physically abusive person with a violent response. While most East Africans will quickly resort to indirect speech to avoid problems and control the situation, if they are provoked enough, they can become angrily confrontational. In this sense, an abusive family analogy doesn't quite fit.

Cultural Insights/Principles

- Requests for financial help are often framed in the presentation of a problem to the listener, and the expected response is to offer assistance to solve the problem.
- Problems in relationships are often communicated to the offending person by a third party.
- The more important an event is, the more time and talking (communication) spent on it.
- The abundance of speakers is intended to enhance the significance of an event – often with speakers lined up in order of importance from least to the greatest.
- Officials, who must sign important documents for you, may inform you of an important fundraiser they are supporting. This

seemingly unconnected information is an indirect request to pay something monetarily to get your documents signed. Declining the invitation to support the cause may severely complicate your process.

• A church, project, or business leader may stand up in front of his colleagues and communicate a significant problem in front of everyone. Instead of being angry at the public complaint, recognize his delicate function of having to balance informing you of a problem (as a third party) while pacifying the frustration of the group. Thank him for bringing the problem to your attention and request a specific time frame to address the issue thoroughly.

• Patiently attending to problems that arise, no matter how many offices you must visit, allows opportunity to build new friendships. Don't overlook the opportunity to build friendships even when solving a problem.

• Learning how to answer a question indirectly with a story or example entertains your audience and builds friendship bonds.

• Try not to pack a schedule so much that you have to cut a meeting short. Allow plenty of time for group discussions.

• East African culture expects the host to receive his guests, direct their actions in his home, and then release them after all of his plans for hospitality are completed. If food is included, it may take time to complete all of the cooking, especially if the visit is unannounced. A good guest will not pressure the host to let them leave early.

• If you need to leave early, first express how much you wish you could stay and how much you value everyone's friendship and that you must reluctantly leave for a pressing issue. Express how much you look forward to the next meeting.

Proverbs

"A speaker of truth has no friends" – African Proverb
"Stumbling with the mouth is worse than stumbling with the foot" – African Proverb
 "Wisdom consists of ten parts: nine parts silence, and one part a few words" – Arabic Proverb
"Examine what is said and not who is speaking" – African Proverb
"A man who uses force is afraid of reasoning" – African Proverb
"Silence is also speech" – West African Proverb
"Perhaps you do not understand me because you do not love me" – African Proverb
"He who shouts most may be the one in the wrong" – African Proverb
"The art of being a good guest is knowing when to leave" – Kenyan Proverb

Chapter 28
Foreign Assistance: Guidelines for Avoiding the Con Man

One day a man came into my office seeking help. He sat forlornly in front of me as he told me his string of bad luck that culminated in his desperate plea for help from me. At one point, this man in his forties looked at me and said, "You must help me because I am just an orphan without anyone to help me." His claiming to be an orphan shocked me. "Who is an orphan?" I thought, and "How is 'orphan' defined?" Is it a child or an adult? Isn't an orphan a child without both father and mother? What if one parent is living? What if both are living but just unwilling or unable to help their children? The definition of an orphan is not at all consistent among the multitude of international organizations or cultures. One may define an orphan as someone without parents and no identifiable extended family. Another defines an orphan as having no parents but who lives with a grandparent or uncle or other relative. Another counts a child an orphan if their father is dead or missing but the mother and extended family are caring for them. Still other organizations may call a child an orphan if both parents are living but have abandoned the child to extended family. Many Westerners do not contemplate the definition of an orphan. For them, the small child with the sad face is the familiar "orphan" who adorns many brochures and TV ads seeking financial assistance for just a few dollars a month. The emotional appeal of forlorn images touches Americans in particular because they know they are fortunate and they have a desire to help.

Many visitors to East Africa are struck almost immediately by the economic gap between them and their gracious hosts. Though the East African countryside is beautiful and fertile and the people hospitable, poverty is more visibly prevalent than in the visitor's home nation. This economic gap intensifies when a visitor is asked for help. Should the Western visitor provide aid? If so, what is the best way to assist? Is every need that is presented legitimate? What cultural dynamics are in play with requests for help? How can the visitor gain a better cultural understanding so that they are able to engage successfully without creating in the needy an unsustainable dependence on help?

Con Man or Saint?

Western visitors often come with an open and sincere heart to help. They may have a religious reason, a social cause, or they may feel guilty about being so rich when there are so many in East Africa who need help. With this sincere motivation comes a naïve belief that every poor person is honest, humble, and only needing resources to turn their life around. There is no way, they believe, a con man can run an orphanage or start a clinic. Surely his testimony and work proves he is a good man with a good heart.

If first impressions count, then Sam Wandiba was a standout. Sam appeared above average in many respects. He spoke English well enough to show his education, but he retained a rustic East African accent that captivated Western visitors. Sam owned a house in Mbale, Uganda plus a farm to which he drove in his own van. He established a medical clinic that served Buyinza, and he raised foreign support for more than 50 orphans. On top of all this community service, Sam professed to be a Christian possessing a powerful conversion story which he told to me on our first visit.

Sam said he was riding in a car with a bishop of the Anglican Church back in the 70's. Idi Amin was in power in Uganda at the time, and the bishop was on the army's wanted list. On a trip to Kampala, the bishop's car was stopped by soldiers, and the bishop, along with Sam and several others, were arrested and taken to a nearby prison in Jinja. The group was kept for several days without food. Soldiers came in periodically to torture and scare the prisoners with threats of death. After several days of this, the soldiers entered one morning and seized the bishop and another prisoner. They were led out into the courtyard and executed. Sam closed his eyes as he recounted hearing the gun shots from his cell. After a few hours, more prisoners were taken out to the courtyard leaving only a few in the cell with Sam. The second set of prisoners were also shot. When the door opened the last time, Sam by instinct jumped behind the door to hide. The soldiers, in a drunken frenzy, did not notice that one of their prisoners was missing. They were enjoying their game of killing prisoners too much to keep records. As the remaining prisoners were taken out to be executed, Sam snuck out of the prison and made a mad dash for the fence. He was almost at the fence when soldiers spotted him running. They opened fire on him. Sam was hit in the shoulder and the force knocked him to the ground where he rolled up against the fence. Sam says, by God's grace, the fence was not attached at the bottom, and he slid out into a bushy field where he ran under cover for a long time. He tells the story passionately, and it always moves people to tears as he recounts how his friends were slaughtered before his eyes.

To sponsors of projects, Sam Wandiba is a dream come true. He is obviously successful. He is educated. He presents himself well. He has founded a clinic and an orphanage from nothing, and he has a knockout testimony that is impactful in any brochure. This is the image of Sam held by all of the many visitors who come over to visit him for 7-10 days at a time in Mbale, Uganda. Sam picks them up at the airport, drives them to his clinic and orphans' home. He feeds them and tells his story and speaks of things he wishes he could do to help his community if only this or that were provided. Sponsors increase their gifts and go home to write powerful reports with big colorful pictures about the work they are doing in Uganda.

To those of us who lived in Mbale, Sam presented a different picture. When I was surveying Mbale as a possible place to work, one missionary (now gone) advised me to stay away from Sam Wandiba. The missionary said Sam was bad news and had caused a lot of trouble for previous mission personnel. He recounted one story of how he had to help a missionary escape the country only hours before Sam and 17 policemen came for him. He told me Sam was good at getting missionaries to come over, then Sam would falsely accuse them of something before government officials to get the missionaries kicked out of the country, and then Sam would seize their property. This missionary told me how he had actually witnessed one such incident. I was experienced enough to listen to that missionary's advice.

Within a three-year period, I had several unexpected meetings with Sam. One time he came to my house for a visit. We sat on my veranda and drank tea as he told me his testimony and spoke of the dreams he wanted to see come true. He invited me to visit him and to speak at the orphanage he had started. I thanked him for the invitation but mentioned my busy schedule and declined for the present. I said, "Perhaps I could come in the future."

On another occasion involving Sam, a former missionary from America, Larry Dean Smith, came to visit some of the Christians he had worked with in the 80's. By chance, Larry ended up staying with us. We discovered he had worked closely with Sam and had even loaned him $20,000 to buy a van. Larry and Sam had even made a legal contract through a lawyer stipulating that Sam would repay Larry for his personal loan. I was present when Larry Smith asked Sam about the money for the van. Sam gave many excuses saying that hard times had delayed him from paying. However, he was confident that God would bless him to pay back all the money in full. Sam had paid nothing in the 8 years since the loan, and he offered to pay nothing to Larry then. Two years after that, Sam still had not paid anything. In fact, Sam expressed surprise that Larry Dean Smith had even come back to Mbale.

My third meeting with Sam occurred when another American visitor, Al Hamilton, came to Mbale about six months later. He knew Larry Smith and had worked with him on some projects. Al Hamilton had made Sam angry. So, according to Al, Sam went to the police and bribed them to arrest him and throw him out of the country. Al Hamilton claimed he had spent a lot of time trying to convince the police and Central Intelligence Division (CID) that he was an honest man only wanting to help Ugandans.

Besides these personal missionary testimonies, it was known in Mbale and around Sam's area that Sam divorced his first wife and married one of the older female orphans. He did not tell the sponsors that he did this, so he continued to receive aid for an orphan that was really his wife. It was also rumored that many of the orphans he sponsored were actually relatives. Those relationships did not come up during the seven-day tours that sponsors received. I wondered if the Australian sponsors knew that Sam also had American and English sponsors as well? I also wondered if all the sponsors knew they each sponsored the same children?

About a year later, Sam received a shipping container full of clothes and goods for his clinic and orphanage. The talk around town was that Sam had switched his church to another denomination so he could receive support for it. He traveled to Kampala to confirm the container's arrival, and then he came back to Mbale to inform his wife. On his return trip to Kampala, the taxi he was riding in collided with a man on a bicycle. The driver lost control of the vehicle and rolled the taxi several times. The bicyclist and driver were killed instantly. Sam, who was sitting by the passenger door, was thrown from the taxi and killed when he hit the ground. I understand the taxi partially rolled over Sam as well. Four died at the scene of the accident. Several more of the taxi passengers died over the next few days in the Mbale district hospital.

Sam's death obviously brought numerous ramifications. What happened to the clinic and the orphans? Did the sponsors find out what had been going on? Will a brother or other relative step in and take up Sam's mantle? What happened to his orphan wife who is now a widow? Sam had enrolled her in a nursing school as one of the orphans. Now that Sam is dead, will she make any claim on his farm and possessions? There is a tangled web of deception and many problems to be sorted through. I suspect Sam's extended family will fight several legal battles with his orphan wife in order to gain control of all of his land and wealth.

The Struggle of Helping

A large amount of research shows Westerners often help too much, in unwise ways, even to the point of hurting rather than helping. African authors like Dambisa Moyo and her book ***Dead Aid*** (2009) have noted that more than one trillion dollars of foreign aid has flowed freely to Africa for decades with no measurable results. Poverty is a complex problem with many contributing factors. Money is only one facet of poverty. Thus, a wise, comprehensive response to poverty is much more complicated than just the transference of funds.

There are two important attitudes that should be embraced by Westerners who visit or live in East Africa. These will go a long way in reducing the emotional stress which comes from requests for financial assistance. First, whatever a visitor's purpose for being in East Africa, they should not look at a request for help as an interruption of their trip. Instead, consider it an opportunity to build a friendship, make an impact, or change a life. Second, the visitor should determine ahead of time a goal for their visit and if they wish to give any assistance. Do they have in mind to help an orphanage, a church, a project? The visitor should consider an amount and how it should be utilized BEFORE additional requests come. In this way, the visitor can explain their limited resources and why they cannot respond to other pressing needs. The visitor should not allow the numerous needs around them to force them into giving beyond their means. Helping should be purposeful and not reactionary.

Cultural Keys to Helping

When considering whether or not to help, it is extremely important to recognize that cultural matters shape the request and presentation of the need. Navigating through these cultural nuances is very difficult for the inexperienced visitor. The following cultural keys should assist in determining the legitimacy of the request, the size of the need, what exactly is being requested, and how to properly respond.

It Never Hurts to Ask

Where I was brought up, it was important to "pull your own weight," "provide for your family," "work hard," "live within your means," and it was a shame to ask for help. Or, you asked only when it was absolutely necessary. It took me a long time to realize that those with whom I worked in East Africa lived by a very different cultural value. To them it was not shameful to ask, nor was it bad to ask even if they did not really need it. Asking for assistance from a rich person is wise because there is a possibility of expanding a personal network of friends and resources. There is a saying that accurately portrays this thought, "It never hurts to shake the mango tree," meaning a little shake may produce falling fruit. So, just because a person asks for help, does not mean he actually needs something, and it does not *obligate* the visitor to give. In fact, it is important to remember that East Africans have survived without the aid of a visitor, and will continue to do so. There should be no guilt in politely explaining to anyone who comes forward with a need that you currently have no disposable income to help.

The Hook of Giving Advice

Another cultural form of gaining resources is through seeking advice or counsel from the visitor. In East Africa, when a person gives advice for someone to follow, then that advisor obligates his own resources to help the seeker fulfill that advice. For example, if I encourage a youth to finish secondary school, then I have culturally obligated myself, as a rich person, to help pay school fees. At first, I was honored that so many came to me for advice. I thought people respected my wisdom and counsel. I realized later the hidden cultural hook of expected financial assistance that goes with providing counsel. The same hook exists for providing counsel concerning medical treatment, business advice, career choices, project needs, and non-profit enterprises.

Another hook in the request is how much of the need is revealed. Often a petitioner may hide part of the problem in order to hook the visitor into initiating support. Then afterward, the deeper, larger problem is gradually uncovered. It is wise for a visitor to ask the petitioner to state, comprehensively, the entire problem and all that is required. Then, if the visitor wants to help, they can stipulate exactly what they are willing to do and what limits they have with help.

The best option is much harder for Western visitors. Rather than arrogantly assuming they have wisdom to counsel all problems, Westerners need to humbly direct those who seek advice to their own cultural leaders who have a much better understanding of the intricacies of the problem and can provide the best financial and cultural solutions.

Do I Help or Assist?

Western visitors need to learn the cultural meanings of the English words "assist" and "help." Especially in Uganda, these words mean very different things. "Assist" means to add your own strength and resources to the petitioner's efforts. "Help" means the petitioner is unable to go any further, and your strength and resources must take care of the rest of the problem.

If the Westerner is inclined either to "assist" or to "help," it would be wise to have the petitioner state clearly what they have done and what kind of resources they are seeking. The visitor can place stipulations on any help given such as requiring the petitioner to complete step one by himself, raise a certain amount from friends and relatives, or achieve some goal or grade, etc. Then if the petitioner fails to keep his part of the agreement, the visitor has a reason for not using any more resources on that need. This kind of response is normal for East African parents who have limited resources for school fees. If they are unable to help all of their children, then they put their resources on the children who are doing the best in school and stop fees for underperforming children.

Do Not Ask the "Visitor"

There is a cultural double standard practiced against Western visitors concerning how to ask for help. In many of the cultures in East Africa, it is extremely impolite for a host to ask for personal help from a guest. They would never do this to each other. The polite way to show honor and respect in relationships is for the petitioner to go to the home of a friend, relative, or neighbor, and ask as a visitor for help from their host. However, because Western visitors are not culturally knowledgeable about this practice (and their East African hosts are unable to go to their visitors' homes), they are frequently asked for help while being the guest. Often they are insulted further by being asked for assistance in front of a large group of people. This is calculated to put more pressure on the visitor to respond positively. It is best, when trapped in this situation, to suggest that the petitioner come to the house, office, or hotel of the visitor, as a guest, rather than shame himself and the visitor in front of everyone by going against his own cultural values in relationships. This suggestion is a polite way of informing the petitioner the cultural guidelines for requesting help is known and that the public request can be offensive.

What is the Backstory?

Dennis, my Kenyan friend and mentor, shared a known secret among East Africans. They know Western visitors are wealthy and generous. So, they purposefully stage a situation for the Westerner to experience. When a visitor comes, a host may gather many of his relatives' children and have them dress in their work clothes. Then instead of using a regular soccer ball, they have the kids play with a ball of plastic bags tied up with string. While the kids play, the host shows the visitor the children 'suffering' with a plastic bag ball. "If only…," the host says, never finishing his thought. The Western visitor asks how much a ball costs, then he goes down to the store and buys a new ball. Everyone is happy. Giving a soccer ball creates goodwill which morphs into an additional clothes' drive for those poor children, which becomes a feeding program, and then all out sponsorship. In a short time, the East African host has found sponsorship for all of his relatives' children earning him great respect as being clever, resourceful, and generous.

On one occasion, I was visiting an old man who was complaining about a poor harvest and a string of bad years in crop production. During a break in our teaching session, I noticed an old woman neighbor next door hoeing her potato patch. Her command of English was impressive. When I expressed sympathy for the bad harvest and string of bad years, she stopped hoeing and looked at me strangely. She said her crop had been very good that year, as it had been for many years in a row. I realized, once again, my host had not told me the true backstory of his situation.

Sometimes a neighbor, government official, or stranger who has nothing to gain may be the best place for getting an objective evaluation of the situation. Relying solely on those who would benefit from any help is a major mistake of the visitor. Determine the true state of affairs before plunging in to save the day.

How to Say No Without Hurting Relationships

Keep in mind that requesting financial help is a cultural sign of building friendships. So it is extremely important to answer wisely without alienating yourself from the petitioner. In Kenya and Uganda, it is never good for a Western visitor to say, "No," to any request for assistance. This does not mean the visitor must agree to every request. What it means is the visitor must learn how to respond in a way that does not harm relationships. The visitor must hear the petitioner's entire, sometimes convoluted story, empathize with him, and even agree that his situation merits assistance. The longer a visitor can listen and empathize with the petitioner the better, because spending time is an important friendship indicator. Then if the visitor is unwilling or unable to help, he/she must explain in great detail, and at length, why their personal circumstances do not allow them to help the petitioner **AT THAT TIME**. The visitor should never answer, "No." Instead they should explain why they can't help at this moment. It would be good for the visitor to explain their desire to help and that if they had available resources they would want to help. Unfortunately, at that time, and because of financial constraints and personal circumstances, the visitor is sadly, unable to help. Without doubt the Western visitor can seriously damage East African relationships by adamantly saying, "No" without offering any explanation.

Reciprocity

A key component for handling requests for financial assistance is understanding the cultural principle of reciprocity. I mentioned in a previous chapter, the begging system of the Turkana of Northwestern Kenya. True, it is an elaborate system of begging from their neighbors that really signifies a financially intricate form of friendship where a family's wealth is spread among friends to avoid financial ruin in one unfortunate event. However, there is a reciprocal principle to this system. When asked for a goat by someone, the first thing a Turkana man may think is, "Do I want this man to be my friend? Is he honest? Is he a man of integrity? Will my friendship with him improve my social status or bring problems upon me and my finances?" These questions reflect a reciprocal system that ties friendships together with finances. No one in East Africa can continually ask from his neighbors without being asked in return. Reciprocity culturally means that whatever size of request the petitioner is seeking, he is giving his neighbor permission to ask for that same size of request in return. Not agreeing to such reciprocity breaks friendships and brings public shame. Such reciprocity is the key balancing element to all relationships, and it keeps one party from taking advantage of the other.

Most Kenyans and Ugandans that I know will be careful not to over-extend themselves with any neighbor for fear of a financial backlash. Since Western visitors do not know or practice financial reciprocity, petitioners press for assistance without fear of reciprocity. One of the best ways to keep assistance requests in check is to develop a way of asking for something in return. The greater the request made to the visitor, the greater the request the visitor can make. If the East African fails to fulfill his part of reciprocity, he can be gently reminded of his failure the next time he asks for additional help. Simply reminding him of his past failure to fulfill his obligation can express the strain in the relationship and be a reason for your inability to help him presently.

The petitioner may not be able to pay back in kind, so the visitor may need to be creative in what is asked for in return. The Western visitor's reciprocal request should be fairly equivalent to the initial appeal for help. Make the return favor difficult enough to make the petitioner hesitate to ask again. For example, the Westerner may ask someone to travel to the capital on public transport to accomplish some organizational errands. Giving two or three days of their own time (with expenses covered) to care for the Westerner's matters would be a show of mutual support.

Or, a Westerner could enlist the help of one or more to mobilize a group for a specific community or project meeting or task. Setting a specific number of attendees and having the volunteers meet that number would ensure mutual reciprocity. If the Westerner receives excuses or reasons for failure in the task, then it would be culturally appropriate to give excuses upon that person's next request for help and politely remind them of their past failure to help. Follow that reminder up with another opportunity to help the Westerner. Those who always seek help but give excuses for not helping in kind, need to be weeded out of any organization or project.

Proverbs

"A lie has many variations, the truth only one" – African Proverb
"The betrayal of trust carries a heavy taboo" – African Proverb
"Do not follow a person who is running away" – African Proverb
"One falsehood spoils a thousand truths" – Ghanaian Proverb
"Unity is strength, division is weakness" – Swahili Proverb

Additional Resources

- ***Dead Aid: Why Aid Is Not Working and How There Is a Better Way for Africa (Reprint Edition, Kindle Edition)*** *by Dambisa Moyo*
- ***The White Man's Burden: Why the West's Efforts to Aid the Rest Have Done So Much Ill and So Little Good (Kindle Edition)*** *by William Russell Easterly*
- ***Poor Economics: A Radical Rethinking of the Way to Fight Global Poverty (Kindle Edition)*** *by Abhijit V. Banerjee and Esther Duflo*
- ***When Helping Hurts: How to Alleviate Poverty Without Hurting the Poor . . . and Yourself*** *by Steve Corbett and Brian Fikkert*

Chapter 29
Handling Requests And Asking for More Details

Several years ago, I received an email from a friend in the United States of America. He had received a very informative letter from a Kenyan evangelist seeking financial assistance. He forwarded the letter to me and asked for my advice. He was inclined to help but wanted my response first. Since many people in the U.S.A. receive such letters these days, I thought it might be helpful to include portions of the letter along with my suggestions on how to respond.

Advice I Wish I Had Received

Letter of Request

Dear brother,

You have been introduced to me by brother XXXXXX. I would also like to introduce myself to you. My name is John Bingle Barasa. I am a Christian man 52 years old. I am married to Silvia Nekesa. God has blessed us with three children.... My parents are both still living... in Uganda.

I became a member of the Lord's Church on **15th May 1978** in the city of Nakuru, Kenya. **In 1988,** I went to Bapton School of Biblical Studies in Bungoma, Kenya. I graduated **5th August 1990** and came back to... and continued to preach for the Reformed Church in...

In **May 1992,** I went to Tanzania as a missionary with my family... I helped to establish three congregations around Arusha.

On 24th Dec. 1996, I arrived in Busia, Kenya... I started a Bible School for all people to come to learn the word of God. We have also established 17 new congregations of about 10-30 members in Busia district.

Due to the spiritual needs in Uganda we are starting a new work in Tororo on the border of Kenya and Uganda. I will be working with the Teso people who are in three districts. The three districts have about 1,500,000 people who need to be saved from their sins.

We plan to start a School of Evangelism. It will be a two-year program in which the students will be in class for six months in the first year and four months doing evangelism in the villages. In the second year, each student will be required to start a congregation during this period. A student who fails to establish a congregation will not graduate.

During this time, they will be doing personal work, they will also be learning a trade or self-help projects. The school will be working with government centers where they can learn these skills. The school will be paying these learning expenses. Students who graduate will be helped with some funds to start their own projects so that they can have an income as they preach the word of God.

When these brothers are taught skills to financially support themselves and helped with funds to start, they will have an income and not depend on American money monthly.

The churches in East Africa are still too poor to support their preachers.

Our operational needs for the school will be $280 dollars per student per month. We will have 10 students in the first year and 20 in the second year. You can assist by supporting one or more students per month.

We also need your assistance with our one time set up cost. The one time set up costs are…

My Response to My American Friend

First, let me say thank you for including me in the request and consideration of John Bingle Barasa's proposal for a combination Bible and Polytechnic School. So many American Christians receive such proposals (Internet is an amazing communication tool) and make their decisions without consulting Westerners who are on-the-ground. This has led to great disappointments for some who become discouraged from ever helping again.

Before I comment on the proposal, let me say that during my time in Kenya and Uganda I have helped start (along with my teammates) two polytechnic schools, two clinics, one orphanage, one primary school, many nursery schools, one Bible school, and one university. I am very familiar with government regulations and procedures concerning the establishment of such schools (in Kenya and Uganda) and the steps to get them going. I have served as chairman for an orphanage, teacher for Messiah Theological Institute, Chancellor of LivingStone International University, and board member for Nairobi Great Commission School and Good News Productions, International. The work we do extends from Western Kenya to Southern Sudan to Northwestern Tanzania.

Now, let me divide my comments about Barasa's proposal into several categories.

Government Regulations

To establish a licensed polytechnic school, the government will require at least the following things:

1. A piece of land large enough to hold the school, dormitories, kitchen, latrines, garbage disposal, offices, and recreation area
2. A certified site plan showing the current and proposed buildings
3. A health inspection and occupancy certificate for the school
4. A bank account in the name of the school showing proper financial accounting
5. A school manual for discipline, rules, curriculum, authority, and fee structure
6. Certificates and documents of all government-certified teachers in their areas of training
7. An established school committee made up of sponsors, teachers and parents
8. A rationale for the school's existence

The process for registration requires all the above things, plus more. It takes time and money to get all of this together. Additionally, if such a school is functioning under the name of the Reformed church, then John Bingle Barasa would have to produce:

1. Minutes from the Executive Board for the Reformed Church giving approval of the school

2. Minutes from the Executive Board and the local school board identifying the trustees of the school

3. The Tax Identification Number (TIN) of the Reformed Church

4. A copy of the Reformed Church's current certificate of registration

Financial Guidelines

Author's Note: All financial amounts listed in numbers 1-3 were current at the time of my response. They do not reflect current salaries of teachers or school fees in Uganda.

1. While it sounds low to American ears, John Bingle Barasa's request of $280 per student per month is quite high for Uganda. A professional teacher for high school with an associate degree receives less than $150 a month in salary according to Uganda's current pay structure. This means Barasa's request of $280 is almost twice the amount of money received by a teacher in Uganda.

2. Currently, polytechnic schools charge less than $350 per YEAR for a student. The highest quality secondary schools that provide room and board charge about $720 per YEAR. Against this fee scale, $280 per student PER MONTH looks very suspicious.

3. We run a school, a tertiary institution under our Ugandan registration, less than 40 miles from Busia. As I write this email, we conduct courses in which 110 students are attending. Of those students, 29 come from Kenya, 5 from Tanzania, and the rest from Uganda. We have hosted courses since 1992. After conducting more than 100 such courses, we currently calculate that a 20-course curriculum on our Basic Certificate Program costs $200

per student for a TWO-YEAR program. That means we charge about $10 per course to cover food, lodging, materials, and in some cases part of the transport to reach the school.

Other Considerations

I do not know John Bingle Barasa in the Busia, Kenya area, but I can say the following things:

• We already have about 10 project groups around Busia who come to our courses in Mbale, Uganda. We teach courses in English and Luganda. We also provide extension courses that can be taught in Lugisu, Japadhola, Lugwere, Ateso, Kupsabynyi, and Langi.

• If Barasa insists on Swahili for courses, then we can accommodate him in Tongaren, Kenya or another school in Kisumu, Kenya less than an hour away from Busia. Our contact in Kisumu also oversees a correspondence course school with over 1000 students currently enrolled. It is an excellent way to receive teaching at a fraction of the cost of attending a school in Busia.

• If Barasa insists on courses in Luganda, then a sister school in Jinja will offer excellent courses with a newly established dormitory and lecture hall. It is also less than an hour away.

• The fact that John Bingle Barasa does not mention already existing schools and groups in his area makes me think he either does not know about them or that he chooses to remain disconnected from them. You may need to learn which it is.

Suggestions

You have several options available to you:

1. Go ahead and provide him with the money he is asking for without further clarification.
2. Work directly with John Bingle Barasa but seek more proof through the confirmation of all the government requirements and paperwork to show that his school in Busia, Kenya is following the correct procedure for establishing a polytechnic school. This also includes asking for clarification on $280 per student per month, teacher qualifications, and what structure is being used to determine who gets the sponsorship.
3. Provide an alternative solution by suggesting that you partner with him through scholarships. You could offer scholarships to individuals for polytechnic training and Bible instruction at a fraction of the cost John Barasa is requesting. We would be glad to help you bank any scholarship funds and confirm that the money is used for the purpose stipulated in the agreement. Remember, $200 is enough for a full TWO-YEAR scholarship at our school in Mbale, and $350 is enough for ONE YEAR at a local polytechnic. We provide clear and accurate financial reports, digital pictures of the students, a bio, and a scholastic update.
4. You can tell John Bingle Barasa that you are unable to help him at this time.

Cultural Considerations

There are several cultural matters to be aware of.

1. Please do not write to John Bingle Barasa and accuse him of wrong-doing or inflated prices. It is better to say something like, "We have heard that local polytechnic prices are about $350 per year. Why is your figure so high?" Asking for clarification is less damaging than accusing him.

2. Please do not use my name as a source for the information on high prices. By doing this, you will create tension between him and me that I do not need. If you do not help John Barasa and tell him my advice was the reason, then I will never be able to befriend or work with him or his family.

3. The best way to preserve a relationship is to either explain why you cannot help at this time, or provide an alternative way of helping that you feel comfortable with, i.e. scholarships, etc.

4. East Africans work on a completely different grid concerning asking for help. We (Americans) value independence, self-sufficiency (financially speaking), a high work ethic, and would not think of asking for help unless we really needed it. Also, we feel obligated to assist someone who asks for help, because we know this is not the norm (in our culture) and something must really be wrong. Conversely Ugandans and Kenyans see no shame in asking. They may be doing fine with life, but if they see an opportunity to ask something from someone with resources, then they will ask.

5. Kenyans and Ugandans have no problem about asking for financial assistance for one thing, but when the money comes in, they may decide to use it for something else. They believe that once you give up the money and they get it into their hands, then they have the right to change their minds about what it is used for. They do not consider this deceptive or deceitful. They believe

ownership and purpose change when they come into possession of funds given. It is much like a fisherman using a lure. Once the fish bites, the fisherman can decide the fate of the fish. He may use different kinds of lures to catch his fish, but ultimately the fisherman can decide what to do with any fish that comes his way.

6. You need to be aware that East Africans have discovered the Internet. There has been a rush of individuals to obtain a free email account and start searching the Internet for their church of choice (a lot of webpages out there provide all kinds of information). Numerous, less scrupulous, people are posing as reputable evangelists, principals, founders of baby homes, etc. and preying on the sympathies of wealthy Westerners. You need to go into any partnership with East Africans having done your homework and with verifiable responsibilities on both sides.

I am sure I have not covered everything, and perhaps my own comments have created more questions. I am ready and willing to provide additional information should you choose it. Let me end by saying that there exists in Uganda and Kenya numerous opportunities to engage in mission work that will be a blessing to the Christians here and to your own home congregation. The biggest problem is identifying legitimate places to work. Take your time, seek lots of counsel, and begin in small stages. Test the waters and add to your help once you have established your relationships and the legitimacy of the endeavor.

Proverbs

"When one begs for water, it does not quench the thirst" – Soga Proverb from Uganda.
"A man who cries all the time is not heard" – African Proverb
"He who pursues an innocent chicken always stumbles" – African Proverb
"It is not rushing that is important, it is making sure" – Masai Proverb from Kenya
"He who timidly requests, invites refusal" – African Proverb

Chapter 30

Crusades: The Destructive Force of Visiting Foreign Evangelists

One day while sitting in a local restaurant, a Western visitor came in with several Ugandans in tow. She ordered food for all of her charges and looked around and spotted me. She came to my table, introduced herself, and then began a five-minute talk about who she was, what she was doing in Uganda, and how important her work was. She called herself a missionary even though she had only visited Uganda six times for about two weeks each time. She gave opinions of the climate, political situation, and the spiritual strengths and weaknesses of the folks she had met. She assumed I was a visitor like herself and so proceeded to tell me the best places to shop and eat in town. Only as she briefly took a breath did my friend interrupt her and casually mention that I had lived in East Africa for more than 25 years. Her demeanor changed, and she quickly excused herself back to her guests. She never allowed me to introduce myself. She never asked me a question, or gave me the chance to give her any advice.

Just as I was misjudged by the talkative Western visitor in the local restaurant, an even greater disconnect exists between the visiting Westerner and his East African hosts. Without realizing it, many Western visitors arrive in East Africa with preconceptions, a sense of superiority, and a large amount of cultural baggage to which they are often blind. They make flawed assumptions, judgments, and interpretations through their home cultural lenses without recognizing such lenses can be significantly dissonant with East African culture. The arrogance of assuming their Western ways are best, can be extremely disastrous for whatever they attempt to do. Nowhere is this more evident than in the visiting Western evangelists arriving to conduct a local crusade. Do the visiting evangelists know anything about their hosts? Are they aware of the traditional practices, beliefs, and needs of the people to whom they will be preaching? Do they know how best to answer local, cultural, and spiritual questions? Do they know how to conduct a crusade that would benefit their East African Christian hosts?

An Evangelistic Disaster Befalls Bupoto

Not long ago the archdeacon for the Church of Uganda in Bundidugyo, Western Uganda contacted the archdeacon in Bupoto (South Bugisu - close to Mbale) and told him of a small group of missionaries from England who were doing evangelistic crusades. He recommended them highly and encouraged the archdeacon in Bupoto to invite them. The archdeacon was excited about the prospects and made arrangements for this group to come and hold a week long crusade.

Now the Church of Uganda (Anglican Church) in Bupoto is the largest church of its kind in the entire Mbale district. It was established by English missionaries in the 1930's, and some of its oldest buildings are still used today. It is a traditional church with conservative practices. The Church of Uganda leans toward a more structured "high church" worship service. They have old, traditional songbooks which they use. They downplay the emotional and concentrate on form and substance. Their emphasis on baptism by sprinkling, and church government is rigidly hierarchal. Nevertheless, Bupoto has been effective in outreach and ministry, growing into a large and active congregation. It was into this context that a group of English evangelists came to do a "crusade."

On the very first day things started going awry. The English visitors were extremely modern in their approach to worship and evangelism. Even though they were from the same church background, the English evangelists began to introduce new worship practices immediately. They encouraged the Bupoto members to clap during their English choruses, and they told the members not to just stand there but to move around a little. They encouraged members to show some excitement when they sang. The visiting evangelists told them it was even okay if they wanted to dance a little bit, and they demonstrated it for them by dancing around in the front of the building.

The archdeacon of Bupoto had invited numerous Church of Uganda leaders from the entire Mbale district for this special crusade with evangelists from England. So enthusiastic was his invitation that, many National high church officials came to meet and worship with the visitors. However, the new practices the evangelists encouraged offended the Mbale Church of Uganda leaders. They were alarmed by what the English were promoting. Yet, these East African leaders, bound by their cultural politeness and relationship values, could not publicly tell their guests to stop. They did the only thing they could do culturally – they got up and left. There is a saying in East Africa that "Africans vote with their feet." They will not tell you they disagree or will not support something. They just don't show up to participate. Such was the case for the Mbale church officials in the Church of Uganda. They left and never returned to the week-long crusade. They left the archdeacon of Bupoto to fend for himself as his visitors tore down his carefully constructed, well-running church work. The English evangelists seemed to be oblivious culturally to this turmoil. In fact, they reportedly considered their evangelistic work as "correcting outdated methods" and "reviving a passive congregation." They were insistent and felt spiritually justified in their ministry.

After each worship service, the evangelists encouraged the people to break with tradition and come forward for prayers. Sick members were especially entreated to come and receive prayer. They introduced loud and expressive prayers to chase away demons. They taught about the baptism of the Holy Spirit, and they emphasized baptism by immersion. On one day of the revival, they showed the American film production of Jesus' life and ministry. It had been translated into Luganda but remained a very American portrayal of Jesus.

The people who had attended the Church of Uganda in Bupoto for years were confused. They could clearly see that the English evangelists acted differently than their own church leaders. They introduced new teachings and encouraged more emotional expressions of worship. In fact, what these evangelists encouraged was no different than what the Pentecostal churches around them had been doing for many years. The Bupoto Church of Uganda members began to question what they had traditionally been taught. Have we been lied to? Have our church leaders been deceiving us? Is this the real way we should be worshipping? One older woman I interviewed said she saw Jesus in the film being baptized by immersion. She said she had been sprinkled but now wanted to be immersed. "How can I fight against Jesus?" she asked.

I am sure the English evangelists went home feeling as though they had conducted a wonderful week-long crusade. I am confident their pictures and reports of the crusade showed large crowds, clapping and dancing audiences, people kneeling and receiving prayers of healing, and lots of people watching the Jesus film. They may have even felt good that they were able to revive a stuffy old church and praised God for the opportunity to minister in Bupoto.

I visited a village adjacent to Bupoto two weeks after the crusade to teach a small group of students. They reported to me what had happened at the Church of Uganda in Bupoto and the results of the crusade. The actual outcome was much different than the English evangelists could have imagined. The Church of Uganda in Bupoto suffered a massive exodus from its membership. Disillusioned members left their home church in search of other churches where "true" worship and doctrine were being practiced. Many felt the Bupoto church leaders had, at best, neglected them and, at worse, deceived them on purpose. Everyone blamed the archdeacon for bringing the English evangelists to Bupoto. The small group I was teaching actually had a few of the original Bupoto members in it. One told me he went to another church to be baptized. Then, I discovered that he had been one of the preachers for the Bupoto Church of Uganda. He was ashamed of what had taken place and blamed both the English evangelists and the Church of Uganda leaders for allowing such a crusade to take place.

Western evangelists are not always the source of conflict and confusion. Sometimes Western evangelists are the victims of a well-rehearsed East African crusade. The Mbale Church Leaders' Fellowship is a consortium of about a dozen Protestant and Independent churches in Mbale. They have registered their organization with the government, have officers, hold meetings, and generally are a very tight-knit group of church leaders. They do not seek to gather all leaders together. You have to be the right kind of church leader and you must go through a vetting process that is unclear and not outlined. The Mbale Church Leaders' Fellowship is also a "Ugandan's Only" association. They will not accept foreign missionaries into their group. So, in a sense, MCLF leaders speak of an evangelical and ecumenical fellowship, but it is by invitation only. There is a good reason for this secretive behavior.

The one thing this group is good at is holding an annual crusade in Mbale. All of the church leaders in MCLF reach out to find a foreign evangelistic team who is able to come to Mbale and hold a week-long crusade. They seek a group that can pay for the expenses of holding the crusade. The expenses are outlined by the Mbale Church Leaders' Fellowship in communication with the foreign evangelistic team. If they agree, then dates are set, and the Mbale group springs into action. They get permission to use the municipal soccer ground to hold the crusade. They construct a wooden stage and bring in huge speakers and a sound system. They print brochures and flyers with crusade information. They visit all the churches in town and even get on the radio to promote the event. Most importantly, they push all of the MCLF churches to attend the week-long event, which produces a fairly respectable crowd. The foreign group comes in, preaches and teaches, local choirs sing and dance, and Mbale Church Leaders' Fellowship leaders emcee everything while directing the visitors to and from their hotels, arranging food, and even a little sightseeing to and from Kampala, Uganda. Many of the church members raise their hands and either receive Jesus or rededicate themselves at the crusade each year. From all appearances to the visiting evangelists, it was a successful crusade.

However, not all of the churches in town participate because they know what is really happening. They know the true character of the Mbale Church Leaders' Fellowship. So, very few people from "outside" churches attend. They also know the secret purpose of the crusade – foreign fundraising.

The Mbale Church Leaders' Fellowship sets the budget and outlines the expenses to the foreign evangelistic team in advance. The field, which may cost $50 dollars to reserve, is budgeted at $500. The sound system and huge speakers come from one of the churches but are "rented" for the crusade at $1200. For each item, the costs are exaggerated. MCLF sends a proposed budget to all of the churches in town and pressures them to give. If they do not, then the rumor mill cranks up, and horrible things are spread about the non-participating churches. The platform, brochures, hotel expenses, food for the guests, radio time, transportation, chair rental, and so many other things are listed as crusade expenses and handed to the Western evangelists to solicit their help. The foreign evangelists hand over a huge stack of money to facilitate the crusade and do their preaching, and the Mbale Church Leaders' Fellowship pays its meager bills and then divides its windfall among the close-knit fellowship leaders. The foreigners go home with pictures and numbers of people who raised their hands and will be discipled by the local leaders. The MCLF leaders start looking for their next foreign evangelists who can come and hold a crusade. There is money to be made in holding crusades!

There are numerous trips made each year to East Africa by Western Christian evangelists and church groups. Their goal is often to complete a youth camp, construct a building, hold a crusade, or provide volunteer work for some church-based project. Such groups come with little or no cultural training to help them bridge the gaps between their home culture and the one in which they seek to work. Without recognizing it, they engage their short-term ministry with all of their Western lenses and values intact and work, teach, counsel, and preach with little understanding of how their words and actions impact their East African hosts.

Western Evangelists often assume a superior understanding of Scripture because of their university studies that offer little training in cross-cultural communication. They confidently teach and answer questions from their East African audience. They do not know the cultural dynamics at play. Sometimes a person in the audience may ask a question about leadership that is actually a back-handed, cultural criticism of their local leaders. Not picking up on the complaint, the Westerner uses his Bible to provide a theological answer. In another instance, some in the church may not like how money is kept and used by only the pastor, so they will ask a question about transparency, accountability, and record keeping. The Westerner actively answers. He does not know he has set a fire in the group that will flare up after he has left. An East African man who agreed to pay a bride price for his wife but who is behind in payments, will ask the Westerner if paying bride prices is a good Christian thing to do. He knows the Westerner will disagree with paying bride prices, and he will use it against his in-laws after the evangelist is gone. He will ignore his initial agreement to pay the price and hide behind the unknowing answer of the Westerner. Another person may stand up and ask whether or not it is good to eat bats, then he will point to a passage in Leviticus chapter 11:19. The Westerner will struggle to answer an Old Testament question for current diet restrictions but may end with a suggestion that eating bats be avoided for health reasons. What he does not know is that the question was intended to criticize some in the audience from a tribal group who traditionally eat bats. The East African just got the Westerner to criticize a dietary practice of another tribal group. I could give many illustrations, but the point is clear, there is an absolutely huge minefield of dangerous questions ready to be asked of the foreigner who knows nothing of the context and cultural backgrounds attached to the innocent sounding inquiry.

Without cultural training or knowledge, the best a Western evangelist can do is stick to his Bible stories and lessons and help interpret what the Bible has to say. The Bible has many trans-cultural principles such as love, kindness, gentleness, respecting others, humility, generosity, and many others that can be taught and encouraged. However, when it comes to application and how to answer a cultural question, the Western evangelist would do well to defer to local church leaders to answer. Additionally, the Western evangelist should insist upon local leaders to arrange worship services and meetings, and only stand to speak or preach at the appropriate time. They should inquire ahead of time from the church leaders about local practices so that they avoid introducing new teachings, customs, worship styles, or church polity in a better or modern way.

Additionally, Western visitors do not know enough about East African legal matters to know what kind of questions to ask. Is the church building they want to help construct on land owned by the church or by an individual who may later claim it as his own house? Does the Western group have government permission to hold a meeting, construct a building, hold a clinic, or hold a crusade? Have the proper authorities been notified? Is the church project legally registered? How can the visitors know gifts given to the project will be used for that purpose? The number of complications is almost endless, and novice visitors are often clueless about the problems. I must add one other note concerning frequent visitors. For some reason, Western evangelists and church groups become cultural experts after only two or three week-long visits. Unfortunately, their limited experience makes them feel more knowledgeable than they actually are. Such attitudes can create some explosive problems.

Should We Abandon Crusades?

One must ask what is the lasting benefit of crusades led by foreign evangelists in East Africa. Most of the posters I see printed and distributed in the towns and villages in Kenya and Uganda have pictures of large crowds participating in singing, praying and preaching. The pictures include promises of spiritual blessings and list large numbers of converts and results. But what is the long-term effect? What really happens after the microphones are put away and the tent is folded up? Are crusades an opportunity to reach large numbers of unbelievers, or are they a lot of froth that whips up the already converted into a frenzy that dies down after the meeting is over? My personal, long-term experience is that little change is seen after the crusade has moved on, but that could be the fault of follow-up and not the crusade itself. For Bupoto, the crusade led by culturally insensitive evangelists was disastrous.

Yet, crusades should not be abandoned, just refined. Western evangelists need to offer their preaching, teaching and resources in a humble learner-posture. They should come as partners in kingdom work, not superiors. They should ask for guidance and counsel from local leaders on what and how to teach and how to "assist" financially. The Westerners should never be the ones paying all the bills. In fact, it might be best if Western evangelists provide their own hotel and transportation and allow local leaders to cover the costs of the crusade. Cross-cultural evangelism and fellowship are vital to gaining a larger picture of God's kingdom and how His church lives and thrives in different cultural settings. Both the Western visitors and the East Africa hosts will grow in their appreciation of the global church through these meetings. Most importantly, the crusade should never be the final goal of any visit. It should be developing long-term relationships and partnerships in kingdom work, of which the crusade is a tiny part.

Cultural Insights/Principles

• Any Western evangelist or volunteer group going to East Africa should seek basic cultural training to prepare them for cross-cultural interaction. Mission organizations, missionaries on the ground, and a few cross-cultural training seminars are available to train Westerners in cross-cultural evangelism.
• Western visitors should not go with a superior attitude or a hero's complex seeking to "rescue underprivileged peoples."
• Westerners should not take selfies as though they are doing something great.

• Westerners should be diligent to avoid creating a negative image of their hosts or people in East Africa.

• All visitors should go with a learner-posture having the belief they will learn more than what they teach.

• Building relationships is more important than the amount of work done, seminars taught, bricks laid, or orphans held.

• If possible, investigate the legitimacy of the organization, church or project you are attempting to help through Internet searches, interviews with local government officials and neighbors, and other expatriates who live nearby and may have insights to share.

• Avoid private meetings with individual leaders who may take advantage of the lack of witnesses to ask for personal help.

• Avoid letting one church leader complain about another church leader. Do not agree to become the mediator of a cross-cultural dispute.

• Ensure, if possible, that any funds given for a project or crusade are used accountably. The best way to do this is to put funds into the hands of a committee rather than a single individual. Multiple people handling the money and gathering receipts increases accountability.

• Avoid making promises to send money or items back from your home country.

• Do debriefing meetings with everyone in the group each day and several times after the trip to help everyone process their experiences, conversations, insights and difficulties. Such meetings provide opportunities to explain unusual cultural behavior, what to do with requests for help, how to address poverty or hospitality, how to help in a good way, how to maintain a learner posture, how to respond to different worship styles and lessons, etc.

All of these proverbs address hidden complexities in relationships that are especially meaningful to Westerners visiting East Africa.

"When sugar is mixed with sand, the elephant doesn't get it, but the ants do" – African Proverb
(Westerners will miss the nuances of speech, actions, introductions, and many other cultural practices that the East African audience will catch. This is especially true of how their messages are translated into another language.)

A spider's cobweb isn't only its sleeping place, but also its food trap"
– African Proverb
(The offices of government officials are not just a place of obtaining permission for meetings, but it is a source of income for the official. Special fees often accompany any permit for an evangelistic meeting.)

"You have little power over what is not yours" – Zimbabwean Proverb
(While Westerners may give money for specific items during the crusade, once it changes hands, they are no longer in control of how it is spent. See the chapter on money and friendships.)

When you befriend a chief, remember that he sits on a rope" – Ugandan Proverb
(Because friendships are reciprocal, befriending a chief will entangle the Western visitor into additional obligations he is not expecting and unprepared to handle.)

"Beware of the naked man who offers you clothes" – African Proverb

(It is not uncommon for East African evangelists to promise big results and not deliver. This is a common trait among politicians, construction companies, hardware goods, etc.)

Chapter 31
The Wisdom of Witchdoctors Applied to Practicing Western Medicine

While living in Mbale, Uganda, an American visitor of mine became extremely sick. I called a friend who was a Ugandan doctor. He came over to my house around 9:00 PM and diagnosed my ailing visitor. The doctor scribbled a list of medicines for me to purchase including a bottle of saline, needles, and tubing. I ran off to a side street clinic and purchased everything without a prescription. Back at my house, I watched the doctor start an IV and hang the bottle on the door of my closet. After going over the medicine regimen again, the doctor started to leave. I asked him when he would come back to take the IV out. He said he would not come back. He instructed me to watch the bottle and when it was almost empty to pull the needle out, bandage the hand, and dispose of the bottle. Just like that, I was a practicing nurse. Evidently I did a pretty good job, because our visitor recovered and flew home a few days later.

It is not uncommon for Westerners to travel to East Africa to serve in a medical clinic. However, being trained in Western medicine may not adequately prepare the doctor or nurse for the cultural context of practicing medicine in East Africa. What kind of questions should a doctor ask to obtain accurate information? What expectations does a patient have of the doctor? Should the spiritual realm play any role in determining the best course of treatment? How can Western doctors and nurses provide the greatest treatment and patient satisfaction? What concerns are there with medical and government regulations and ethics?

An Interview with Three Witchdoctors

Melissa Owen (a two-year volunteer teammate), James Luchivya (a national coworker), and I traveled to Kang'inima for a dual purpose. We first taught a combined session of three local groups, and then after lunch we visited with three former witchdoctors who had recently become Christians. On a previous visit to Kang'inima, I witnessed these three men burn traditional clan shrines, dig up buried medicine pots, and pull all the charms, medicines, and witchdoctor paraphernalia from their homes and bodies. On this visit, we believed Melissa, a nurse working in Mbale, could increase her effectiveness in medical work by learning the techniques used by witchdoctors. We were especially interested in doctor/patient relationships, medical questions, patient expectations, medications, and patient satisfaction. Following are some of the medical insights we gleaned from our hours-long conversation with these witchdoctors.

Question: What percentage of patients visiting a witchdoctor come for healing?

Witchdoctors: About 60% come for healing from sickness. Another 20% ask for fortune telling, and the remaining 20% seek protection from curses or to cast a curse on someone.

Question: How long does one train to be a witchdoctor?

Witchdoctors: That depends upon how much money an aspirant has. An apprentice pays older witchdoctors to reveal their trade secrets. If an apprentice has a lot of money, he can learn a lot in a short period of time. If not, then small amounts of money bring slow advancement. Also, witchdoctors depend upon spirits to help them practice their witchcraft. Among the Bagwere people, the mayembe spirits (literally meaning "horns") are sought for healing powers. Other, more evil spirits such as the nkuni and walugono are more expensive to obtain and are used for curses, protection, etc. There are two kinds of mayembe spirits. One is passed down through the family from generation to generation becoming stronger with each transition. This kind helps the family and does not require a sacrifice. There is another kind of mayembe spirit which can be purchased for a great price. Besides money, the future possessor must agree to give a human sacrifice. The person selected may be a wife, father or mother, or child. The possessor does not have to kill the person himself, just allow the mayembe spirit to take that person's life. It is believed the person selected for sacrifice will die shortly afterward. After paying a lot of money, two horns are filled with special medicine and wrapped up as a symbol of the possession of a mayembe spirit. The possessor gains the ability to divine sicknesses through this spirit. He becomes a witchdoctor capable of healing.

Question: Do you believe these spirits exist and are powerful?

Witchdoctors: Yes, they exist and they are very powerful. However, we must warn you. The spirits are tricky. They will always try to blame a sickness on a curse from someone else. Even if it is only malaria, they will claim a curse has been cast. The witchdoctor will agree with these spirit claims because he will be able to increase his profits if the patient's problem also includes the spiritual realm. Money is a driving force for a witchdoctor's practice because he has no other source of income. Essentially, the clan supports him by their seeking his help.

Question: So what does a patient visit include?

Witchdoctors: For healing, the witchdoctor will place the patient in a completely dark room. Then the witchdoctor will call upon the mayembe spirit to manifest itself and provide guidance for healing. The mayembe spirit will appear in the form of small lights (like lightening bugs) that move about. They will speak audibly to the patient and divine the problem. The witchdoctor is considered an expert in both physical and spiritual remedies.

Note: These former witchdoctors, turned Christians, confessed to not only seeing these lights but to even conversing with them. They affirmed these spirits are real and they have witnessed their powers.

Principle One – Do not attempt to separate the physical reality from the spiritual reality. The East African believes them to be intertwined, with the spiritual realm able to affect the physical realm. Any Westerner who openly debunks the spiritual realm undermines their ability to provide medical treatment. An East African would think the Westerner's treatment covers only half the problem. A Western medical missionary would do well to study the difficult passage in James 5:14-16 that speaks of a relationship between the spiritual and physical – a belief embraced by East Africans. "Is anyone among you sick? Let them call the elders of the church to pray over them… And the prayer offered in faith will make the sick person well… Therefore… pray for each other so that you may be healed. The prayer of a righteous person is powerful and effective." This Biblical passage links physical healing with spiritual confession of sins, which may be a closer reflection of East African thought than Western. Additionally, the missionary doctor should cover his practice in prayer seeking God's protection and claiming greater power in the Almighty who rules over all demons and spirits.

Question: What interview procedure does the witchdoctor follow with his patient?

Witchdoctors: He will begin by asking questions. Do your arm joints hurt? Do the joints in your legs hurt? Do you suffer from headaches? Does your chest or back give you pain? Have you been unable to sleep? Are you having nightmares or wild dreams? The witchdoctor will listen carefully to the patient and even draw out more personal information as the patient responds. At the same time, the patient will strive to give the most accurate information possible because he knows the mayembe spirit will detect his lies. If necessary, the witchdoctor will ask about the physical conditions surrounding the patient. Do you have peace in the house? Have you fought with a neighbor or relative? Are you troubled about something? Answers to these questions may provide insight into possible curses cast upon the patient. The witchdoctor has an advantage over Western doctors because he lives in the same village as the patient and may have already heard about a family problem.

Principle Two – Ask questions of the patient. Allow them to explain their pains and sufferings, even if it involves a long story. Ask about their surroundings and their emotional well-being because patients believe everything is connected. It may provide additional information that will affect that person's mental health and abilities to follow medical directions. Do not discredit their conclusions or beliefs.

Question: What kind of medicine does the witchdoctor have and use?

Witchdoctors: Witchdoctors tend to mix their own herbal medicines from a variety of sources such as roots, leaves, bark, and other items they learned from previous witchdoctors. A minimum of seven months is spent learning about a large variety of herbs used for treatment of a multitude of sicknesses. It is important to remember that a witchdoctor's learning process never stops. A witchdoctor will continue to learn from other witchdoctors all his life. The witchdoctor does not reveal what herbal mixture he uses. He will not give it a name. He wants the patient to be dependent upon him, and to return should their medical problems persist. The witchdoctor's future source of income comes from return clients. So, he will not tell the patient what they suffer from or what kind of medicine they are given. The patient is only given instructions on how to take the medicine. NEVER will a patient leave the witchdoctor without getting some kind of medicine. The patient will always take something away with detailed instructions on how to ingest it. Invoking a curse on someone may have difficult instructions such as purchasing a black goat, putting it in a boat and rowing out to a small distant island and sacrificing it there.

Principle Three – East African patients will always expect to be given something from the medical practitioner. If the Western doctor says they are suffering from the flu and refuses to give the patient some medicine, then the patient will leave believing the doctor is not wanting to help. If the Western doctor says he has no medicine for the flu, then the patient will believe the Western doctor is weak and unable to cure his sickness. Instead, he will go to the witchdoctor who promises relief from any sickness, and who will give him medication.

Principle Four – Western doctors are trained to name the sickness, explain its symptoms, discuss treatment options, and even give timetables or percentages on recovery. The East African patient, generally, is not accustomed to expecting explanations concerning his sickness. In fact, he is warned not to ask (by witchdoctors and East African medical doctors alike). The patient does not expect or WANT the Western doctor to explain the nature of his sickness. The patient will feel much better having a powerful advocate/intercessor who can discern the sickness and provide medical treatment. This desire to have an advocate becomes a big obstacle for teaching preventive health care in the villages. They prefer a respected doctor or witchdoctor do this. The only way to overcome fear of self-diagnosis and treatment is to first provide quality practical medical attention and healing to confirm the doctor's knowledge and skills BEFORE he gives instruction.

Question: Do witchdoctors always give genuine medicine?

Witchdoctors: No. They know that sometimes a person is just suffering from stress. However, the witchdoctor will never tell his patient this. He will make up some vague malady and still give a small amount of medicine with instructions to follow. The witchdoctor believes the patient's confidence in him is a major reason clients will always return to him even if symptoms would have abated in due course without any treatment.

Principle Five – A major part of the patient's trust in the doctor will be psychological. This will be gained by the doctor fulfilling the patient's expectations, i.e. questions about ailments, questions about personal situations, giving medicine and instructions on how to take it, connecting the malady to the spiritual realm, and experiencing some amount of healing.

Question: What if the patient does not get well after being given medicine from the witchdoctor?

Witchdoctors: The witchdoctor will blame the patient for not following his instructions correctly. He will say the patient took too much at a time or too little, or not at the proper intervals. He will then increase the price for additional treatment. A second round may include a goat sacrifice and more money. Repeat visits for the same sickness will force the witchdoctor to raise his prices so high that the patient will leave that witchdoctor and try someone else. This allows the witchdoctor to claim he always provides a cure. Failures are the result of patient error.

Principle Six – The doctor is always right. If the Western doctor admits he does not know the ailment or the proper medical treatment, then he seriously undermines his credibility to the East African patient. Such patients will likely seek out traditional medicine men for treatment.

Question: How can the Western doctor gain the East African patient's trust?

Witchdoctors: The Western doctor must first provide results before the East African will listen to him and follow his instructions. (At this point, others in our group spoke up and gave examples.) Melissa treated a women's swollen foot at Namiyembe by putting medicine and a bandage on it. The foot healed. The residents at

Namiyembe now BELIEVE Melissa KNOWS how to treat such sicknesses. On another occasion, Melissa taught a group of women how to make a rehydration drink at Kang'inima. One mother used it for her sick child and the baby became well. Now, all the mothers in Kang'inima pass around the teaching Melissa gave on the rehydration formula.

Principle Seven – To gain a listening, believing audience, the Western doctor must first prove his ability to bring about healing. When East African patients truly believe he can, then they will listen to his instructions. It will be helpful if the Western doctor first learns these principles and starts where the people's expectations are. He will have to bridge the gap between his Western medical training and the East African patient's expectations for treatment. If he cannot do so, then a great opportunity to heal and to make an impact will be lost.

Question: Where do Africans go first for treatment?

Witchdoctors: They will try the hospital or clinic first. If they do not see tangible results within two days, then they will go to the witchdoctor. Relatives may pressure parents of sick children to consult a witchdoctor claiming that if they delay they will be killing their children. East African Christians normally rely on the hospital. In cases where the hospital does not seem to be working, some Christians may secretly resort to witchdoctors. Non-religious or traditional East Africans may seek treatments from the hospital AND the witchdoctor AT THE SAME TIME.

Principle Eight - Make sure the patient is not double dipping on treatment. This could complicate healing and provide the witchdoctor with an excuse to blame the Western doctors and their medicine for prolonging a sickness. Pressuring the patient to confess a visit to the witchdoctor or use of their medicine may help in identifying complications or unusual symptoms.

Summary

East Africans are not all rooted in traditional medicine practices. Like all cultures, there is a range of belief and practice. This range will be affected by residence in a rural or urban context, education, economic status, and the strength of tribal practices. There will be some East Africans who are highly educated, urbanized with no roots to the traditional tribal beliefs and who know nothing of witchcraft. Others will be enmeshed in the traditional beliefs and practices while outwardly looking very modern.

One other category of medical practitioners needs to be mentioned. There are a number of people who began medical training but either dropped out because of a lack of scholarships or because they could not pass the exams. Whatever the reason, these former medical students know enough to go into villages, set up clinics, and pass themselves off as professional medical clinicians. They purchase and prescribe medicines, offer minor surgical assistance, and often mix in traditional healing methods with herbal and spiritual emphases. These kinds of clinics incorporate some of both worlds to enhance their attractiveness to potential customers. However, they practice without medical certification and can potentially cause more harm than good.

Essentially, the witchdoctors' interview provided a history/tradition of medical practice and beliefs that build an invisible foundation of understanding and expectation in many East African patients. Western medical personnel are uninformed of this background and often assume that patients speaking English, wearing modern clothing, and driving a vehicle will think exactly like them in medical matters. This kind of assumption is a mistake.

So how should a medical team, or Western doctor prepare for service in East Africa? They must address the many tensions that exist between Western health and healing practices and East African practice and expectations. It would be best for the Western doctors to consider how to respond to the following questions?

Note: These questions are not comprehensive, but provide a sample of the kinds of questions a Western medical doctor should consider before engaging in any medical clinic or work in East Africa.

1. Truth, sharing information, and a genuine desire to educate the patient for self-diagnosis and self-treatment concerning many medical needs, is contrary to the expectations and traditional medical practices of East Africans. How should Western medical personnel who emphasize preventive medicine respond to patients who only want treatment for their sickness?

2. If the East African patient does not really need a prescription for medicine, should the Western doctor provide a placebo, vitamins, worm medicine, etc. so he can fulfill the East African's expectation of receiving help?

3. Western doctors, trained heavily in the sciences, normally resist incorporating any aspect of the spiritual realm in their efforts to treat East Africans who do not separate the physical and spiritual. How should the

Western doctor respond to patient expectations for a spiritual element to treatment?

4. Western doctors will often acknowledge to their patients that they do not know the exact sickness without proper testing first. This confession of a lack of knowledge in East Africa erodes the patient's confidence in the doctor and the clinic. How can a Western doctor maintain his integrity and seek additional help without undermining the patient's trust in him?

5. Western doctors, trained in Western forms of patient/doctor relationships will struggle to identify with his East African patients' personal and communal life and medical expectations. How can a Western doctor interview a patient in a way that provides the necessary information for diagnosis AND satisfies patient expectations?

Cultural Insights/Principles

• East African countries, like any other nations, require practicing medical personnel to be certified with the government. Westerners should not practice medicine in East Africa without proper documents and permission from the local Medical Officer of Health (MOH).

• Do not hold a clinic or do medical work without the "written" permission of local government officials. If possible, get them to participate in the clinic.

• Develop a system of stations for any clinic where a patient's history, vitals, etc. can be ascertained and written down before seeing the doctor.

• When interviewing the patient, determine if another treatment has been given for the ailment or if they have sought help from a witchdoctor. Emphasize the necessity of knowing all treatments sought for the ailment.

• Most patients in East Africa carry an exercise book – a children's ruled notebook for studies – in which doctors have written the patient's medical history and treatments. If they have such documents, examine it first and then write in information from their current visit.

• Consider providing some kind of "medicine" for every patient such as: vitamins, worm medicine, aspirin, iron or calcium supplements, etc.

• If the clinic is going to be in a rural area, consider the possibility of non-literate patients. Pill instructions would be better with pictures for time of day.

• Consider how to incorporate the spiritual principles listed in this chapter to any clinic work.

• East African governments have become very sensitive about Western agencies, charities, and companies dumping expired medicines on them. Anyone bringing in expired medicines can get into some serious trouble.

• Most medicines can be purchased for a fraction of the cost inside the country.

Chapter 32
How to Navigate Being a Patron in a Patron Society

Several years ago, President Daniel Toroitich Arap Moi of Kenya visited the town of Kisii. During his visit, he presented the municipal officials with a brand new bus that was to be used for public transportation needs from town to the surrounding areas. The municipal officials stood up and praised the President and told him that now they knew for sure that he loved the people of Kisii and was concerned for their welfare. At the time, I thought it so odd that the municipal officials treated the bus as a sign of the President's concern for the people. I just didn't understand the dynamics of a patron society. What is the relationship of the wealthy to the poor? How do they interact? What is the purpose of giving assistance and how do the recipients of help respond? Understanding these dynamics will greatly enhance a Westerner's time and efforts in East Africa.

Who is This Ali Muniafu?

Ali Muniafu is a typical Mugisu man, short and muscular in stature, with a round face that possesses a big, bright smile. We did not notice him first, he noticed us. A few years back, my coworker, Ian Shelburne helped lead a funeral ceremony for a friend in a small suburb of Mbale called Moni. While Ian focused on conducting the ceremony and burial, he did not know or notice all the faces in the crowd. One of those faces with sharp eyes, was Ali Muniafu. This Moni funeral started one of the most confusing relationships I ever had while living in Mbale, Uganda.

A few days after the funeral, Ali showed up at my house wanting to talk to me. He didn't speak English and I didn't speak his native Lugisu, so we compromised and spoke Swahili. He said he had attended the funeral in Moni. He had been impressed by the way the Christians had cared for one another and he was surprised that Ian, being a stranger to the community, was so willing to participate in such a difficult service. Even though Ali was a life-long Muslim living in a mostly Muslim community, he pleaded with me to set a day and time to come to his house. He had something important to discuss with me. His flexibility on day and time made it impossible for me to say no. So, without knowing him at all, I agreed to go to his house which was only about four miles from mine.

On the following Friday, I began my drive up to Nabisolo, located just beyond Moni. I did not know what Ali wanted to talk about, and I was afraid I was going to end up hearing a long list of things he wanted me to do for his community. Friends of mine told me that Nabisolo was a strong Muslim community without a single church in its sub-county. Since I was a Christian, I felt a bit uneasy being invited into a Muslim community. Ali's house was nestled on the foothills of Nkokonjeru, the high cliff that overlooks Mbale and makes up part of Mount Elgon's base. As I drove up, I came close to three waterfalls cascading from the cliff, and I gained a beautiful view of Mbale lying on the edge of a large flat plain that stretched out to the west. Storm clouds gathered on the mountain and some distant rumbling suggested we would receive rain in a few hours. I was skeptical of the steep, already muddy road I was traveling and anxious about my return trip.

The heavy rains of the past few days had made the waterfalls larger than normal. They were swollen and white against the darker cliff walls. The green of the vegetation was vibrant in the morning sunlight. Everywhere I looked, I saw food growing.

In a small trading center half way up the cliff, I turned right at a sign for Nabisolo Nursery and Primary School. The path was slick with mud and my truck tires spun a little as I navigated the steep incline. I drove about 400 yards down a winding foot path and parked in a small school yard teeming with preschoolers. From the car, I walked about 100 yards down the side of the hill to Ali's house. Already a small group of older men were waiting. They were sitting outside in the sun visiting with one another. I noticed a large amount of white hair. A couple of men had thick-lensed glasses.

Ali met us at the edge of his compound. He grabbed my hand with both of his and shook vigorously. It was easy to see that he was genuinely happy to see me. He escorted me to a metal chair outside with the other men, but I didn't sit long before he took me inside for "breakfast." I climbed the broken step into Ali's living room. It was a mud-walled room with wooden shutters for windows and a wooden door. The room was barely large enough to have two couches against opposite walls facing each other with a small coffee table in between. There were no pictures on the walls. A small table at the end of the room had an unusual collection of stuffed animals, wooden carvings, and knick-knacks. Still, the sofa sets gave me the impression that Ali was a little wealthier than the average Ugandan. Buzzing around like a bee, Ali shouted out something to an unseen person in the back. Within a few minutes, hot, milky tea was brought to me. A tray of bananas and sliced bread also appeared from outside. Then to my surprise, another bowl of roasted chicken was set before me. I was the only one eating. All the other visitors sat outside patiently waiting for me to finish. Ali busied himself with household chores. He came and sat to visit with me several times and stayed the last time as I finished eating.

Back outside, Ali gave everyone a chance to introduce themselves. Each person stood and gave his name and where he lived. Nearly all of them mentioned being a Muslim. When they finished, Ali gave a speech. With as sincere a voice as I have ever heard, he said that he had heard of our mission and he requested that we come to his home area and start a church as soon as possible. He believed we would be a benefit to his community. He would help organize the gathering and even offered to find a suitable place in which to meet. He believed our work in Mbale was good, but that it was difficult for people living around him to walk the four miles into town to attend. He hoped we would consider starting something nearby.

As we walked back to the truck, the whole group pressed me to come back next week. They said they wanted a regular, weekly study to begin at 9:00 AM each Saturday morning. They showed me a place under some trees where they wanted to meet, and they introduced a man who would make sure the place was swept and clean. By this time, I was so overwhelmed by the sincerity and generosity that I agreed to return on Saturday.

My friendship with Ali was just beginning. At first, Ali's actions were confusing to me. He, almost magically, was able to find me every time I went into town. Wherever I got out of my truck within a few minutes Ali would see and greet me. Then he would ask me for something small. One time he asked for two dollars' worth of airtime for his phone, so he could keep in contact with me. Another time he asked if I would buy him a soda at a local restaurant because he had just completed an important errand for someone else. Another time he told me his wife was sick and asked if I could purchase some medicine he had written down on a slip of paper from the clinic. As I thought about it, he asked how my wife was doing. He was an ever-present request machine. Yet, there was something about Ali that made me want to help him. He was always pleasant, always respectful, and always genuinely happy to meet and greet me. If he saw a friend of his on the street passing by as we were talking, Ali would forcibly stop his friend and give him a long, complimentary introduction of me. He would praise me for what I was doing, exaggerate my importance, and insist that his friend greet me and become a participant in my work.

On another occasion, Ali appeared abruptly and found me coming out of a shop in town. He rushed up urgently and said, "Please come with me right now. I have someone I want you to meet." I did not want to go with him. I had other things to do. However, Ali insisted so emphatically that I gave in and followed obediently. We walked down the street into the main municipal building, up the stairs and within minutes I was sitting in the office of the District Security Officer – one of the most powerful people in the entire district. There Ali introduced me to this important person who for some inexplicable reason knew Ali Muniafu. Ali showered me with honorific titles, embellished my work and achievements in Mbale, and impressed upon the District Security Officer how good it would be if he knew who I was. The District Security Officer patiently listened to Ali, then turned to me and asked a few questions. We exchanged phone numbers, shook hands, and within minutes I left his office. Out on the street, Ali turned to me and in passing mentioned his daughter was behind on school fees. He turned his joyful eyes toward me and asked if I could help with ten dollars to supplement his efforts to keep her in school. I reluctantly succumbed and helped. Then Ali turned and was off in a flash.

This same kind of meeting happened often. Ali would find me in town and press me to follow him. In this way, I met the Regional District Commissioner (RDC) one time. He is the top political figure in the entire area. Another time, I met the mayor. On one occasion, Ali took me into the police station, greeted all of the policemen by name, walked through the offices without asking for permission and took me straight to the police commissioner's office. Ali knocked politely and then immediately opened the door. Inside the Police Commissioner called Ali by name and motioned for us to sit down.

Ali gave his short speech about how important of a person I was and that it would be good for the police commissioner to know me. We exchanged phone numbers, and then we were out of the office in a few minutes. Out on the street, Ali asked if I could help his son with a soccer ball for their team in Moni. Without hesitating, I walked across the street and into a sports store and bought a ball.

Many times Ali showed up at my office on Tuesdays. He drank tea, ate peanuts, and sat in the outer office. When he got a chance, he would slip into my office and inform me about some political problem, a robbery, or some matter that he wanted me to know so that I could be safe. He wanted me to also inform the others in our organization.

Over the years, I never knew what to do with Ali. He was infuriating in one way because he always wanted something from me. Yet, he always showed concern for our personal safety and the progress of our organization. Once, when we were being falsely sued by a couple of men, Ali showed up and insisted on me following him to the court house. He took me into the personal chambers of a court clerk who gave me advice on how to handle our case. On other occasions, I met businessmen, civic leaders, municipal councilmen, and village elders. All of the meetings seemed awkward to me. Everyone knew Ali. Once, a policeman gave Ali some money in front of me, said something in Lugisu, laughed, and then sent us on our way. While walking out, Ali told me he was a good policeman who could help me if I ever needed assistance.

For years, I never understood what Ali Muniafu did for a living or what role he played in society. When I first met Ali, he told me he was a businessman who sold maize meal and sugar and other basic commodities in shop 36 in the Mbale municipal market. Later he left that work and seemed to float between odd jobs. On another occasion, and in broken English, he told me he was a police informant. I was unsure if he knew what that meant to someone like me. Yet, that made more sense than anything else he did, because Ali was always on the move and always knew what was going on in town and the surrounding suburbs. In fact, immediately after our house was robbed a few years ago, Ali Muniafu was at our gate within the hour wanting to know if we were safe. He also worked with the police to see if he could discover the path the criminals took after robbing us. After years of thinking about it and learning more about East African culture, I have finally been able to understand my confusing relationship with Ali. Within the context of a patron society, Ali saw me as his patron and himself as my client. Had I known then what I know now, I could have appreciated Ali's efforts to expand my reputation and social network, and I could have utilized his willingness to help me in exchange for the financial favors I provided. Ali would have been less confused about our relationship, and together we could have produced so much more results had I actively and perceptively participated.

Without mentioning it specifically, I have described certain aspects of a patron society when I wrote about hospitality, gender roles, poverty, indirect communication, and money. Yet, I never stepped back to talk about the larger cultural context in which these smaller cultural characteristics fit. Ali's relationship with me provides the foundation to describe what is often called a patron society.

Let's begin by defining a patron society. In the simplest terms, a patron society is an asymmetrical reciprocal, relationship between a superior party (the patron) and an inferior party (the client). This relationship is asymmetrical in that the patron has extensive resources, influence, and power at his disposal, and can use his wealth and resources to protect and provide for his clients' survival, well-being, and promotion. Clients seek to build relationships with patrons in order to develop a resource network that can be accessed when needed. This relationship is reciprocal in that the patron provides resources and influence while the client responds with displays of esteem, gratitude, solidarity, and compliance.

Western cultures are less familiar with the patron form of cultural interaction. Western cultures mostly use a fiscal currency to access goods and resources. Westerners can purchase food, buy clothing or a car, or take a trip by using their own money or credit cards. Items or events have a posted market price, and the purchaser's receipt shows there is no debt or obligation to the seller. If there is a need for financial capital beyond the individual's abilities, Western societies have established banking institutions to extend funding resources for a percentage price. In such societies, there is no need for individuals to develop social networks with wealthy patrons. Individual access to public financial resources removes any need for cultivating relationships or building a social resource network.

Most cultures of the world fall into a category that is often called "Majority World" (including East Africa). These countries and cultures generally have limited access to financial currency, so there is a great need for and dependence upon the more important social capital. Many majority world cultures have a huge financial resource gap between the wealthy and the poor, and this gap is almost impossible to bridge without significant help. Thus, the poor are trapped in a lower economic living condition with little opportunity for advancement or upward movement. The poor also have almost no access to independent funding. Banking institutions are not receptive to the poor because they have no collateral upon which to borrow money. Poor people often do not even have a bank account or proper paperwork for any traditional family farm. The only place the poor can turn to for help are the wealthy. The poor, as clients, seek vertical relationships with those who are more powerful and wealthy. Thus an asymmetrical relationship system develops.

A wealthy person becomes the patron (benefactor/sponsor) of a group of poor people depending upon the size of his own resources together with his personal objectives. If he has little money, then he will sponsor just a few clients. If he has extensive wealth and social or political ambitions, then he may utilize his vast resources to promote himself and his social goals though his numerous clients. To cultivate clients, he uses his wealth and social resources to provide the poor with access to funding, help in times of need, and protection for the poor's well-being. The poor, unable to repay the money, offer instead their respect, gratitude, solidarity and compliance to their wealthy patron's actions and agenda. They will support and praise him publicly, and increase his reputation and influence within the larger community.

While a middle class is developing in East Africa that functions more like the Western individual economic currency, the traditional cultural system among the larger poor segment of East Africa functions more like a patron system. Historically, chiefs held all the land and cattle in his hands. He would distribute wealth among the clans as he saw fit and in turn received social deference and obedience. When chiefs were benevolent, his subjects would give gifts to express their appreciation. This traditional culture was relationship based asymmetrical in that the chief/patron was all powerful and granted land and resources to his followers. It was reciprocal in that the followers/clients offered their obedience, allegiance, respect, and solidarity to the chief.

What I didn't know or understand at the time was that Ali Muniafu was operating on the patron society model. He showed great respect, praised me publicly, gave small gifts, showed support and solidarity with me, and I gave financial resources to him to fulfill occasional needs. However, Ali was confused in that I did not respond as he expected. I did not seek his admiration, sometimes refused his gifts, brushed aside his concern for my family, and did not assign him tasks to perform. Whenever his needs became too great for me to meet and in turn brought me dishonor, Ali would use his network to be a facilitator or broker for my benefit. He would introduce me to powerful and respected people in his society. By connecting us together, all three of us benefited by the new connection. Yet, I did not understand Ali's purpose, or value his efforts as much as I should have. I could have maximized his network of friends much more than I did and brought greater honor to Ali and a better resource network for myself and my organization.

All visitors will benefit greatly by understanding and utilizing the principles and social networking of the East African patron society. To neglect or refuse it will confuse your hosts. To practice it humbly, graciously, wisely and generously, will maximize your relationships and work.

In spite of my misunderstanding Ali's initial intentions and actions, we became good friends. A church was established near his home within the Muslim community, and a building was constructed. The most amazing thing still today is that whenever I fly back to Mbale, Uganda and walk the streets, Ali Muniafu will find me, ask about my family by each individual's name, and then ask for something small from me. These days, I respond differently. I buy his lunch and ask him about local leaders and how our work could be advanced best within the community.

Cultural Insights/Principles

- Western visitors may not realize friendliness and hospitality may be precursors to a patron relationship.

- Helping anyone is potentially the beginning of a patron relationship.
- Think twice about to whom and how you provide resources.
- Failure to seek reciprocity (within their means) distorts the patron relationship.
- If a "client" only praises you in secret and not in public, then be suspicious of that client.
- Employing someone to work should not be become a patron/client relationship. Employees will bring their personal problems to work and seek assistance from their employer, so employers need to establish boundaries of how they can help and up to what amounts. Otherwise, employees will borrow great amounts of funds against their future salary. Then when the debt becomes too great, they will quit and move on to another job.
- If police are helping you with a problem, it is not unusual to have them ask for some money to purchase airtime, or fuel for the truck. Your response will greatly affect their work for you.
- Refusal to provide any form of resources will undermine any communal effort that a Westerner seeks to lead or organize.

Proverbs

"We start as fools and become wise through experience" – African Proverb

"The sun does not forget a village just because it is small" – African Proverb

"You cannot tell a hungry child that you gave him food yesterday" – Zimbabwean Proverb

"Poverty is slavery" – African Proverb

"Poverty never visits a husband without visiting his children" – African Proverb

"A rich man who does not know himself is worth less than a poor man who does" – African Proverb

"The biting fly has no friends" – African Proverb

"The firewood in the rafters should not laugh at the ones in the fire" – African Proverb

Chapter 33
Accusations and How They Signal Broken Relationships

There was no denying it, Juma had stolen a camera, some money and a couple of other things from our office. When confronted with overwhelming evidence, Juma denied it vehemently. I had to remove him from our mission even though he was a close friend and confidant. It was my first-time firing someone, so I was shocked to discover his response. Since he was caught stealing, I wanted to be sensitive to his embarrassment by letting him go quietly and help him save face. I was later astonished to discover that he took advantage of my silence by spreading numerous rumors and accusations about me personally, our mission, and he even managed to upset a couple of churches. All of this festered for a couple of weeks before it exploded into a huge problem for us. Once I learned of the false accusations, I was able to speak with the churches and explain what really happened. The members understood, and we were able to resume our work without additional hardship. However, Juma's actions left me confused. Why did he spread rumors and falsely accuse us? Why didn't he realize the truth would come out and just add to his shame? I didn't understand at that time how East Africans respond when relationships are broken. Nor did I realize the purpose of his accusations. Westerners visiting or moving to East Africa will benefit greatly in their friendships and work by understanding the deeper purposes of accusations and how best to respond to them.

How to Respond to Accusations

It was a letter no one really likes to receive. The government seal on the outside was combined with the Police Department letterhead. Inside, I found an official letter summoning me to the private workplace of the Officer in Charge of the Police Department (OCPD), the top policeman in the entire Mbale District. I was to be in his office the next day at 10:00 AM to answer serious charges brought against me by a group of local citizens. I did not sleep well that night and hardly ate any breakfast the next morning.

I arrived a few minutes early and sat briefly in the outer office with a stern-looking secretary. She was slowly reading a local newspaper. She looked bored and barely acknowledged my entrance into her office. Within a minute, another woman came in and talked to her about a meeting downstairs that was to begin soon. The secretary stood up, opened the second drawer of her filing cabinet, and pulled out a pair of bright green high heel shoes. She dropped them on the floor, ably put them on her feet, and then both women walked out leaving me by myself.

After another couple of minutes, an assistant in the OCPD's office opened the door, looked around the empty room, and called me in. I was surprised to find his office already full. At one end was the Police official sitting behind a huge desk with a picture of President Museveni behind him. There were numerous files stacked everywhere. In front of his desk was a line of four chairs on each side of the room positioned in such a way as to face each other.

To my surprise the four chairs nearest the door were already full. Four old men who were friends of our mission in Mbale occupied them: John Wanjala, Zacharia Warera, Hemon Wasike, and Albert Makhokha. All these men were frequent visitors to our office. Each Tuesday they came in to drink tea and eat peanuts which were offered to every guest, and to ask for financial assistance for their personal needs. As a mission, we had helped each one numerous times as a sign of respect. Then when funds grew short, we explained to them that we could only help them on the first Tuesday of each month. They came every week to drink tea and visit with guests. However, they never missed the first Tuesday of the month when we gave them a small financial gift of help.

This day in the police office, all four men sat sternly, not even greeting me as I entered the room. Instead of the weekly smiles and laughter, I felt animosity. At the opposite end of the room from the policeman were ten additional chairs that had been brought in from other offices. These chairs held several of Zacharia's family including his daughter Mary, her husband Alfred Mangasi, several of their children, and a few other people I had never seen before.

I sat by myself in one of the four chairs on the opposite side of the room from the four old men. The office assistant ran over to the desk and deferentially bent his head down close to the policeman's ear and whispered something. He then handed a file to the police officer who placed it in front of him. The eyes of everyone in the room watched as the policeman slowly opened the file, read something from a note on top, and then looked up to address the group. He skipped all the normal greetings to emphasize his superior authority and the seriousness of the meeting.

He said, "Thank you for coming this morning. I have become aware of a serious problem that has arisen within my area concerning these men to my left. They have come to my office on two different occasions this past week to bring accusations against you (the officer finally looked at me) and your mission. Instead of this becoming some kind of court case, I thought we might solve this issue with my help." At that point, the officer looked at me and asked, "Is this all right with you?"

With probably wider eyes than I wanted to show, I told him I was unsure why I was even there, but I would be glad to address any issue that someone might have with me. At this, the officer looked over at the four men as though he was adjusting his assessment of the old men. He turned to me again and said, "I will let these men explain why we have come together today." At that he looked at them, waved his hand nonchalantly, and asked them who was going to talk.

Zacharia spoke up first. He politely greeted the policeman and thanked him for intervening in this serious problem. He praised the policeman for being a good leader for Mbale and expressed his confidence that he would guide all of us to a worthy solution. Zacharia did not greet me or extend any kind words toward me. In fact, he did not acknowledge my presence until he began his list of complaints.

Zacharia finally looked at me, called me by name, and told everyone that when I first came to Mbale I was kind and very helpful to him and the others. However, these days, I show no respect to them, refuse to greet them, and have stopped helping them financially. In my mind I thought back to last Tuesday when I greeted all of them and wondered why he was saying all of this.

Then Zacharia looked at the policeman and told him he had worked for our organization for several years but had been let go abruptly, without notice, and without severance pay. He said he refused to be chased away without receiving what is legally due him for his long employment and service to our mission. In truth, Zacharia was never an employee of our mission and any work he did was on a two or three-day contract to paint a room or two. However, he told us several months before that he wanted to "retire" because he was getting too old to work. We agreed to find another painter. Evidently, Zacharia thought our mission should pay him years of severance pay even though occasional contract workers were not legally able to claim severance. I started to interrupt Zacharia to clarify his work status with us, but before I could get a sentence out, the policeman stopped me quickly with a hand up, a stern look, and a quick reminder that I was there to listen to this older gentleman.

Zacharia then introduced his son-in-law, Alfred, to speak. Alfred had helped us with cooking for special occasions, but he had been terminated for constantly fighting with our employees. He treated them badly, and he was a relentless rumormonger. We released him about two years back on bad terms with our mission. Alfred looked at me as though he had been hurt deeply. He told the policeman that he was the very first person I met when I came to Uganda. He had helped me settle in, guided me in my work, counseled me, and was a good friend. Then, for no reason, I had chased him away from his employment, thrusting his family into poverty and forcing him to find minimal work for someone in Iganga some 60 miles away. He too wanted to know why I had not paid him severance from all the years of good service. His wife, Mary, Zacharia's daughter, at that point, cried out, "Why, Shawn, did you do this to us?" and she started weeping. I sat there dumbfounded by the absolute lies being thrown out before the policeman and the absurd demand for money. Again, I started to say something. Again, the policeman interrupted me. I began to suspect that everyone in the room had sat together in a pre-meeting discussion to determine how this gathering would go.

As Mary cried loudly, Hemon spoke up. His words were less respectful and more venomous. He said the old men knew we received funding from America for the four of them, but that we refused to give it to them and that we were "eating" those funds which were rightfully theirs. I couldn't help myself before shouting, "What?" Again, the policeman held his hand up toward me demanding silence. There was a look of frustration on the policeman's face toward me. Hemon claimed to have seen our organizational records of funds coming in and that there had not been any cut in monthly income. They believed our reduction of funding to them was purposeful, malicious, and unethical. He demanded immediate payment of all back funding that they were entitled to.

Now my mouth was as wide open as my eyes. I could not believe what I was hearing. These men had been recipients of mission benevolence, but none of it was specifically designated to them. They knew this very well. I was struck that they would tell such a blatant lie in front of the police.

The policeman sat passively, slowly encouraging every person on that side of the room to speak any words they had. Many of the people in the room simply repeated the accusations already thrown out. Of course, the repetition of the accusations was intended, culturally, to underscore the depth of hurt and seriousness of the breach of relationship which these four men felt. At that moment in the office, that cultural context of accusations was lost on me. I was overwhelmed by the hostile accusations, the lies and exaggerations of positions and service, and the twisted stories of events and funding. After 90 minutes of complaints, accusations, and demands, the policeman finally drew their talk to a conclusion and thanked them for bringing this to his attention.

At this point, I was exhausted, angry, and sweating profusely. I felt betrayed by people who I thought were my friends. I could not believe they were saying these things in the policeman's office. The policeman finally looked at me and asked what I had to say about all the words these respected older men and good citizens of Mbale had related. It seemed obvious to me that the policeman was completely on their side. I felt alone facing a hostile mob.

As I began, my anger caused my words to come out choppy and forcefully. My voice raised as I corrected, refuted, and dismissed every detail and accusation that had been brought up against me. The entire group sat passively except for Mary who continued to weep and cry out my name occasionally. As he listened, the policeman looked pained as though I was hurting him as well. His countenance confused me and made me think he was pressuring me on their behalf. I was determined to hold my ground and go to court if necessary. I knew I was innocent of these false accusations. I talked for a while but eventually ran out of words.

At this point, the policeman did something surprising to me. He looked at the men and at me. He scolded us all for bringing this to his office. He believed we were good people and that we should be able to settle this matter in private without the aid of the police. He counseled us to select a neutral mediator and meet on the following Monday in my mission office and talk through the matters by ourselves. He encouraged us to find a solution without going to court. If we were unable to solve this, he told the old men and me to come and report to him again. Almost on cue, the office assistant came in quickly, bent down and whispered something into the policeman's ear, and then left the room. The policeman informed us that he had been called away to an urgent police matter in Namatala. He dismissed us and quickly left the room leaving all of us staring at each other.

Years later looking back with a greater understanding of culture than when that meeting took place, I realized that I could have interpreted that meeting differently, understood the function and goal of the policeman, and found a better way of expressing myself.

Westerners do not understand the purpose of accusations made by East Africans. Westerners become engrossed in trying to defend themselves and explain how the accusations are not true. They listen to identify false statements and erroneous facts, and then present evidence to the contrary to dispute the words of the accuser all for the purpose of arriving at the truth of the event or circumstance. Westerners will go to great lengths to show how the accuser was misinformed or honestly confused, misheard a conversation, got his facts wrong, or didn't understand the agreement, action, or conversation.

When Westerners react in this way, East Africans are confused and frustrated by our response. So, they will ignore the explanation or refutation and begin listing different accusations that seem even more wild than the first set. The Westerner normally intensifies his response with anger and shouting and focuses entirely on the statements and words of the accuser to argue his point, stand his ground, and insist on the truth. The Westerner believes setting things right in the minds of the East Africans is the only way to clear the matter up.

The East African is most concerned about relationships and not necessarily reporting accurately the truth of the matter. They will subjectively exaggerate or embellish the Westerner's mistake to emphasize broken relationships. They will leave out agreements, terms of service, or pertinent facts because the accusation is not about the truth. It is an effort to show the Westerner that a relationship has been damaged. The goal of accusations is to clearly express their hurt and anger at a perceived problem in the relationship. Accusations demonstrate how concerned and alarmed they are at the perceived brokenness of the friendship. In other words, accusations are intended to be an alarm bell for the accused to do something about repairing the *relationship*.

If the Westerner does not know this, then he will run down the path of correcting falsehoods, misunderstandings, and providing proof that the accusations are false. He will interpret the accusers as hypocrites and liars who are willing to tear down any sense of friendship with this "betrayal." The Westerner totally misses the real purpose of the meeting. He focuses on the words of the accusation and not the relationship.

When Westerners press for corrections and try to prove their innocence, the East African will, to the Westerner's consternation, sit there and deny our logic, reasoning, and proofs. He comes across to the Western visitor as looking completely foolish, because he obviously is standing on untruth, but he is unwilling to budge. The East African, on the other hand, is completely confused by the Westerner's reaction to his accusations. Instead of sitting down to work on the relationship, the Westerner goes off on some unimportant tangent and starts babbling about truth and proof. The African will refuse to recant the accusations because the real problem about the relationship has not even been addressed.

Perhaps the hardest situation comes when an East African feels the relationship is irreparable. If he sees no way to restore it or has abandoned his desire for reconciliation, then he will lash out in anger and try to hurt the Westerner and undermine his reputation and work. His accusations will be calculated to maximize damage. The accusations will be mean-spirited. They will be exaggerated. They will contain a lot of lies. They will be very, very hurtful. The best way for a Westerner to never experience this is to pay attention to relationships and to always emphasize their importance both now and in the future. Even when things look bad now, express hope in a future restoration of relationship. Never closing the door on a relationship may cause an angry East African to show restraint in his response.

I could have done a better job with that meeting. I realize now that the policeman had no intention of pulling us into a court case.

He realized the accusations of the old men were probably not accurate, but he agreed to help facilitate a "serious" meeting to get the thick-headed Westerner to wake up to the broken relationships. He had planned all along to allow the old men to vent their frustration and to express their hurt and concerns before me to their fullest. He knew they would appreciate being respected by him and heard by me. The policeman had hoped that I would listen to the accusations and realize the seriousness of the broken relationships. He hoped I would respond with alarm about the old men being offended and that I would offer some means of repairing the friendships. He pushed me in that direction by suggesting we meet by ourselves to work on a solution, and he wanted to add the power of his office behind his admonition to work on the relationships.

I should have started out by expressing my respect for the policeman and his wise decision to bring us all together to receive his counsel and direction. I should have thanked him for letting us use his office and for his willingness to spend so much time with us to help solve "our problem." Then I should have spent a great deal of time ignoring the accusations presented by Zacharia and others, and instead speak about how much I valued the old men, their wisdom, and the friendship they had extended to me. I should have expressed alarm that our relationship had been damaged in some way, and that I was ready and willing to talk more about how to solve this broken friendship in the very near future. In fact, I could have offered to bring in a neutral party to help us discover the best path forward. I should have extended an open invitation for the old men to meet me in my office on any Tuesday, or to offer a special meal where we could gather and talk about the length and strength of our friendships.

I didn't know the purpose of the accusations at the time. I focused on the wrong things, and it took a lot longer and a much harder path to get resolution. I unintentionally turned a small problem into a bigger problem because I missed the cultural cues that were clear to everyone else present.

It is extremely difficult to go against our cultural instinct, but there are some important things Westerners must do when facing this kind of situation.

1. Do not get caught up in trying to prove your innocence or address every untruth. Recognize this as a relationship problem and address that first. If needed, talk about the accusations AFTER the relationship is restored.

2. Try to ascertain what the motivating force is BEHIND the accusations. Did something go wrong? Was a promise broken? Did someone not get assistance? Was someone unintentionally shamed? It will take great detective work to figure this out, but discovering the root cause will keep everyone from wasting time on superfluous accusations.

3. Try to figure out who is making the accusations. Is it an individual? Or is one person speaking on behalf of many? Or is everyone speaking on behalf of just one? When Westerners get into a group session where complaints are aired, spend less time on the accusations and more time identifying who is accusing you and who may be defending you. This will help a lot in knowing where to go for deeper information. The one defending may be able to provide Westerners with inside information or the cultural scoop that will save a lot of headache.

4. Do not be too quick or rash. Westerners should not go into a discussion angry. Anger is considered a shameful response to any situation. Westerners will do better to

keep a cool head even during difficult sessions. It will be best to listen to all the accusations and then, if needed, request a short period of time to consider how best to respond. There may be a need to communicate with the home office, seek permission, gain guidance, or gather more information so that any response is comprehensive and satisfying to all involved. However, do not leave any meeting where time is given without expressing how valued all the relationships are.

A lot of times, when East Africans fight each other, time softens the problem. When an East African does something very bad to another, he will slip out of sight for months before showing up again. He will purposefully meet the other person on the street to carefully test the waters to see if his former friend is still angry. If he is, then the offender will disappear again until the air is clear. The Bagisu have a proverb that says, "Brotherhood is like blood from the tongue; you have to swallow some of it." It means friendships have good and bad times, and we must persevere through the hard times to enjoy the good.

This "cooling off" period is not a recommended way of handling problems, but it is the way of many East Africans. Westerners need to be aware of it. It also means that a real troublemaker who has run off may show up again in six months, a year, or even two. Be ready for him.

Proverbs

"If you want to know how the true story goes, wait till the arguments start" – African Proverb

"If you and a fool have an argument, he succeeds" – African Proverb

"Hot tempers cause arguments, but patience brings peace" – African Proverb

"Who I am is not what you call me, but what I answer to" – African Proverb

"Peace is costly, but it is worth the expense" – Kenya Proverb

"The ax forgets, but the cut foot does not" – African Proverb

"Ashes fly back into the face of the one who throws them" – African Proverb

"Silence is also speech" – West African Proverb

"For the beauty of the rose, we also water the thorns" – African Proverb

Previously, I shared an experience where I failed to respond positively to accusations. However, there were many times when I was able to navigate accusations and disputes successfully to resolve the conflict. As I grew in understanding of the East African cultural value of relationships, I became better at overlooking the accusations and focusing on the point of contention. Pushing down the desire to defend myself, I sought first to repair relationships. The following story illustrates an emphasis on relationships where we judiciously limit the carefully prepared accusations. I must note that the participants in the story below were Christians and that their faith impacted their cultural response to our "church case." Still, Nakalira's story remains one of the most moving reconciliations I have ever experienced.

Solving a Dispute at Nakalira

For a while there had been a problem at a church in Nakalira about 30 minutes south of our home. Two older men, both headstrong and desirous of being in charge sought to gain the control of the church. Both men gathered individuals to their side, but neither could overcome the other. Both tried to chase off the other, but neither succeeded. It became obvious that the group was evenly separated into equal camps of strength and determination. When nothing traditional worked, the two men, Emmanuel and Zacharia, requested that someone from the mission team come listen to the problem and then decide, as a neutral party, who was going to be the church leader of Nakalira.

Mike Schrage and I volunteered to go to Nakalira. Neither of us was looking forward to it. We knew the meeting would be filled with accusations, complaints, petty arguing, and multiple witnesses on both sides interrupting to tell their stories. It was going to be a long, difficult day. On top of that, no matter who we chose, the other would pull his friends out of the church, and it would suffer for it. It seemed like no matter what we did, there would be a loss.

As we drove down to Nakalira, Mike and I talked about what to do. Do we listen to their complaints like judges? Is there some way we could interrupt their pre-planned, constructed arguments against each other? Was there any way we could salvage the situation and save the church from splitting? We thought, talked, and prayed about it.

As we drove closer, a strange idea came to us. We decided that we would turn the tables on the accusers. Instead of allowing them to talk for a long time about how the other person was bad and did horrible things, we would only allow each person to stand and explain how they had contributed to the division in Nakalira. It was a bold idea and totally against cultural norms, but we were desperate to try anything to avoid the long session of complaints that was before us.

As we drove into the Nakalira church compound, we saw Emmanuel on the roadside of the building with four men huddled around him. He was talking quickly and emphatically while jabbing his finger into the sky. We drove around to the other side of the building to park the vehicle in some shade. There, we saw Zacharia with a group around him. He was leaning into the group and talking quickly as well. It was obvious both men were setting up their plan on how they wanted the meeting to go, who was going to say what, and when. Our hearts sank further down as we saw the grim determination on their faces.

Mike and I walked slowly to the church building, greeting everyone who came to us. The crowd was larger than usual, no doubt, because they all wanted to hear what was going to be said and how we were going to decide. By the time we sat down, the room was packed. We could feel the animosity in the atmosphere.

Without the usual greetings, everyone sat down and quieted themselves. We were given the opportunity to take control of the meeting immediately. So, we did. We told them how much we appreciated all of them. We counted them as dear friends. We were proud of their accomplishments up to this time, and we spoke of a bright future for everyone. Then we asked the group to forgive our clumsiness in handling the coming meeting because we were Westerners and unfamiliar with the traditional methods of handling disputes. So, we asked the group if they would allow us to try an unusual way of addressing the problem. The crowd fidgeted a little, maybe with excitement, and readily agreed. After all, they could complain and redirect it if we missed the goal of the meeting.

I stood up and initiated our plan for the meeting. I explained that we knew everyone had prepared to stand and make statements about the dispute in Nakalira. We knew that both sides had planned how to present their case. However, we were not interested in such long discussions. We did not want to hear bad things spoken about by anyone in the room. We did not want anyone to be shamed by having others speak badly about them. We, instead, were interested in finding a solution to the problem without having to judge and decide between Zacharia and Emmanuel. We confessed that making any decision on our part in the current format would be divisive and hurtful to at least half the church. So, we wanted to try something different. At this point, people were listening intently and even leaning forward.

We told them that we were going to allow people to speak, but they could not say anything bad about another person. They could not make an accusation or complaint. Each person could only stand up and confess how they had contributed to the division that currently existed within the church. I told them that I was prepared to shout them down and force them to sit if they persisted in saying anything bad about another person. I asked them to forgive my boldness in speaking this way, but I was determined to find a better solution to this problem than sitting as a judge. I repeated the outline. Anyone can stand and speak, but they can only say how they themselves have done wrong and contributed to the division. I asked everyone if they understood our directions. Everyone nodded their heads. With great fear and trepidation, I sat down and told the crowd we were ready to begin.

Mike and I sat for more than a minute without anyone standing up. It was the longest minute I ever spent in East Africa. Then suddenly, Emmanuel, who wanted to be the church leader, stood up. His countenance was softer than before. He looked at Mike and me and said in a quiet voice, "I see what you are trying to do. There is great wisdom in this process. So, let me try." At that, he confessed that he wrongfully wanted to be the church leader in Nakalira. In his pursuit of that position, he had tried to push everyone out of the way, even Zacharia, his good friend of many years. He confessed to being angry at Zacharia for standing in his way. Today, he realized his mistake. He had hurt Zacharia and realized he had been ready to split his church for the position. It was wrong culturally and from a Christian perspective. He renounced his desire to lead the church, and he was willing to listen to any decision we made. I was stunned by his humility and speech about his heart and attitude.

As soon as Emmanuel sat down, Zacharia, who was also vying for the leadership, stood up and began to talk. Zacharia, with tears in his eyes, spoke of his anger against Emmanuel, his friend, and the bad words he had spread about him. Zacharia was sorry for his actions and words and wanted everyone to know that he was withdrawing from any effort to be the church's leader as well.

After Zacharia sat down, there was a flood of people who wanted to stand and speak. One by one, everyone in the building stood and confessed to having some part in the fight and division. Everyone agreed to stop the fighting and reunite. The session went over two hours because part way through the meeting, people stopped confessing about the division between Emmanuel and Zacharia, and they started talking about not respecting their husbands or neighbors or not working hard enough to help their wives. It was one of the most amazing, cathartic experiences I have ever witnessed.

When the meeting finally ended, Mike and I praised the church for their good hearts and willingness to work together. We told them we had never seen such a display of humility and willingness to work hard and stay together. They would always be an example to us. We dismissed, and everyone immediately began hugging each other and laughing. As we drove off, I looked back to see Emmanuel and Zacharia hug each other and laugh, shake hands, and then hug again. That experience in Nakalira will always remind me that good really can come out of the ugliest accusations.

Chapter 34
Bride Prices – Bidding Wars, Negotiations, and Family Agreements

In my first year in Kenya, I was asked to perform a wedding ceremony for a young couple. I was so proud of being asked that I naively agreed without checking with both families and confirming the full support of all. Right in the middle of the ceremony, the father of the bride stood up and interrupted the proceedings. I didn't know what to do. I stood silently, as he informed everyone that the young man had not come to him to talk about marrying his daughter. He had not come to talk about the bride price, and therefore, the bride's family was angry and not supportive of going any further. I had never had such an interruption before. I turned to the groom and asked if it was true. He nodded sheepishly that he had not talked to the bride's family. I mentally kicked myself for not being wiser. I asked the groom if he was willing to negotiate the bride price. He said yes. I asked the bride's father if he wanted to stop the wedding ceremony and first complete the negotiations or if he would allow the wedding to continue on the promise the groom would come to talk. He consulted his family first, and then said they agreed for the wedding to continue with the public promise of future negotiations. With that agreement made, we continued the ceremony. I learned an important first lesson about East African culture concerning bride prices.

Contrary to Western beliefs that paying bride prices means a young man is literally purchasing his wife, East African bride price practices are founded upon a social contract binding not just two individuals together, but also their families. The cultural intricacies of extended family introductions and negotiations and the verbal and monetary agreements build a strong social and financial obligation that is mutually supported. East African bride prices create a large network of marital support and encouragement that is often lacking in Western cultures.

South Sudan Bidding

Zacharia Munyok, my Sudanese friend, talked with a full mouth as he picked apart the fish head we were served for lunch. The Nile River was less than a mile away in Nimule, South Sudan, and the fish had been purchased that morning from fishermen who had worked all night for the catch. He was describing how a young woman gets married among the Dinka people of South Sudan. Zacharia spoke with firmness and assurance as though his Dinka cultural practices were unquestionable by outsiders. It was just the way life was, there was no other way for a respectable marriage to begin.

According to Zacharia, the young woman and her parents determine when it is time for her to marry. She cannot begin the process without her parents' approval, and the parents are wise to give their daughter a say in the timing of the event. When both determine the time is right, the father will tie a white flag on a long pole and secure it high up in a tree near their house. The white flag is a traditional cultural sign that there is a marriageable young woman ready to initiate the bidding process.

Traditional bride prices among the Dinka are tied to cattle which once was the preferred currency in a non-cash society. Cattle were often exchanged for pieces of land, market goods, and to pay debts and bride prices. As some tribes moved away from cattle to farming, bride prices changed, but among the Dinka of South Sudan, cattle still hold a prominent place in bride price negotiations.

The white flag in the family tree instigated a traditional response from all of the young men interested in the young woman. Each young man decorated a flag to represent himself, and he wrote the number of cattle on it he was willing or capable of paying for the prospective bride. Over a designated period of time, the tree became decorated with colorful flags representing the interested suitors and their bids.

The father and his daughter paid close attention to the young men who came to place flags in the tree. The daughter obviously looked for a handsome, intelligent young man with a broad smile, good personality, and promising future. The father looked for proof of sufficient wealth to ensure his daughter would have a comfortable life, and more importantly that the young man came from a family of good reputation. To the father, marriage was not just finding a husband for his daughter, it was the joining of two extended families together by a traditional marriage bond. The father did not want to join his family to a quarrelsome family that would bring trouble to his home. He sought a strong family that would enhance his own.

The surprise of this tradition is that the young woman does not automatically go to the highest bidder. The father and daughter discuss their options and come to a mutually agreed upon decision that satisfies both. It may happen to be the highest bidder, or it may be one who was in the middle of the suitors but who promises the best match, family, and future for all involved.

Such a cultural practice struggles to remain intact as the civil unrest and fighting take their toll on the traditional lifestyle of the tribes in South Sudan. In such turmoil, cultural practices adapt to the unstable situation and find new and creative ways to complete the important functions and rites of passage of its people.

The Negotiations

Gabriel met Sylvia when she began work as a receptionist at Mount Elgon Hotel. Gabriel was the assistant event coordinator who organized the room and meal plans for large functions often held at the hotel. Gabriel enjoyed his work and he excelled at it. He enjoyed meeting government officials and the numerous international guests who stayed at the hotel. It was quite a change from his earlier, agrarian life in the village. About 18 months into work, Sylvia was hired to receive guests, give directions, take payments, and often become the extra help for large meetings. It was the latter overlap that put Gabriel and Sylvia together.

Both Gabriel and Sylvia were Bagisu by tribe and had grown up in neighboring sub-counties of Manafwa District just south of Mbale, Uganda. Gabriel was a year older than Sylvia, but they shared a common Christian faith, interest in sports, and they loved their families. The friendly banter between Sylvia and Gabriel grew into fondness which resulted in a few dates and a deepening relationship.

Six months later, during the Christmas holidays, Sylvia invited Gabriel to visit her family near Bubulo. He readily agreed because he wanted to spend some time away from work with Sylvia, but he also knew that meeting her parents put their relationship on a much more serious level. There would be many questions to answer, and everyone in Sylvia's family would be making assessments and sharing their opinions about Gabriel. Sylvia was ready to introduce Gabriel to her family as a potential future husband. After all, at 23, her grandmother was already asking why Sylvia had not yet married.

The holidays went exceptionally well and Gabriel and Sylvia found themselves spending more time together. They attended the same church in Mbale, and their talk soon turned to the subject of marriage. Both liked the idea and felt that sooner was better than later. This mutual agreement put the responsibility on Gabriel to take the next step in their marriage plans. He must meet with Sylvia's family in what is called an "introduction" to discuss marriage and bride price arrangements.

At the "Introduction" Gabriel was not the main speaker. His brothers and a few friends spoke loudly and confidently of Gabriel's character and why he would be a good husband to Sylvia. Her family responded with numerous brothers and uncles who praised Sylvia's good qualities and why she would be a worthy partner in marriage. Occasionally, Sylvia's father, who sat quietly to one side, would call a brother over and whisper something in his ear. Then the brother would jump into the discussion and bring up another great quality of Sylvia. Once all of the praise and qualities were mutually agreed upon, Gabriel had to identify the girl of his intentions. In a playful manner, Sylvia's family brought out three young women, but Sylvia was not among them. Gabriel was asked to point out the girl he sought to marry. He confidently informed everyone that she was not among the girls standing before him. At this, Sylvia's family laughed loudly and brought out another group. The second group of three women came out dressed nicely in Gomesis, the traditional ceremonial clothing for women, but again Sylvia was not among them. Again, Gabriel informed everyone that Sylvia was not to be found. Again, the family laughed and sought to find more girls to present. The third group was very fashionably dressed and Sylvia was among them. When Gabriel pointed her out as the one he wanted to marry, there was much jubilation. With a successful introduction completed, the more important meeting for determining the bride price was set.

For the bride price meeting, Gabriel selected his pastor from church, his maternal uncle, and two of his brothers to accompany him for his talks with Sylvia's family. Since both families were Christian, the traditional meal with roasted beef and an extravagant amount of locally brewed beer was replaced with roasted chicken and cases of cold sodas and mineral water in plastic bottles.

As discussions began, again Gabriel did not speak. Instead, his brothers and his pastor recounted how Gabriel had met Sylvia, how their friendship blossomed into a serious relationship, and how they both wanted to honor their parents and extended family by going through the traditional bride price negotiations. Gabriel's brothers and pastor all spoke about Gabriel's character, intelligence, family, and work. They also explained his work and salary and emphasized that he was only beginning his career. Money would be hard to find for the bride price, but Gabriel would promise to faithfully pay his fair price in a timely manner.

After Gabriel's brothers finished, Sylvia's brothers and an uncle spoke of their fondness for Sylvia. They recounted how she grew up, where she went to school, her skills and talents, her Christian faith, and her new work. Sylvia's brothers also spoke of various events or characteristics of Sylvia that would be worthy of respect. Sylvia's father also wanted her brothers to stress the amount of money he had invested into her education and training so that she would be a valuable partner in any marriage. She would be able to gain employment and contribute to her new family's financial welfare. Sylvia's faith, character, education, and career opportunities would increase any bride price that Gabriel sought to offer.

Gabriel, already familiar with such negotiations had already counted the potential amount the bride price would be, so he was ready to bargain. As food, sodas, water, cookies, and roasted peanuts were served, the two sides engaged in a friendly banter of negotiations. The rounds of talking not only narrowed the price, they built relationship between the two families that would certainly be valuable for future marriage ties.

A specific number of cows was one of the first items to be established. With age, education, and employment opportunities, Sylvia brought a higher price than other young women who had not completed secondary school and had no professional skill sets. Some traditional bartering items were thrown in to honor the past art of negotiations. Gabriel agreed to add four wool blankets, a jerry can of kerosene, six goats and four chickens. A traditional payment of a specific amount of beer was not necessary for either family. The hardest part of the negotiations came with the final amount of cash that would be given as well as how it would be paid. Gabriel's goal was to negotiate with the bride's family a mutually agreed upon plan for the size of payment installments and the schedule of when they would be paid. Gabriel's brothers and pastor contended passionately that the young couple would have serious financial strains in finding a place to live in Mbale, setting up a new house together, and establishing their marriage. They pleaded for an extended payment plan. Sylvia's family sought the largest amount of cash possible up front in order to test Gabriel's financial limitations, his family's wealth, and Gabriel's sincerity in marrying Sylvia. In the end, the two families completed their bride price agreement. It was written out by a local council chairman, who served in the role of a traditional village chief, and the document was signed by representatives from both families and the chairman who witnessed the agreement.

Instead of the traditional payment ritual, where some weeks later cattle would be herded to Sylvia's home and Sylvia escorted by Gabriel's family back to her new home, the two families agreed upon a more modern, Christian version. Gabriel would bring the cattle to Sylvia's home, but the couple would meet and take marriage vows in their home church in Mbale. Both families agreed to this arrangement and a date was set. Of course Gabriel would have to pay for getting Sylvia's family to the wedding and feeding everyone after the service. After all, no wedding is successful unless everyone goes home full of tasty food.

With the bride price settled, Gabriel spent weeks building up his funds to make his down payment. He sought donations from friends and well-wishers to pay for the coming wedding. Gabriel succeeded. With both families and the church backing their efforts, Gabriel and Sylvia started their marriage with a lot of emotional, spiritual, familial, and social support.

The Shortcut to Bride Price Negotiations

An older man and woman rushed into my office upset and in a state of panic. Skipping the important formalities of greetings, they began immediately to tell me their problem. Their daughter had gone missing, and they could not locate her. All of their searching had proven futile. They had gone to relatives and even visited the boarding school where she was enrolled, but no one knew where she was. They were anxious for their daughter's safety and circumstances. My eyes widened and my mouth dropped open as I listened to their story. My heart pounded in my chest as I thought about how I would respond to the disappearance of my own daughter. My mind raced through possible scenarios. Had this couple's daughter been kidnapped? Was she being held for ransom? Had she been raped, killed, and secretly buried somewhere? Was there a family enemy who had abducted her for vengeance upon the family? For some reason, I thought of an American milk carton from years past where they placed the photos of missing children. I was greatly troubled by their story.

As they finished their story and all three of us were in a state of agitation, I suddenly realized all of the staff around me were going on with their work as though nothing was wrong. I was astonished that they were not reacting with anxious hearts and the wringing of hands of this father and mother? Why did they appear so calloused and unconcerned?

I called in a Kenyan coworker to help me know what to do with this serious problem. He sat down calmly across the desk from my frantic visitors and hesitated before asking the first question. His experienced manner and laser questions proved he had seen this very scenario played out before. "How old is your daughter?" my friend asked. The couple said she was 18 years old. "Was she in a boarding school?" my friend asked. Both parents nodded yes. "Was she doing well in school?" The father said, "No, she had performed poorly last semester and complained about having to go back." My Kenyan coworker asked, "Did she ever talk to you about dropping out of school and getting married?" The father said, "Yes, she mentioned a boy, but we forbid her from seeing him and told her she must complete her secondary schooling first." My Kenyan friend asked, "Was the boy someone she met while attending school?" The mother responded first saying, "She told me the boy was from a neighboring boarding school for boys only." One more question came to my friend's lips, "Did you talk to your daughter's friends at school or the boy?" The father, looking down and said, "The headmasters looked for them but they could not be located on the school campuses. They did not know where the boy had gone."

By now it was becoming clear that the young girl had chosen a traditionally familiar, well-trodden, short cut to marriage. This path is often taken by girls who perform poorly in school, don't want to continue studies, but whose parents force them to return. Such girls are more interested in getting married and moving on with life. However, when parents become an obstacle rather than a help with marriage options, girls will take matters into their own hands. They will run away with a young man, live with him long enough to get pregnant, and then return home to the parents and essentially tell them, "Solve this problem." This forces the parents to sit down and negotiate a bride price with the young man's family to complete the marriage arrangement imposed upon them by the girl.

My Kenyan friend, looked at the couple. They did not look as desperate as before. In fact, they looked a little ashamed. He told them that their harsh response to their daughter probably caused her to make a choice between school and marriage. She was probably staying with the young man somewhere near the school or in his home area, and that their daughter's school friends were probably in touch with her and could tell them where she was. He suggested they return to the school and talk to her friends. If they failed to discover her location, most likely she would return home within a few weeks with news that she was pregnant and ready for marriage. The couple looked down in shame and meekly accepted the counsel of my coworker. It was a learning experience for me too. For years after that, I had numerous couples run into my office seeking help for a missing girl. In every instance the girl turned up pregnant within a few weeks. I learned to respond the same way as my coworkers by calmly asking a few pointed questions that revealed the now common circumstances and probable cause of the girl's disappearance.

Western Considerations

Upon hearing about bride prices in East Africa, the average Westerner is often intrigued and repulsed. Bride prices, like slavery, may give the impression that a person is being purchased. Even more sensitive to Western ears is the idea that a female may be controlled and regulated to something akin to property or chattel. How can any financial amount be placed upon a female human being and negotiated over like livestock by the males of two families? Thus, Western visitors almost immediately condemn the traditional practice of bride prices. However, a deeper understanding of East African culture may help change such perspectives and allow Western visitors and residents to evaluate and address cultural issues less partially.

There is a sense where a bride price is a financial sum paid to the bride's family for the approval to marry. The price even varies according to the girl's own physical and personal qualities as well as how much the bride's family has invested in the girl as in education and the acquisition of skill sets for future employment. However, few, if any of the participants believe the amount negotiated reflects the true value of a human being. The exchange of money, in essence, is not the purchase of a female, but a social contract. It is a strong traditional agreement between two families, culturally structured, with mutual obligations on both families, that financially binds everyone to encourage, support, and work for the success of the future marriage.

After the young man and his family pays the bride price to the young girl's family, the cattle, items, and cash are either used up or distributed among the brothers and parents of the young girl. If then, the young girl becomes angry with the young man and returns home, her family will compel her to go back and work things out. If she refuses, the groom's family will come and demand the full bride price be returned. This places financial pressure on the bride's family to encourage the bride to reconcile the marriage. If the young man only makes a down payment and is too slow to pay his part, the bride's family may call her home to demonstrate their frustration with the young man's inattention to his agreed upon obligations. Should the couple find themselves in the midst of a divorce (a rare occurrence), tradition dictates that a bride price must be returned, but a certain amount is deducted for each child produced within the marriage. After a certain number of children, there is no obligation to return the bride price. However, the children traditionally remain with the man who has completed his bride price. Such traditional rules can cause problems. On one occasion, I witnessed a young man lose his first infant child to death. Though he had not completed his bride price, he made arrangements to bury the baby on his farm. However, the bride's family arrived and demanded the body of the baby to bury in their compound because traditionally, without a bride price, the child belonged to their daughter and extended family not the young man and his family. This necessitated an immediate negotiation for some kind of bride price payment to be completed before the burial could be performed.

Within a communal society, bride prices bind two families and by extension two communities and clans, to mutually support the marriage. Just like in a previous chapter where we discussed the importance of building a friendship network through a series of borrowing and lending resources, bride prices function as an exchange of resources for the purpose of building a support network for successful marriages. Consider also that many other non-western cultures use arranged marriages for a similar purpose of creating a social bond between two families to support the marriage.

Are there abuses to the bride price system? Yes, especially if the husband dies and the wife is left to live among the brothers of the husband. Greedy in-laws may chase away the widow without children in order to seize their dead brother's property. Or they may allow the widow to stay in the family home in exchange for sexual favors. Such instances tend to be the exception rather than rule and happens most often when the dead husband's children are too young to assert their rights on land and possessions. It is important for Westerners to not use such exceptions as an argument against a cultural practice lest they find the same argument pointed toward their own home cultural injustices. An abuse or exception of any cultural tradition, institution, or practice does not provide a legitimate rationale to discard that tradition. It does provide rationale to transform it or improve it, but not to completely abandon it.

In most cases bride prices build a socially acceptable way for a woman to leave her home and join her husband's family and clan to build her own home where children and grandchildren are a natural result. Much of this is lost upon Western visitors who only see and appraise traditional bride price negotiations as "purchasing" a wife.

Seeing Culture from a Different Perspective

It was only when astronauts were able to travel to the moon that we obtained a good look at the planet we call home. The first images of this blue marble looking world suspended in space was breathtaking. It provided a perspective humanity had never seen before. It took a long and arduous journey just to get that glimpse. Such is the case with traveling deeper into another culture. The closer Western visitors come to understanding the host culture, the greater possibility they have of looking back at their own home culture and seeing it from a perspective never before possible. Essentially, living in another culture for a long time provides visitors new lenses with which to evaluate their own home culture and practices.

Before Westerners condemn bride prices, it might be wise to understand the importance of financial negotiations and how they play into mutual obligations and relationships. Then it would be good to look at our own cultural approach to marriage and see if our culture has provided a more successful way. An honest evaluation would suggest Western cultural practices focus upon individual fulfillment rather than extended family support. Individuals seek a marriage partner often without the help or input of family members. If parents or family are asked to bless a potential marriage candidate, it is more perfunctory than essential. There is little expectation of future help in relational matters from the family should problems arise. Individuals are left to their own efforts to make or break a marriage. There is normally no extended family support group for marriage problems. It is handed over to professional counselors if the marriage partners agree to go and if they are willing to pay.

The result of Western cultural practices concerning marriage shows a growing number of divorces, broken homes, children passed between households, more women and children living in poverty, and a huge inflation of court cases concerning legal guardianship, child support, kidnapped children, to name just a few. If marriage practices of Westerners and East Africans were measured against one another with all their flaws and problems, it seems Westerners would not have much foundation to stand on to lecture East Africans about bride prices and marriage practices. This deeper understanding of East African cultural practices and a personal home cultural reflection are necessary to more effectively visit, live in, engage, and truly appreciate the people of East Africa.

Cultural Insights/Principles

• Bride prices, in varying degrees, are practiced throughout all African cultures in Sub-Saharan Africa.

• There are few cases of divorce and the return of the bride price because culturally, bride prices are never intended to be reclaimed. Once a woman is married to a man, African tradition deems the social contract to be permanent, even death cannot part them! The woman is expected to continue the lineage of her dead husband by raising his children and remaining a part of his family. Her husband's family and the community traditionally support this practice.

• The modern idea of freedom for a woman after the death of her husband is Biblical and, by African culture, considered Western.

This idea has been handled clumsily by Western missionaries who get caught up in decision making in the church.

• According to East African cultural beliefs, it is almost impossible for a woman whose bride price was paid to become single again and to marry another person. If for some reason she breaks with tradition and marries again, when she dies, her body is often taken back to the first husband's family and buried there.

• If a man marries a woman whose bride price has already been paid by a previous husband, traditionally he will not consider himself to be the proper husband of that woman. Culturally, it is considered an illegitimate marriage. To legitimize his own household, he will eventually marry another woman whose bride price he will pay. Paying bride price is a cultural demonstration of a man's abilities, wealth, and pride. Taking a woman whose bride price was paid by another man does not give him the traditional cultural dignity he seeks.

• East Africa allows polygyny. Men who can financially support multiple wives will strive to do so as an expression of their abilities, wealth and social status. Men who add a second wife without the first wife's consent can create great discord within his home. Surprisingly, some women of past generations preferred a second wife to help with household and farming chores as well as adding a close friend.

• Women also pride themselves on how much of a bride price (resources) they were able to bring for their families. This gives her greater recognition among the others in the family, community, and clan.

Just to throw a wild idea out there, let me propose for argument's sake, that Western cultures adopt the bride price practice with a slight twist. The young man and woman seek parental approval before moving forward with any plans to marry. This honors parents and solicits extended family approval and support. Both families come together to agree upon the marriage, commit to supporting the proposed marriage, and establish an amount of funds to be paid to the family of the bride. As an example, let's say $50,000 dollars is set as an amount to be paid in full or in agreed upon allotments until completed. The bride's family agrees to put the money into an investment for growth. If the young couple successfully completes ten years of marriage, the bride's family promises to give the bride price money and its earnings to the couple. If they do not reach ten years, then the bride receives the money. Would this kind of arrangement show the sincerity of the young man in marriage? Would this strengthen family bonds on both sides of the family? Would it build a greater support system for the young couple? Would it decrease the chances of divorce? Will it ever be adopted like this in Western cultures? Probably not. However, some aspects of East African bride price culture could improve upon Western cultural practices for marriage.

Proverbs

"A happy man marries the girl he loves; a happier man loves the girl he marries" – African Proverb
"It is much easier to fall in love than to stay in love" – African Proverb
"Marriage is like a groundnut (peanut), you have to crack it to see what is inside" – African Proverb
"He who marries a beautiful wife, and he who plants by the roadside have the same problem, insecurity" – African Proverb
"Coffee and love taste best when hot" – Ethiopian Proverb
"The buttocks are like a married couple; though there is friction between them, they still love and live together" – African Proverb
"When husband and wife are in harmony, one piece of yam is enough for their food" – African Proverb
"A husband with a good wife will never be on the road without supplies" – African Proverb

Chapter 35
Circumcision – Rites of Passage and Why We Cut

During our first year in East Africa, my wife Linda and I were driving down the main road of Kitale when suddenly, a huge crowd of pedestrians turned the corner in front of us and completely blocked all lanes of traffic. It was not an angry crowd, but it was a determined crowd. They expected everyone to pull over and allow the dancing, singing, tree-limb-waving group to pass. At the head of this crowd was a group of young men in colorful attire, clanging bells, blowing whistles and dancing. Others in the procession ran out ahead of the slowly moving crowd and directed traffic. Several young girls, with their shirts partially unbuttoned, ran ahead of the boys singing, jumping, and laughing. We pulled our car as far off the road as we could, not knowing what was happening or if there was any danger in our interruption of their celebrations. The crowd danced by, with a few people joyfully shouting at us and waving as they passed. It was unsettling because we had no idea what was happening or how we should react. Little did we know that circumcision season had begun, and we would continue to see these processions several more times. Rites of passage are important markers in traditional cultures of East Africa. They symbolize the community acknowledgement of a young boy or girl becoming a young adult. It is an advancement in status, respect, and responsibilities. It is an important traditional event, but one that Western cultures struggle to understand and often ridicule or condemn. Nowhere is the cultural blindness more evident than in Western attitudes toward circumcision rites in African nations.

The How, the Why, and the Hypocrisy

Every even year, the Bagisu and the Sebei around Mbale, Uganda, as well as many tribes in Kenya, engage in male circumcision rituals. The Bagisu practice only male circumcision but the Sebei practice both male and female circumcision. The ceremonies begin around August of these years and may last until the end of December. Families with candidates for circumcision may decide at any time during these months to perform the circumcision ceremony.

Initially, it is the young Mugisu man himself who decides he is ready for circumcision. He may range from 12-20 years of age. If he gets too old, his father may approach him about it and suggest it is time. The first step is to get approval from the immediate family since his father and family will pay for the food and ceremony. The next person the young man must talk to is the "Khotsa" or maternal uncle. He holds a place of great respect in the young man's life and will eventually give a small cow for the circumcision ceremony. The Khotsa can refuse or delay the process, depending upon his ability to provide the cow. If all is ready, then the young man begins his rituals.

A group of supporters will gather with the young man who is dressed in traditional garments for his journeys. The boy will put on a traditional helmet made of monkey skins (preferably from the Colobus Monkey) called "Lubisi" and wear a cape of monkey skins called "Liabi." He will don a mask called "Ikwena" and carry bells called "Shide."

Of the journeys the circumcision candidate will make, the first one will be to the Khotsa to formally invite him to the ceremony and to receive from him the small cow. While he jogs down the road clanging his bells, a whole host of well-wishers travel with him. Many carry branches or sticks with them and often become so numerous that the road is blocked for all traffic. Everyone dances with him and sings encouraging songs. Phrases like "Imba lu muliro" are chanted which means "circumcision is fire." Explicit words are often shouted referring to his genitals which are the center of attention. Young women will accompany him including his sisters and maternal aunts. In the Mbale area, these women may partially disrobe and often flash the young circumcision candidate enlightening him to what he is to receive after he becomes a man.

Another journey will be made to the graves of his ancestors. The young circumcision candidate will smear himself with goat dung called "Buse" to show the ancestors (they are believed to be able to smell this) his appreciation and respect for them. A sacrifice called "Khurala Tsingani" is made at the grave site to appease the departed spirits so that none of them will curse the young man. A goat or chicken is used for this sacrifice.

Another journey requires a visit to a special river site where "Musambwa" are believed to be staying. Musambwa are the river spirits who are said to take the form of huge snakes. A spying spirit called "Nakonge" often watches the rituals at the river and is often seen in the form of a black sunbird with red markings. At the river, the circumcision candidate must become completely naked and then be ritually mudded. This is called "Mwitosi." Mud is especially placed in the ears of the candidate so that he will not hear any evil spirits. A special mud cap is molded, and a special blade of grass placed on top called an "Ututu" which helps identify the candidate to all the spirits. Also at the river, a container of beer called a "Kumwendo" is sipped, and beer is blown out into the air as a blessing toward the Musambwa. From the river, the circumcision candidate runs naked and mudded back to the place of circumcision. Special songs called "Sioya" (which include culturally crude and erotic references to his male organ) are sung as the candidate is escorted. His father and uncles will form a counsel called

"Khulomelera" in which the young man will be charged concerning his duties as a man. This counsel often includes the young candidate's duties as a man within his tribe.

At the father's home compound where the circumcision is performed, the circumcision candidate will stand within sight of a small grass shelter called a "Namwima" in which ancestral spirits are believed to rest and to watch the cutting. There will also be a "Y" shaped stick called a "Lukangu" on which the heart, lungs and several ribs of a sacrificed goat are placed. These are presented to the spirits to appease and honor them. The young candidate may also be given special herbs or medicine called "Itanyi" to strengthen or encourage the candidate. It is considered a catalyst for courage which will provoke the candidate to stand firm. At the time of circumcision, three actions which bring great shame are feared. It is against these fears that Itanyi is supposed to work. The first fear would be that the circumcision candidate cries out at the time of being cut. If he does, he is shamed in front of all those watching, and he must erase this shame by sacrificing a goat which is eaten by the witnesses. A worse shame would be for the candidate to cry out his mother's name during the cutting. For such an offense, the candidate must sacrifice two goats. The worst shame would be for the candidate to become so scared that he has a bowel movement in front of everyone. For such a shameful thing, he must sacrifice a sheep to remove a potential curse that would come upon him.

The actual cutting is done while the candidate is standing on a piece of plastic. This plastic is used to catch all the blood that is shed. The plastic is later picked up by the Khotsa and secretly buried so that no one can use the blood to curse the young man. If the Khotsa cannot participate, a trusted relative must be chosen for this task. Healing from the circumcision normally takes about three weeks.

Female circumcision ceremonies among the Sebei of Uganda, the Kalenjin tribes of Western Kenya, and many tribes in South Sudan, are not as public as the male circumcision ceremonies. Much of the female ceremony is clouded in secrecy. At Sebei female circumcision ceremonies, men are allowed up to a certain point, then they leave and only women witness the actual cutting. Females do not participate in parades, beer sacrifices and river mudding like the male circumcision events. It is also difficult to give an accurate description because female circumcision differs slightly depending upon the tribe and country. So, unlike the naming of items, events and parades that shape male circumcision rites just before the foreskins are removed, female circumcision focuses more upon the physical cuts of the female genitalia. Older women do the cutting and are most often the ones who push for the young girls to yield to the traditional ceremonies. The Sebei women of Uganda will add four small cuts on the candidate's forearm. These cuts are rubbed with ash to produce raised scars. The scars are a visual sign to everyone that the female has completed the circumcision rite and is ready for marriage.

While Kenya has sought to ban female circumcision, Uganda has not emphasized a need for reform to banish the practice. That may be because only the small Sebei tribe on Mount Elgon practice it. Kenya's medical association has printed much information about female circumcision. According to Kenya's ministry of health, females who have been circumcised may experience adverse medical problems such as recurrent infections, difficulty in urinating and passing menstrual flows, complications in getting pregnant and giving birth, chronic pain, problems with cysts, and higher fatalities during childbirth. There are no known health benefits to female circumcision.

With all this medical information available, why do women continue to practice female circumcision? The answer lies in the strong traditional beliefs and practices of the tribes. Men of these tribes prefer women who have been circumcised. They believe circumcised females will have less sexual drive. This means they are less likely to engage in sexual activity outside the home. Female circumcision is thus seen as a valued demonstration of purity, faithfulness, marital stability. The older women see the ceremony as a source of honor, because they know the preferences of the men in their tribe. To fail to circumcise their daughters and granddaughters may expose the girls to ridicule, social exclusion and potentially prostitution. There is great cultural pressure to undergo the cutting rite.

Westerners who come to visit or live in East Africa may encounter these traditional practices. Many visitors are shocked or appalled by the female circumcision practices and have renamed it female genital mutilation (FGM). Western politicians and activists have put tremendous pressure on East African governments to ban female circumcision. Western countries donate funds for education programs and even tie development funding to East African government compliance on Western goals of eradicating female circumcision. Western nations emphasize the dangers to health and the "subjugation" of women by such crude traditional values and practices. Westerners see themselves as liberators seeking to set women free from such appalling traditional practices.

Here is where I need to be very careful as a Westerner with almost 40 years of East African experience and insight. I need to state clearly and unequivocally that any cultural traditions and procedures that create medical complications for women in East Africa should be scrutinized closely and, if possible, stopped. At the same time, I encourage Westerners to stop for a moment and think about our arrogant display of ethnocentrism when we demean their cultural practices and demand they be stopped because they offend our cultural values. If East African women submit to this procedure because it makes them more desirable to men or more respected in their society, and they know the medical dangers of doing it, then should Westerners be asserting their own values and beliefs into the cultural practices of East Africa to ban this process? Additionally, do Westerners recognize their own hypocrisy in this female cultural issue?

Women in Western nations spend billions of dollars each year on risky, unnecessary medical procedures to enhance their own self-esteem and physical attraction to others. They pay for face lifts, tummy tucks, liposuction, breast implants or reductions, butt implants, nose, eye, jaw and throat reconstructions, and engage in diets, exercise regimens, cosmetic enhancements, fashion purchases, and wear uncomfortable high heels that damage feet when worn too long. Women suffer from anorexia, bulimia, depression, drug abuse, horrible body image, and even ridicule and shame from OTHER WOMEN, if they don't conform to the cultural ideals of beauty held and pressed upon them by their own culture. In what East Africans would consider genital mutilation, Westerners submit to sex change operations where a person's physical attributes are chemically and surgically altered. Such operations do far more cutting than the female circumcision rites of Uganda, Kenya, and South Sudan. Such activities are not without physical risk. Western women experience medical complications, hospitalization, and sometimes death because of their beauty or medical "procedures." Do Western nations condemn and try to eradicate these practices at home? No! Westerners not only embrace these cultural beauty practices, but they also encourage and promote them through every form of media, advertisement, business sales, and even turn these "beauty" medical procedures into TV shows for entertainment.

Western cultures, with their political and economic clout, cry loudly about the "suffering" of women in female circumcision rites. East Africans are polite in that they will not argue with the visitors, and poor government officials will parrot the words of the rich Western diplomats to obtain international funding. However, East Africans are shocked by the apparent hypocrisy of Western cultures that overlook what would be considered mutilation and oppression of women in Western cultures while condemning the female circumcision rites of East Africa.

In fact, the height of hypocrisy comes when Western cultures use political influence together with international aid to force East African nations to ban female genital mutilation. They seek to use government power to override cultural traditions and personal female choices. Yet, in their own Western countries, women loudly proclaim, with the support of political groups, the right of choice over their own physical bodies especially when it concerns abortions, sex change operations, and sexual activities. They claim the government has no right or authority over the bodies of females. It is a tremendous irony that these Western women who fought government laws and gained freedom to control their own bodies and reproductive systems, have no hesitation to use government power to ban women's cultural practices in East Africa.

To have a powerful voice in East Africa, Western visitors must acknowledge and address their own cultural issues concerning beauty and women's rights at home before pursuing radical cultural changes in East Africa. They must learn the deeper meanings of East African cultural rites of passage, especially when they pertain to sexual attractiveness, social status, desirability, marriage, and beauty. What is the old saying? Those who live in glass houses should not throw stones. Here is where a deeper understanding of the host culture will bring new insights into the home culture of the Westerner.

Cultural Insights/Principles

- Some cultural groups in East Africa do not practice any form of circumcision – male or female – and thus will not have this cultural problem.

- Traditionally, male circumcision is done every even year.

- Male circumcision, as a rite of passage, is structured to inculcate the young candidates with a sense of honor, duty, obedience, respect for authority, and especially unity among those being circumcised.

- Since everyone must face life on their own, male circumcision teaches bravery by bearing the pain of cutting without the aid of any anesthetics. Bearing the pain without crying out shows the candidate's ability to face the pain of life that will befall him.

- In some communities like the Maasai of Kenya, the foreskin is not entirely removed, (on some young men) but left hanging on (they call it a tie), as a reminder that there is nothing as painful as circumcision that one would face in life.

- Candidates who successfully complete the circumcision rite are given a special name. This group name will be used for eight years to identify a generation, and then a new name will be given. Among the Bukusu, for example, there are 12 names or generations. After all 12 names are used, the first name will be recycled since none from the first group will still be alive when the first name comes back around.

- Traditionally, young women were married off in the odd years, but with the introduction of Christianity and church weddings, young women are now given in marriage at any time.

- Christians seeking to avoid the beer, sacrifices, and ancestral rituals may take their sons to a medical clinic and have them surgically circumcised before the extended family puts pressure on the father to follow traditional methods.

- Part of the change in modern circumcision practices comes from a growing understanding of medical cleanliness and the possibilities of infection from the traditional ways of circumcising.

- While male circumcision is done openly and in front of a mixed crowd, female circumcision is done secretly with only women present. I am not aware of any medical clinics that perform female circumcision.

- Should a circumcision party block the road, do not try to drive through or around it. Pull the vehicle off the road and allow them to pass. Some may come up and shout in the window or sing loudly, or even hit the car lightly, but they will pass. Remain calm and respectful.

- If invited to a male circumcision ceremony, be aware that much traditional medicine and witchcraft are utilized. Your presence may be seen as endorsing the practices.

- Churches sometimes offer alternative circumcision rituals that teach moral living, family responsibilities, sing hymns, and provide a licensed medical officer to perform the cutting.

- Do not agree to attend a female circumcision ceremony because you may be seen as endorsing a highly controversial practice. Your presence could be used by political opponents to create trouble of which a foreigner would be the central focus for anger.

- If asked for a contribution, determine whether you want to donate to all forms of circumcision rituals or just those incorporating religious principles or using medical professionals.

Proverbs

"Ugliness with good character is better than beauty" – Nigerian Proverb

"If there is character, ugliness becomes beauty; if there is none, beauty becomes ugliness" – Nigerian Proverb

"The one who loves an unsightly person is the one who makes her beautiful" – Ugandan Proverb

"Three things cause sorrow to flee: water, green trees, and a beautiful face" – Moroccan Proverb

"A beautiful thing is never perfect" – Egyptian Proverb

"Judge not your beauty by the number of people who look at you, but rather by the number of people who smile at you" – African Proverb

"The most beautiful fig may contain a worm" – Zulu Proverb

"There is always a winner, even in a monkey's beauty contest" – African Proverb

Additional Resources:

African Study Bible *by Oasis International Limited (The Study Bible contaians more than 120 Theological and Cultural Articles and Learn Notes written by African authors. There is an article on "Dreams", p.1274.)*

Chapter 36
The Power of Dreams and Guidelines for Interpreting Them

It was late in the evening when I heard a knock on my back door. As I opened it, I found an older man whom I had met the previous week at a new place where we had just begun teaching. The man expressed faith and wanted me to rejoice with him because he had received a dream from God. He said he had been praying to God for school fees for his three children. With the biggest smile on his unshaven face, he shared with me that God had told him in a dream that I was going to pay for his children's school fees. He had rushed over to my house to share this wonderful dream with me and to ask when I might be able to help. Having had numerous brushes with people having dreams already, I smiled, clapped my hands, and expressed my joy and excitement with him over his dream. I told him I was thrilled that God had shared that dream with him, and I said that just as soon as God shared the same dream with me, I would pay the fees. The man's smile froze. He stopped clapping and jumping around. His eyes silently searched my facial expressions for any indication of my inner thoughts. With no smile, he asked when I might be able to help. Without a smile on my face, I said it would come after God gave me the same dream. He went away frustrated but without reason to accuse me. I did not deny his dream and I readily agreed to obey it once I had similar confirmation. I never received that dream. He never got his school fees from me.

Moses Musalima is a small man of five feet one or two inches. If he weighed 120 pounds, I would be surprised. He is thin and the shirt he wears drapes over his shoulders as though it was meant for a much larger person. But size never stopped Moses. By the time I first met him, Moses was already 47 years of age. He was married and had ten children. The oldest two daughters were already married, and I assumed Moses was a grandfather. He was prosperous. Moses had a large farm where crops were planted. Neat houses decorated the roadside portion of his place. To his extended family and his community Moses had earned respect and honor, because he had proven himself to be of stable character and actions. He spoke and people listened. But in the midst of his everyday life, something spectacular happened to Moses.

Moses related to us that in July of 1992, he was working in the lower part of his farm down in the swampy area when a leopard jumped out of a bush and attacked him. Being small in stature, Moses instantly feared for his life. At one point, Moses broke free and started running away, but Moses tripped and fell into a ditch. As he lay there, he thought his life was over. However, Moses related, the leopard strangely passed over him and ran off. His life was spared. This whole event with the leopard was witnessed by a neighbor.

In December of that same year, Moses was working in the same part of the farm when a Pied Crow came and began flying around his head as if trying to land on him. The bird flew so close that Moses was able to reach up and grab it. Moses took the crow home and called his relatives together. His father and a visiting sister, who was a member of a Pentecostal church, suggested they pray about the matter. After praying, they let the bird fly free.

People here will quickly point out, "In Africa, there is no such thing as an accident or a coincidence." Traditionally, two strange events happening in such a short period of time, would indicate that something evil is happening. Many would assume that a jealous neighbor had put a curse on Moses and a trip to the witchdoctor would be necessary to purchase medicine strong enough to ward off some impending danger. Moses was unusual in that he turned to seek God rather than run to the witchdoctor. Moses did not join a church; he just began praying.

As Moses tells it, several years later he had a dream. He dreamed that he was walking along in that same part of the farm, and without knowing why, found himself following a person in a long white kanzu (long tunic). As they walked, a large snake appeared. Moses pulled out a machete and chopped the snake up. Walking a little further, the same snake reappeared alive and well. As Moses approached the snake to kill it again, the stranger turned and told him to leave it alone. He said, "I am the one who brought it back to life." At this, Moses asked the stranger, "Who are you? I am following you here in the field and I don't even know who you are." The stranger, holding a piece of clothing, responded, "I am the Lord. Here take this garment and wash it in the clear water." Moses looked at the swampy water where the Lord was pointing, and it had somehow become crystal clear. Moses took the dirty garment and washed it in the water, and it came out sparkling clean. The Lord also showed His church house to Moses which miraculously appeared in Moses' field just by the swampy area. The Lord also said one other thing that puzzled Moses. He said, "You need to think, to know, and to understand. A white visitor will come to your house soon and he will tell you what you need to do." From that time on, Moses felt he should become a Christian. He believed that the washing of the garment meant he should purify his heart and the Lord's house was the place where God wanted Moses to construct a church building. Oddly enough Moses did not go out and search for a church organization to join. Instead, he sat in his house, did his daily work, and waited for the white stranger to come to him.

A few years later, Moses received word of two church organizations interested in coming to his house. He eagerly invited both. He also prayed to God asking that the first group to arrive be the right group. A few weeks later, I drove up to Moses' door because a nephew of Moses' had implored us to visit his village home.

Before I even got out of my vehicle, Moses came up to the door and waited impatiently for me to get out. As soon as I did, he grabbed my hand in both of his and shook vigorously. He was very strong for being such a small man. He kept saying over and over again, "I am so glad you have finally come. What took you so long to reach my house." Obviously I was confused as to why we were considered late. We lived only 30 minutes away and we arrived a little earlier than we had promised.

Without another introduction, Moses grabbed my arm and pulled me along a path. He said, "Come, I want to show you where we are going to construct the church building." Moses bypassed all of his family and neighbors who had gathered, and pulled me down toward a swampy part of his farm. In excited words, he related his story of the leopard, almost acting it out as he pointed at the bushes and the ditch into which he had fallen. He spoke of the bird and reenacted how the crow had tried to land on him and how he reached up and caught it. He talked about taking it to his family and praying. He pulled me over to a piece of land already cleared and said, "This is where we will put the church building."

Then Moses took me back to his house and sat me down under a brush arbor he had made specially for this meeting. He sat me in front in a place of honor, and then turned to the growing crowd of neighbors and friends. He reminded them of his dream about the

Lord sending someone to teach him what he needed to do. He professed before everyone present a heartfelt desire to follow God and a willingness to do anything to please him. He expressed publicly a readiness to give up land for a church building and to spend his own money to get it built. He even turned to me and asked permission if he could do this. He then pointed at me and said to the crowd, "He has come just like my dream said he would. He is going to tell us what we need to do. He has been sent by the Lord."

I have been to countless villages and never have I had a reception quite like this one. Moses sat down expectant of some great wisdom to pour from my mouth. I had come with my usual presentation and outline about what we do and do not do. I normally talked about our programs, goals, objectives, and how we work in local groups. It was obvious that kind of speech was not what Moses was expecting to hear. I threw my notes aside, and spoke from the heart.

Moses believed his dream was real and that we were the answer to it. He repeatedly expressed his strong resolve to be a Christian and work for the church. His belief in dreams is not uncommon among East Africans. In fact, most East Africans believe dreams are one way to connect to the spiritual world. In the larger context, the majority world believes in dreams and they will seek interpretations of dreams that keep recurring.

Western cultures have pushed the spiritual realm far from their daily existence and sought to explain and understand the world and dreams from a completely physical reality of laws and principles. With no credence given to the spirit realm, dreams are explained in scientific ways. In the December 1987 issue of **National Geographic,** an article on sleep listed some modern, Western theories on what dreams were. Mark W. Mahowald, Director of the Hennepin County Medical Center in Minneapolis at that time said dreams: (1) Reveal one's hidden thoughts or tensions, (2) Manifest the random firing of neurons in the brain, or (3) Clear our brains of useless material. More current explanations for dreams include: (1) To manage emotional stress, (2) To rehearse for future obstacles, tests, or confrontations, or (3) To organize and retain memories. Other Western theories suggest dreams are simply the result of something one ate.

In many religions, dreams were considered the way in which God communicated with human beings. Many stories in the Bible speak of dreams. Jacob and Daniel of the Old Testament, and Joseph and Paul of the New Testament are just a few prominent characters who had dreams and acted upon them. The questions for Western visitors to East Africa today is: What does one do with someone like Moses Musalima? How does one respond to someone who says we are the answer to their dream? How should Westerners handle and respond to the dreams of their East African hosts?

In Moses' case, he became a Christian along with his entire household and many neighbors. He built a church on his property, and now many years later Moses is still active in that church. So, was Moses correct or mistaken about his dream and his response?

As a Westerner gains a deeper understanding of East African culture, new lenses will allow them to reexamine their own home culture concerning dreams. Scientific and rational principles are skeptical of dreams having any connection to a spirit realm. Yet in Western culture, popular movies and TV shows often incorporate dreams into story lines insisting they have spiritual or even evil meaning. Western culture dismisses dreams, but fails to realize that the majority of the people in the world still hold to some spiritual significance for dreams. Are Westerners, the tiny minority in this view of dreams, the only ones who are right? Or is there the possibility that dreams are used to communicate news, warnings, instructions from a realm beyond the physical?

Guidelines for Dealing with Dreams

Westerners either visiting or living in East Africa, may encounter hosts who believe in and share dreams. A tourist may have a guide that shares a dream or drives a different route in the game park because of a gruesome warning that came to him during the night. Business people may have an East African associate who may insist upon an odd time to meet or require unusual agreements to accommodate a recent dream about international business. Workers, friends, and even Christian associates may come to the Westerner to share a dream, ask for an interpretation and advice, or give a warning. So how should we respond? Westerners can lose tremendous credibility with their hosts and even hinder their own personal, organizational, or business goals if they immediately reject the legitimacy of dreams and in any way demean the person who believes in them. The following guide should be helpful in responding in the most effective way to anyone who shares a dream.

How should we respond when someone shares a dream that seems to be significant?

1. LISTEN to the dream. Do not be dismissive.
2. Ask questions to draw out additional details and information. Determine if the dream is recurring.
3. Encourage the dreamer to consult wise and mature leaders and/or their local pastor for counsel on the interpretation of and obedience to the dream. No dreamer should self-interpret and obey without consulting others. If no meaning becomes apparent after a period of time, then the dream can be dismissed.
4. If someone's dream involves you in either a project, business matter, or personal response, make sure any interpretation of a dream is consistent with the laws of

the country. No appropriate dream that requires obedience should instruct someone to steal, lie, cheat, commit adultery, divorce their spouse, or perform some illegal act. Any dream instructing the dreamer to violate the law should not be considered trustworthy.

5. If someone shares a dream that requires a religious group to act upon it, make sure the interpretation of the dream is consistent with the religious teachings of Holy Scripture. God would not require a believer to do something contrary to His already revealed will. Additionally, if the dream instructs the dreamer to do something against faith or that would bring harm or hardship to family or friends, then that dream should not be viewed as credible.

6. If a dream suggests the dreamer is going to receive or experience something or must do something, but no time frame is given, then the dreamer should be patient and not force his dream's results. Do not allow the dreamer to pressure you into making the dream come true. If the person is religious, he should give God time to work out the details as God wills.

7. Be especially cautious of any dreamer who shares a dream that requires others to obey. Such a dream is controlling and gives the dreamer power over others. It is a common tactic of insincere religious leaders or those involved in witchcraft to share dreams that require others to do or give something. Such dreams should be prayed against and cast aside as false dreams.

8. If a dream does not come true, the dreamer should not be discouraged. You may remind the dreamer that not every dream has a special significance. Not every dream is a message from the spiritual realm or a word or instruction from God.

9. If Western visitors find themselves in a situation where dreams are highly regarded and some in the group have many dreams while others do not, it may be important to note that not everyone has dreams. Having or not having a dream does not determine a person's worth, abilities, or spiritual maturity.

In relating my two (of many) experiences concerning dreams in this chapter, I may have sounded skeptical in the first example about the dreams expecting help on school fees, while I remained non-committal about Moses' vision in the second. Actually, my response to dreams has evolved over my years of living in East Africa. At first, I did not believe dreams had anything to do with the spiritual realm. I, like Charles Dickens' character Mr. Scrooge, initially thought dreams and apparitions to be "an undigested bit of beef, a blot of mustard, a crumb of cheese..." more gravy than a message from the grave. I mostly believed dreams reflected an unsettled mind about circumstances I was currently facing. However, my East African experiences have caused me to move to a more balanced position. Do I still dismiss every dream told to me? No. Do I now believe every dream is a significant message from the spirit realm? No. Could there be merit in a dream that follows the guidelines I laid out above? Yes. I do not encourage dream sharing, nor do I avoid it. I listen. I ask questions. I measure every dream against common sense, government laws, and Biblical principles. Even after scrutinizing a dream, I counsel a wait-and-see policy. Still, I meet people like Moses Musalima who confound my own cultural understanding of dreams, and force me to rethink what I believe and how I should respond. What I have seen and experienced has helped me bridge the gap between my home culture and my host culture concerning dreams. It is a bridge I must cross on occasion to engage my East African friends and to understand their worldview and response to things they encounter.

Proverbs

"You can share the same bed, but you can't share the same dream" – African Proverb
"There are no witnesses to a dream" – African Proverb
"Dreams are voices of the ancestors" – African Proverb
"Dreams are related to the past but connected to the future" – African Proverb
"Return to old watering holes for more than water; friends and dreams are there to meet you" – African Proverb

(All young children are given the chore of carrying water. Young boys eventually take on other responsibilities, but the smallest ones carry water. It is during youth that all children dream of what it will be like in the future when they are adults. They dream of the future. Also, during the collection of water, there is a daily opportunity to visit friends and neighbors. The proverb captures the communal interaction and youthful dreams of those who most often collect the water.)

"Thoughts and dreams are the foundation of our being" – Nigerian Proverb
"A woman possessed by demons dreams of toads in red dancing shoes" – Nigerian Proverb
"One cannot stop sleeping for fear of bad dreams" – Ethiopian Proverb

Chapter 37
Witchcraft: Is it Real or Fake?

In Nigel Barley's humorous book, ***The Innocent Anthropologist***, the author talks about the anthropological study he conducted among the Dowayos of Cameroon, West Africa. Barley's response to the local rain chief is a classic illustration of the gap between Western cultural beliefs and those of many Africans. After he worked hard for months to convince the rain chief to let him see his rain stones (his most prized possessions), the witchdoctor finally agreed. Barley speaks of the arduous climb to the top of a bitterly cold mountain, where he finds a waterfall. He writes:

"A watercourse issued from above, and beneath the icy spray was a hollow in the rock. Within were large, lumpy clay pots like water jars; inside these were stones of various colors for male and female rain. The rain chief splashed them with the same remedies he had spat on me and held the rocks out for my inspections. There was one more thing. We splashed through the water to a large, white rock. This was the ultimate defense of the Dowayos. If he removed this, the whole world would be flooded, and all would be killed" (Barley, 1986, p. 160).

On their descent, the rain chief asked Barley if he was happy. Barley said he was but that he still wanted to see the rain chief make it rain. The witchdoctor asked if he did not see the remedy that he splashed on the rocks. The rain chief confidently predicted it would rain on them before they reached home. Again, Barley writes:

"The storm hit us at the very worst point of the descent, where we were executing goat-like leaps across the fissures. Granite becomes slippery when wet. At one point, I was reduced to crawling on all fours. The rain chief was sniggering and pointing to the sky. Had I seen it now? We were shouting above the storm to be heard. 'That's enough,' I cried, 'you can make it stop.' He looked at me with a twinkle in his eye. 'A man does not take a wife to divorce her the same day,' he replied" (Barley, p. 161).

Barley's visit to the mountain, his secret glimpse of the rain stones, and the heavy downpour on the way home did not convince him of the rain chief's powers. In fact, he admits, "I, of course, would never believe anything so against the grain of my own culture without much better evidence than this. I -- like they -- see what I expect to see" (Barley, p. 161). Barley's response illustrates one of the fundamental obstacles to understanding another culture. Our own culture conditions and trains us to see and interpret events through our own cultural framework. We consider our conclusion to be the truth, but people of another culture may experience the same event and come to a different conclusion. So, which is true?

In another instance, Barley speaks of his first glance at the tools of the local rain chief. His response highlights another misunderstanding among Western cultures concerning objects dedicated to witchcraft. He writes:

"The rain chief showed me his portable rain kit… He took me off into the bush and we crouched down behind a rock with much extravagant looking around and scanning of the horizon. Inside was a plug of ram's wool. 'For clouds,' he explained. Then came an iron ring. This served to localize the effect of the rain: if, for example, he was at a skull festival, he would make it rain in the middle of the village until the people brought him beer. Next came the most powerful part of all. This was a great secret that he had never shown anybody. He bent forward earnestly and tipped up the horn. Slowly, there rolled into his hand a child's blue marble such as one might purchase anywhere. I moved as if to pick it up. Horrified, he withdrew his hand: 'It would kill you'" (Barley, p. 157-158).

The Cultural Gap in Understanding

To help understand the difference between typical Western understanding of witchcraft and that of animists, consider what makes an object holy. The Biblical root words for holiness mean to separate, divide, earnestly dedicate, devote, and consecrate. Holiness is not inherent in creation. It comes by God's dictates. He sanctifies or sets apart someone or something, such as the Sabbath, Israel and its priests, their firstborn, and sanctuaries.

In the Old Testament, objects dedicated to the Lord or for his purpose were designated as holy. Some of these objects were temple furniture, priestly clothing, real estate, money, animals, oil, incense, and water. Achan's sin in Joshua chapter seven was to take something dedicated to God from the spoils of Jericho. The spiritual significance of Achan's theft is spelled out in devastating clarity in Joshua 7:10-12, and Achan was not the only one who died because of his disregard for holy things.

Barley makes the mistake of evaluating the rain chief's tools by their form and substance and not by their dedicated purpose. He recognizes the common form of a child's marble but fails to realize it had been dedicated to the spirits and work of rain making. Sometimes, Westerners fall into the same trap. Because they can see that a certain witchdoctor's medicine is simply a piece of bark, some powder, a shell, a tree root, or some other seemingly innocuous thing, they are too quick to dismiss the object, the witchdoctor, and witchcraft as bogus. Westerners overlook the object's significance as having been consecrated to spirits for some task.

Turn this around for a moment and consider a non-religious person's response to the form and substance of Christian rituals. Baptism, a spiritually significant washing away of sins, is humorously viewed by some as merely submerging a person in the water with all their clothes on. Prayer means nothing more than closing your eyes and speaking to no one. Communion, an important remembrance of fellowship in the death of Christ, may be seen as a somewhat curious meal of bread fragments and sips of wine. In the 2nd century, some unbelievers made the malicious claim that Christians were cannibals who ate the flesh of their savior. The form and substance of these rituals seem inconsequential to the unbeliever, but they have tremendous importance and power to the believing participant and severe consequences when neglected.

Does consecration work both ways -- to righteousness and to evil? More specifically, can a simple object dedicated to evil spirits bring harm? Consider God's commands to the Israelites in Deuteronomy 7:25,26 where it says, "The images of their gods you are to burn in the fire. Do not covet the silver and gold on them, and do not take it for yourselves, or you will be ensnared by it, for it is detestable to the Lord your God. Do not bring a detestable thing into your house, or you, like it, will be set apart for destruction. Utterly abhor and detest it, for it is set apart for destruction." It seems from this passage that even the silver and gold dedicated to making the idols carried a punishment for its possessor. In fact, God uses the phrase "set apart for destruction" as an antithesis for something set apart for righteousness. Paul uses a similar argument in his teaching to the Corinthians about things devoted to idols. He said, "…the sacrifices of pagans are offered to demons, not to God, and I do not want you to be **participants** with demons. You cannot drink the cup of the Lord and the cup of demons, too; you cannot have a part in both the Lord's table and the table of demons. Are we trying to arouse the Lord's jealousy?" A Westerner should not underestimate the significance or the power behind charms, shrines, idols, talismans, or tools of witchdoctors. What may only look like a root, or feathers, or powder, maybe "something set apart for destruction." Might a person become a participant with evil spirits by possessing or using such an object?

Is The Supernatural Real?

Western View

Westerners have, at best, a confused idea of the spirit realm and witchcraft. Social scientists from the late 1800s and early 1900s developed views that the practice of magic and belief in spirits was simply a model of "evolutionary development (from magic to religion to science), a psychological coping mechanism, a pre-logical explanation of natural events, or a sociological phenomenon that helps define and sustain community roles" (Kuemmerlin-McLean, 1992, p. 470). These views still heavily influence contemporary thinking. In fact, the social scientific view has had its greatest impact on the medical, judicial, and educational systems of America.

Many Westerners consider people who conduct séances, read palms or Tarot cards, or make astrological predictions as phony. They assume a belief in spirits is primitive, pre-logical, or unscientific. The media often represents witch covens as eerie kooks and social misfits who perform secret animal sacrifices. Yet many classic children's tales involve magic. Supermarket tabloids often scream headlines of ghostly or angelic encounters, and many popular movies contain themes based upon demons, Satan, angels, curses, or witchcraft. The result of such a confluence of thought, is that witchcraft, demons and the supernatural have become interesting and even entertaining topics, but not real enough to merit a place of serious thought or value by Western cultures.

It is this kind of mixed view of the spirit realm and witchcraft that Westerners carry with them to East Africa, and it becomes a tremendous stumbling block when engaging people who honestly believe they live within a spirit realm and see witchcraft as a means to utilize the spiritual within the physical.

Biblical View

The Biblical view is very clear. The supernatural is real. God, angels, Satan, and demons are the very basis of religion. Human interaction with the supernatural is guided by spiritual laws given by God within the Bible itself.

There are terms referring to practices of the supernatural and magic throughout the Bible. The most specialized vocabulary, however, appears primarily in the Pentateuch when God is commanding the Israelites not to adopt the evil practices of the nations they would conquer. The most basic and inclusive list is found in Deuteronomy 18:10-11.

Instead of teaching that the practice of magic is fake, the Bible accepts it as real and prohibits its use. Egyptian magicians had the power to duplicate, by their secret arts, three of the signs that God commanded Moses to perform before the Pharaoh. On another occasion, the Bible narrates King Saul's consultation with a witch who summons Samuel's spirit for guidance. Simon the sorcerer of Samaria had great power that amazed the people of his area, and Ephesus was a center for learned practitioners of witchcraft who preserved their incantations, spells, and curses on valuable scrolls. The essence of this Biblical view is not denial of evil power, but the insistence that God's power is greater. Throughout the Bible, Scripture encourages the godly to trust in God's strength, and warns them of punishment and separation from God if they indulge in practices associated with witchcraft and idolatry.

African View

In East Africa, strong animistic beliefs provide the traditional cultural framework for most people. Animism has a strong belief in the presence and power of spirits and other supernatural forces in the world. The spirit world exists and interacts with the physical realm. Sickness, death, crop failures, business successes, and many other things are believed to be affected by the spiritual world. Animism provides the lens through which many East Africans interpret all experiences, events, and values. Witchcraft is an important part of this system because it is a means to control the spirits and supernatural forces. Each East African tribe may have special spirits guiding and protecting them. Often there are clan spirits and prescribed sacrifices for everything from rain, crops, livestock, sickness, and protection from evil. The Bagisu people of Uganda keep a special shrine for the rain spirit (Nabende). The neighboring Bagwere people make small holes in their huts so the child spirit (Mukama) can come and go freely. The Sebei people living on the Ugandan slopes of Mount Elgon put a special tree branch over their doors to protect them from measles. Each clan and tribe often have dozens of spirits, and they perform rituals and activities that these spirits require them to do. Some spirits may even have the same name from place to place. The Jinn spirits of the Berbers in Morocco are called Jini among the Swahili of the Kenyan coast and are called Majini among the Bagwere of Uganda.

In 1987, the Luo people of Kenya petitioned the government to return a large python called Omieri which had been moved from their area and taken to Nairobi for treatment. Farmers had accidentally burned the python when they were clearing their fields in preparation for plowing. The clan elders claimed the python's absence would hinder their communication with the spirits and bring disaster upon the area. The government not only agreed to return the snake but did so in a private plane.

Also in the 1980s, a famous Luo lawyer, S. M. Otieno, died (a.k.a. Nyalgunga by his clan name). When his wife (a Kikuyu of central Kenya) announced plans to bury him on the family farm north of

Nairobi, the Luo clan elders sued Mrs. Otieno for the body, claiming the clan spirits would be angry if he was buried outside of their homeland. The case took 52 days in the court, which ultimately ruled in favor of the clan.

Why Is Witchcraft So Attractive?

The same person who would grudgingly give the smallest coin to a beggar on the streets of Kampala might travel 200 miles over several days and spend two months' wages to seek relief from a personal problem from a famous witchdoctor.

On the island of Lufu (Lake Victoria), a witchdoctor might instruct a person with family problems to take a goat in a canoe and paddle out to a distant, isolated island and sacrifice it to the island spirits. The person would sell his possessions to purchase a goat, undertake the long and arduous journey to the island and spend a couple of days performing all the tasks given by the witchdoctor. But the same person would not attend a free, two-hour religious meeting 100 yards from his house on principles for family unity.

Why would people willingly submit themselves to travel long distances, dig deep holes, swallow unknown substances, build costly shrines, burn and sacrifice good food, bury clay pots, hide expensive powders, run around naked in their neighborhood at night, and do all manner of additional odd activities to satisfy a witchdoctor's prescription? Why are people attracted to witchcraft? What is its strong appeal?

First, witchcraft releases the user from numerous personal responsibilities. If the child gets sick, the soccer team loses, a driver has an accident, or a thief is caught, the charm they used simply was not strong enough. Or, others had stronger medicines.

For the wife who thinks her husband is interested in another woman, she can buy a charm to correct the problem. She must do nothing to change. She does not have to look any nicer. She does not have to behave more respectfully or show more honor to her husband. She does not have to work any harder in the house. In short, she does not have to do anything herself to keep her husband around. That is the work of the charm. She can continue to be lazy, disrespectful, dirty, quarrelsome, sexually cold, or whatever other action/attitude that her husband finds difficult to live with. If the husband runs away, it is the charm's fault.

For the man who fails in his business, the charm he purchased was not strong enough to attract customers. He does not have to admit that he tried to cheat customers with price increases, watered down milk, or used unjust scales. He does not have to say that he was rude and showed little concern for customer satisfaction. He does not have to tell anyone that he did not restock his store and that he misused all the money that came in. It is not his fault for mismanaging the business. The charm simply wasn't strong enough. A stronger charm will help him succeed in some future business.

To be relieved of having to accept personal responsibility is a powerful attraction to witchcraft. One is no longer the cause of their own troubles and misfortunes. They do not have to do anything to change. They can continue living as they want. They simply buy charms to ensure that they can do as they please, and if a problem does arise, then it is the charm's fault. They are free of blame.

Second, witchcraft gives users a sense of the power to manipulate people, spirits, and circumstances around them. With a sacrifice or little bit of medicine, users can cleverly bend everything to their wishes. They become the masters of their universe. They see themselves as smarter and cleverer than others because they have secretly made people do their bidding. They have greater power.

They can do more. They are in control of their lives. They do not need to answer anyone else.

Yes, these users of witchcraft will admit that there is a spirit world and that God and spirits do exist. But with witchcraft, they can manipulate the spirits to do their will. They can gain protection from evil or even curse others. Witchcraft can "appease" the spirits and turn their anger away. A sacrifice, a promise to do good, praise, or a contribution at a religious gathering will make God happy and allow the witchcraft user to continue with his own lifestyle. In fact, he will ask for prayers for his sick child and then buy a charm thinking that he has cleverly covered all the bases and provided maximum protection for his infant.

The powerful attraction for witchcraft is that users become their own gods. They set things up to do their bidding. They bend and manipulate everything else to their wishes. They must obey nothing but their own desires. They cleverly control all things. Perhaps this is why witchcraft and idolatry are so closely related in the Bible.

A Life Full of Spirits and Witchcraft

The following examples are by no means exhaustive. They are a composite picture of East African life experiences from the Bukusu, Luo and Kabras of Kenya, the Bagisu, Sebei, and Bagwere of Uganda, and the Lomwe of Malawi. They illustrate that Africans are exposed to witchcraft in every phase of their lives.

Many East African women traditionally purchased charms to help them get pregnant. Among the Bagisu people, there are special waterfalls called nabeke where barren women can go and bathe. The washing ritual is supposed to increase the woman's chances of getting pregnant. Once she is expecting, she will eat a special mixture of animal blood, milk, and pumpkin to make her healthy and protect the baby. In some cases, special ceremonies are conducted as soon as the baby is born. If previous children have died in a Bukusu home, then as soon as the baby is born, it is passed out of the window and laid upon the trash heap. A grandmother picks up the child and brings it in through the front door asking if anyone in the house wants to care for it. This ritual is supposed to confuse the spirits who have caused the death of previous children. If the child lives, he is named Makokha (the Bagisu name is Kuloba) meaning trash heap. Kabras mothers put charms called eyindukhulu on infants to ward off sickness. Babies may be completely naked but wear a string around their waist, a necklace, or a bracelet (hirizi). Before a child can walk, a Gwere mother will dash from her house and lay her infant in the tracks behind a passing vehicle. She believes the energy from such a vehicle will be transferred to her child. The Kabras traditionally laid their infants upon the back of a black cow or strong dog for the same reason. If a Bukusu child wakes up with nightmares from evil spirits, he is fed kimikalo, a special herb mixture to ward off spirits. Bukusu grandmothers conduct special name-calling ceremonies (khutuma visambwa) over a child to identify which ancestral spirit has come back in the form of this child.

Growing up in the home, children see and hear about the spirits that live around them. They learn the names of clan spirits and what each one does. As a sick child, they make visits to witchdoctors for treatment. Among the Bagwere, cuts on the chest or arms are a sign of such treatments. Gwere children watch their fathers sacrifice a chicken and break it up into a small clay pot which he buries in a strategic spot in the compound for protection against all kinds of evil. Additional medicines may be buried at the step of their door. Some Sebei families place medicine for protection above the doorway to keep evil spirits, sickness, or harm from entering with a visitor.

At circumcision time when young men begin their rite of passage, the Bukusu and Bagisu make special shrines called namwima for the ancestors to sit in and watch the proceedings. The blood of a sacrificial chicken is smeared on the circumcision knife and special herbs (etiang'i) are eaten by the initiate to make him strong during the ritual so that he won't cry out and shame the family.

Students may purchase charms to better their performance in school or athletics. Is the town's soccer team or the national team playing poorly? The witchdoctor prescribes a special medicine that is put into the shoes of the athletes. This medicine is designed to attract the soccer ball and to help athletes kick accurately. Additionally, stronger medicine will make the opponent's goalie see more than one ball coming at him. This will make the goalie jump to block mirages and allow the real ball to pass. African newspapers acknowledge that many soccer teams on the continent hire their own team witchdoctors. The Kenyans even claimed in the past that one of their witchdoctors was hired by a German team. One wonders how many competitors wear charms at the Olympics to enhance their performance and abilities.

When Africans are older, they may purchase small roots/charms for their wallet to help them secure a job. The charm costs about two months' wages, but if they keep the charm in their wallet, they cannot lose their job. It must also be kept secret. If others know about it, the charm will lose its power. A Lomwe woman in Malawi notices her husband is spending too much time away from the house. She fears he has a girlfriend somewhere. The witchdoctor instructs the wife to catch a gecko and take its tail which she burns, crushes, and secretly adds to her husband's food. This will make him stay at home. If a Lomwe man is gone from home very much, most assuredly he eats gecko tails in his food. Charms (eyisimbishila) purchased by the bride in Kabras enhance her ability to keep her husband faithful. If he is not faithful, then another woman's charm is obviously stronger to pull him away from home.

The whole community participates in spirit-pleasing sacrifices at funerals. Everything from where the grave is dug to how the body is prepared reflects beliefs in the spirit realm. The family honors the spirits of the dead who are now able to bless or curse them. Shrines are built in clan areas and designated as sacred spots. The Balangira clan of the Gwere tribe in Uganda collects the skulls of ancestors and keeps them in special shrines. The community reinforces such beliefs by the very prevalence of these ceremonies.

Thus, from birth to death, spirits and witchcraft cover every major event in an African's life. If there is a problem with the spirits, troubled relationship, sickness, enemy, fear, or curse, the witchdoctor can sell something to take care of it.

The pressure to conform to these communal beliefs and practices is intense. The clan and extended family can withhold numerous privileges from an unruly member. My friend, Dennis Okoth, a Kenyan Luo, upon his confession of Christian faith, was tied up by his father, beaten, and starved for several days to try to make him renounce his new faith. Mung'ono, a clan priest among the Bagwere, lives on clan land, in a clan house, and receives his entire income through clan donations. If he renounces the clan spirits and becomes a Christian, he will become destitute. Such harsh punishments and family repudiations await many who seriously consider confessing any religious faith. Death is not an uncommon punishment in the most extreme situations. In such a cultural context, it is almost impossible to find an African who is an atheist.

It is into this environment of life-long conditioning, fear of spirits, and family and community pressure, that Westerners come. They bring with them their own cultural, non-spiritual beliefs and are unaware of the social, familial, and economic choices they require

East Africans to make. The most tightly knit, traditional communities tend to resist Islam and Christianity. Syncretism, the practice of embracing and honoring opposing beliefs, is the only way many East Africans can appease the clan spirits, their family, and their Western friends. It is a difficult position to be in, and Westerners need to be aware of this tension as they begin their visit, project, or residency.

Advice for Westerners

In previous chapters on bride prices, circumcision, and dreams, I endeavored to explain the East African cultural values and rationale that support such practices. I attempted to temper Western reactions to these practices by prompting a reflection upon our own cultural values and customs. Then I offered a more sensitive, balanced, cross-cultural response. It has been my goal in this chapter to do the same with witchcraft. In fact, I provided a more in-depth and researched analysis of witchcraft because it permeates every level of East African society. Hopefully these chapters will cause Western tourists, businesspeople, and residents to grow in their appreciation for their East African friends, business partners, and political counterparts and be less inclined to so quickly dismiss or condemn East African cultural practices, or to grow frustrated that "modern ideas" do not gain ready acceptance or take lasting root.

In my effort to explain these cultural traditions, I may have given the impression that I support them. Let me reiterate that I do not condone any custom or cultural practice that physically, emotionally, or spiritually harms someone. In this sense, I must add my personal observations about witchcraft. I believe in the spirit realm and the existence of witchcraft. My own personal experiences have revealed witchcraft to be founded upon a bondage of fear rather than a freedom of joy and love. Witchcraft teaches spirits can be easily offended, and that they have the power to harm or bless the living. Thus, each person must fear and honor ancestral spirits to avoid offending, and they must respond quickly to any perceived offense by appeasing the angered spirits lest some evil befalls the living and their household. Witchdoctors are master manipulators of this fear of witchcraft because they covet financial income from repeat customers. People caught up in witchcraft rely on the power of medicines and charms rather than hard work, sincere speech, and honest relationships. In fact, witchcraft promotes a selfish worldview where the practitioners attempt to bend everything toward their desires even if it is against the will of others around them. This me-first mindset undermines true communal values, creates distrust in relationships, and promotes deceptive business practices.

Denying the existence of demons, spirits, and the power of witchcraft, or espousing beliefs that Western attitudes and values are "better" or more "intellectual or progressive" than African beliefs is not the way for tourists, businesspeople, or residents to engage East Africa. The Westerner's lone voice, in a vast community of East Africans who have years of traditional experiences, will cause East African hosts to judge the Westerner a fool – though they will not openly oppose him to preserve the appearance of relationship. The Westerner will undermine his own credibility for any task he seeks to accomplish and severely compromise his social standing, influence, and friendship network. I am reminded of an American who while visiting the Turkana in Northwestern Kenya in the 70's, confidently announced that Americans had sent men to the moon just a few years before. The Turkana audience, many of whom had not seen an airplane, not to mention a rocket, laughed heartily at this stranger's babbling. His project failed and he did not stay in the area for very long.

An unhealthy interest in witchcraft should also be avoided. I have encountered several examples where Westerners purchased objects devoted to witchcraft and then subsequently suffered sickness, nightmares, prolonged headaches, and in some extreme cases the death of someone in the family. While such incidents may be discounted by Westerners as coincidences, East Africans will quietly attribute such horrible outcomes to the presence of witchcraft within their homes. Westerners would be better off to not purchase any witchcraft items, and to avoid ceremonies, rites of passage, funerals, or other public activities where witchcraft is strongly or overtly present. After all some Africans say, "No one hugs a cobra without being bitten."

Additionally, it would be wise for Westerners who stay long-term, to learn about and avoid art, bracelets, and carvings such as Makonde artifacts and masks. While the seller may point to its fine craftsmanship and downplay any connection to the spirit realm, many oddly shaped figurines represent evil spirits or fertility gods. Certain animal-shaped carvings represent tribal totems revered for protection and blessings. A prime example of spirit carvings among many tribes is the chameleon figurine whose ever-changing color and odd-acting eyes demonstrate fearful characteristics of the ever-present spirits.

The best practice for Westerners living in East Africa is to politely respect the existence of and belief in witchcraft, but to avoid its artifacts and practices that are overtly associated with it. Do not express an unhealthy interest in witchcraft or purchase items connected to it. Stay focused on your work and explain that your lack of participation in anything connected to witchcraft is because of your different Western cultural beliefs.

Advice for Missionaries

The general advice given above is a good place to start for long-term missionaries serving in East Africa. However, it is not enough. Christian missionaries seek to free East Africans from the powers of witchcraft and bring freedom through faith in Jesus Christ. However, such a conversion is complicated and not to be initiated lightly. Missionaries should not be over-confident novices when engaging witchcraft.

Think how Paul approached the Athenians in Acts 17:16-34. He did not begin by condemning their idolatrous practices. Instead, he commended them for their religious interest and then spoke of God by using one of their own altar inscriptions. The missionary will get much farther if he begins by acknowledging the existence of spirits and demons, but then go on to explain where the greatest power of protection and blessing lies. The missionary and East African Christians would do well to preach on Biblical texts that show Jesus' power over evil spirits. Jesus casting out the Gaderene demon named Legion in Mark 5:1-20, will make an East African audience take notice. Casting out demons, healing sicknesses, raising people from the dead, performing miracles, all of these proclaim the power of Jesus Christ in terms that East Africans can relate to. Preaching about those who confess Jesus as the Son of God (including demons and Satan, in his temptation of Jesus) makes an impact on East African listeners as to who is really in control. Jesus promises freedom from the bondage of evil spirits, fear, and curses. This is an "Athenian" opening that missionaries must not neglect.

Reasoning does not work either. I once tried to reason with people who used charms by asking the following questions: "What kind of an explanation can you give if your soccer team, which wears charms to win, is beaten by a team that does not use charms? If you use charms to help you succeed in business, then why is Uganda one of the poorest countries in the world with an annual per capita income of less than $400 per person? If your children wear charms for protection against sickness, then why do people in Uganda have a life expectancy of less than 55 years of age and its infant mortality rate ranks among the highest in the world? If your women truly buy charms to keep their husbands faithful, then why do Ugandan newspapers estimate that adultery affects over 70 percent of the households in the country?" Their answer is always the same. Either the medicine was not strong enough, or, they say, "Just think what things would be like without the charms working so hard."

The first and most important step for East Africans to break free from witchcraft is to become a Christian. Dying to sin, being washed clean and free of sins, and receiving the Holy Spirit and his empowerment are necessary to crush the influence of evil spirits in an East African's life.

The implications of confessing Christ as Lord should be explained and enacted much more specifically than what is usually done in the West. The Greek word for "confess" literally means "to speak the same as." To confess Christ would then mean to speak as Christ would speak. We would speak against the same things Jesus would. We would bless the same things he would. The East African Christian should publicly speak his allegiance only to Christ only and renounce all past association with evil including clan spirits, witchcraft, and traditional spirit practices. The more detailed and extensive this confession and renouncing is, the clearer his allegiance to Christ will be. Witchcraft-related cultural practices that may have happened to him while in the womb or as an infant should also be included in the renunciation. Do not neglect to address generational curses, sacrifices, and beliefs.

A complete cleansing must take place of the new Christian's home and life. The missionary and church leaders must lead the new

Christian in burning all objects associated with the spirits. Remove and destroy all symbols and charms of witchcraft, shrines, sacrifices, and objects of protection. This may involve digging up buried charms, pulling up special plants, cutting off amulets from the body, ripping out charms sewn into clothing, and uncovering all manner of talismans hidden in the roof, bedroom, kitchen, grain storage, and compound. The public confession of evil deeds and burning of scrolls for witchcraft in Ephesus provides an important example.

There is great need to fill up East Africans' life with good now that they have emptied themselves of the evil. Jesus' parable of the evil spirit going out of a man and returning to find the house swept clean, put in order, and empty graphically illustrates the vulnerability of new East African Christians. Removing evil habits and beliefs without filling up their "empty house" with spiritual principles and healthy practices and incorporating them into a supportive community leaves them susceptible to a quick return to old habits in times of difficulty. This Biblical principle is put to good use by Alcoholics Anonymous and other support groups who help free people from addictive and destructive habits. Developing spiritual disciplines and teaching about living a Christian life are crucial for the new convert. Jesus commanded his followers to "make disciples," and this included teaching new converts to obey all of Jesus' commands. Replace the passive confidence in charms with an active participation and manifestation of the fruits of the Spirit. Teach new converts to rely upon of prayer, fasting, Scripture memorization, praise, and fellowship.

New converts should not be left without an encouraging support group or new community in which to root their new identity. They should be incorporated as quickly as possible into a body of believers who will see to the new convert's personal and spiritual needs. New East African Christians will need strength to withstand the family and cultural pressure to return to their old practices. A local church community will be a strong place of refuge as new Christians gain a new spiritual identity, family, and way of life.

The missionary's most important spiritual weapon from a distance will be prayer -- constant and vigilant. Paul mentioned Epaphras in his letter to the Colossians. He said that Epaphras worked hard for the Colossians by "wrestling in prayer that they stand firm." Even from a distance, the missionary can work hard for new Christians. In fact, a missionary's greatest work is not teaching seminars, holding Bible studies, writing and printing tracts, but knee-bending prayer. Mission committees, sponsoring churches, friends, and family should all be recruited for focused prayer covering the mission work.

Years ago, I met a young man who had moved to Kitale, Kenya to teach computer training in a local polytechnic school. He openly told me my mission work undermined local culture and ancient tribal beliefs. He felt that I was doing more harm than good and that I should go home and leave the people alone. I countered his observation by asking if he also should leave. He was shocked that I would say such a thing. I pointed out that his computer training program was introducing a foreign way of thinking, working, and communicating. What right did he have to come and introduce his technology while I had no right to share my religious beliefs? He argued that computers would improve their way of life. I argued the same thing. In the end, he reluctantly agreed that we had more in common than he had previously thought.

Businessmen travel the world to sell their products mindless of how such items will affect local culture. Western political policies are yoked upon financial loans to African countries forcing them to embrace a foreign political view or practice. Tourists visit East Africa and wear what they please, talk and drink as they want, and change no personal habits while touring the beautiful countryside.

They ignorantly demonstrate their cultural values in front of their East African hosts. Hollywood's relentless themes of sex, violence, betrayal, espionage, and so much more are shamelessly portrayed in graphic detail before the eyes of people groups vastly different from California. Yet no cultural thought or sensitivity is used to alter their messages for foreign audiences. In fact, every business, politician, tourist, non-profit worker, environmentalist, etc. seeks to press and bend East Africans to their views and goals. Missionaries should not feel ashamed to stand among the vast crowd of international visitors and workers and share their religious beliefs.

Proverbs

"A Diviner cannot accurately divine his own future" – Nigerian Proverb
"It is the fear of offence that makes men swallow poison" – Nigerian Proverb
"Countries practice witchcraft on one another" – Bantu Proverb

(Should it be a surprise to anyone that countries that practice witchcraft would wield it against other countries? Consider how many athletes wear charms during international and Olympic contests. How many politicians wear charms to enhance their words, actions and positions in the political arena? Have you ever thought about how many witchdoctors live in Washington, D.C. and sell their services to visiting diplomats? Westerners are blinded by their own cultural lenses and cannot see what is happening around them.)

Additional Resources

*Barley, Nigel. **The Innocent Anthropologist**. Middlesex, England: Penguin Books, 1986.*

Beckwith, C. & Fisher, A. (1999). **African Marriage Rituals.** *National Geographic Society. November, 1999.*

Keummerlin-McLean, Joanne K. **Magic.** *Anchor Bible Dictionary. 1992.*

Mattox, F.W. **The Eternal Kingdom.** *Delight, Arkansas: Gospel Light Publishing Company, 1961.*

NIV Study Bible. *Grand Rapids: Zondervan, 1985.*

Vine, M.E. **Expository Dictionary of New Testament Words.** *McLean, Virginia: MacDonald Publishing Company. 1979.*

Wright, David P. (1992). **Holiness. Anchor Bible Dictionary.** *1992.*

100 Years of African Missions: Essays in Honor of Wendell Broom *by A.C.U. Press (Much of my chapter on Witchcraft was edited from my own chapter 15 called "The Gospel and The Spirits".*

Chapter 38
The Adventures and Dangers of Becoming Third Culture People

Several years ago Clyde and Sheila Austin came to hold a special seminar for our missionary team in Kitale, Kenya. As a professor of Psychology with an impressive knowledge about cross-cultural personal and family dynamics, Clyde was especially good at helping us realize what was going on before our very eyes. In one session, Clyde handed us a can of blue plastic clay and another of yellow, and asked each of us to pinch off a piece of each color. When we all had pieces of blue and yellow plastic clay, Clyde instructed us to smash the two together for as long as we wanted, mixing the colors together. When we were finished mixing the colors, Clyde instructed us to fashion a person out of our plastic clay. Each of our clay people were mottled with blue and yellow patches and some green – the result of blending blue and yellow together. None of our clay people were alike. Clyde explained to us that the blue plastic clay represented our home culture, and the yellow plastic clay represented our host culture. How long we lived in and engaged the host culture would determine how much yellow was added and how much mixing of the two colors would be accomplished. Clyde pointed out that no one was perfectly green with a balanced blend of both. He also noted that there were distinct patches where we retained our home culture or adopted part of our host culture. Then as we talked about the mixture, Clyde instructed us to separate the two colors of plastic clay again. It was impossible to accomplish. Clyde made an important cultural point. The yellow host culture will forever change a person's identity, worldview, values, and lenses to see the world so that they will never be completely blue again. Some of the yellow will just not come out. Clyde's simple illustration underscored the effect of living in a host culture for any length of time. Cross cultural living really affects adults, but it impacts children even more. Westerners moving to East Africa for any length of time, must be aware of how the move will forever change them and their family.

The New Perspectives

In the beginning of this book, I informed the reader that all of the topics covered were like pieces of a mosaic. Every individual topic was a single piece of a huge, complex, cultural picture. Each piece or experience made little sense by itself, but added together with others they produce a mosaic of East African culture. The more pieces one has to add to the mosaic, the more nuanced the picture becomes and the greater the understanding of East African culture. The topics included in this book are not comprehensive. They are starting places. They are important pieces that need personal experiences and stories to fill in for definition and refinement. Yet, this limited list of topics serves a purpose. It provides a foundational framework on which to hang personal experiences for greater clarity and understanding. Hopefully, these topics can educate visitors on how to open themselves to new ways of seeing, listening, conversing, and most importantly how to deal with experiences and feelings in your cross-cultural exchanges.

I also used the illustration of a bridge of understanding that connected two very different lands and cultures. It is a bridge that can be built more effectively with the pieces presented in this book. Also in my mind, we move from darkness (ignorance) to light (understanding) as we cross the bridge and begin to engage a new and very different culture and people.

The final point I wish to make is how this journey changes us. We cannot stay the same after building and crossing the bridge. We will see, with newly trained eyes, a beautiful, colorful tapestry of peoples and cultures all mixed into East Africa. They will challenge us, provoke us, tire us, teach us, and grow us. In the process, we will cross over to the other side of the bridge and gain a new perspective of where we came from. With East African lenses, we will be able to examine and evaluate our home culture. If we stay long enough in East Africa, we will be able to see our home culture's warts and flaws much more clearly. We will struggle with this new perspective, but in the end, we will gain a healthier view and assessment of where we came from.

With pieces of blue and yellow and green plastic clay as our new identity, we will feel the pull of two homes, two cultures, two experiences, two loves, all crammed into one heart and head. We will forever be different from those we left behind. We will always be different from the ones we went to live among. We will continually feel both at home and a stranger in both worlds. Such is the life of an experienced, cross-cultural traveler.

Becoming a Third Culture Adult

This morning I woke up in Lubbock, Texas, and put my Ugandan coffee grounds into my coffee pot and waited for my fresh cup to start the day. I opened my cabinet to select a cup and passed over a decorative cup from London, the mug with the world map on it, the cup I bought at Java House in Nairobi, Kenya, and several other cups from East Africa. I settled on a thick white cup with the Jinja Café logo on its side from a favorite restaurant in Uganda. As the coffee brewed, I skipped the local morning news and opened a news app on my phone to search for the latest political news of East Africa. I read an article from an archbishop in Uganda, an economic report on Kenya, and I discovered that there had been new tribal clashes between the Dinka and Nuer somewhere north of the Nuba Mountains of South Sudan.

After breakfast, I passed the African artwork that hangs in my living room, removed a few items sitting on my Kenyan-made coffee table in the living room and set them on a book shelf I built myself from Muvuli wood in Uganda, and made sure my framed batik was straight on the wall. I drove in my car, on the right side of the road instead of the left, to my office and flipped the light switch up instead of down (typical for East Africa) to turn on the office light. All day, I struggled with the short, terse American greetings, and yearned for the extended greetings of East Africa. At another time, I purposefully moved something to my right hand to give it to somebody because that is the polite and honorable thing to do in East Africa. They did not notice my silent gesture of respect. Without thinking, today I bowed slightly when shaking a friend's hands. I also looked away when talking to a female coworker because I wanted to be polite (very important in East Africa), though she may have thought I was bored or inattentive.

For lunch I know where the best Indian cuisine is in Lubbock, Texas. I also frequent a Lebanese restaurant, and often shop at an African supermarket run by a Ugandan woman (we always greet in Luganda). Recently at the African supermarket, I purchased some Mchuzi mix for a meat dish we will prepare soon. I also put in an order for some plantain bananas, and I stocked up on Kenyan teabags for afternoon tea.

After work, I took time to check Facebook, email, and WhatsApp. I had two emails from friends in East Africa – one in Kenya and the other in South Sudan. My WhatsApp group of East Africans was discussing a recent road accident on A104 near Voi while traveling to Mombasa. On Facebook, my friend in Nimule, Sudan, shared pictures of a recent teaching session he had conducted. I recognized some of the faces.

After supper, my wife Linda and I traveled to a store to consider purchasing a new mattress for our bed. We found a style we wanted, but we were unsure of the price. The salesperson would not go away, so we switched to Swahili and discussed our finances in another language. Rather than taking the hint for privacy, the salesperson was intrigued and asked what language we were speaking. We hesitated, knowing that as soon as we answered "Swahili," more questions would arise.

Of course, Linda has been changed as well. She still cooks from scratch since we had no fast food options for most of our time in East Africa. Because of how rare they were in Africa, Linda developed the habit of washing and re-using Ziploc bags. She still does that in America. In Uganda, she stockpiled basic goods because of the constant shortages. Today, our American pantry still has a larger-than-normal amount of goods – just in case. Linda knows how to handle water or power outages. She tends to use items beyond the expiration date, and because medical help in East African rural areas was sketchy, Linda became quite proficient in knowing what kind of medicines were needed for a large array of illnesses. She was and still is our go-to person for sudden symptoms.

Living for 30+ years outside of America causes me to look at my home country through different lenses. I have huge gaps from the 80's and 90's and into the 2000's about TV shows, movies, music, advertisements, and national news. That means I may not understand a common idiom used in speech, or a reference to a music group that thrived and died in that 30-year span. It also means I have developed an outsider's perspective concerning American trends, fashion, movies, pop culture, TV entertainment, and politics (all parties). I tend to see the cultural blind spots Americans have when it comes to the world in general. Americans live in a bubble, unknowing and uncaring of what happens in other countries. As a people in general, we are ignorant of world geography, politics, trends, civil conflicts, famines, and international news. Because of our strong ethnocentrism, we believe our values should be the world's values. So, we use our strong economy and military might to force other countries to adopt our views on politics, women's rights, homosexuality, or whatever our current political or social issue is. Our in-fighting in politics at home and the scandals our newspapers love to expose, presents Americans around the world as childish, selfish, entertainment driven, fickle, untrustworthy, and arrogant. What we call a stabilizing military presence around the world, other countries see as an international bully. Yet, in all of the foolishness, America shows itself to be amazingly free in speech and actions, a land of opportunity through education and hard work, and an escape from much of the oppression and corruption so many people live under in dictatorial nations that make up the majority of the world. Essentially, I develop a broader view of America. I see its warts and am amazed at its attractiveness to foreigners. Living in East Africa helped me develop new lenses with which I now view my own home in a different way. I am truly thankful for the new perspective.

America is where I grew up, but I have two homes. In whichever one I am currently living, I always follow the news concerning the other. I eat a culturally mixed diet, see and interpret everything through two sets of lenses, accidentally throw odd Swahili or Luganda words into my English conversation, wear unfashionable clothing, decorate my house with a collection of international acquisitions, and sometimes avoid telling people I lived half my life in East Africa because they don't know what to do with that. I am a blend of cultures. This makes it hard for me to fit in well at home or in East Africa. I am blue and yellow and green. I am a Third Culture Adult (TCA).

My Third Culture Kids

My son Noah was born in Lubbock, Texas, in 1987, and my daughter Natalie was born in Amarillo, Texas, in 1992. However, both of them took their first airplane ride to East Africa within a few months after their birth. Both spent the first 18 years of their lives growing up in East Africa. My son began nursery school and his first two grades in Kitale, Kenya, where we lived. When we moved to Mbale, Uganda, in 1995, Noah was home-schooled for a couple of years but hated it. He looked as though he was literally dying on the vine. So we agreed to send him to Rift Valley Academy in Kijabe, Kenya, about an hour outside of Nairobi on the slopes of the Rift Valley. Noah thrived there because he suddenly found himself surrounded by kids just like him – Third Culture Kids (TCK's). I still remember him coming home during the first break of his seventh-grade year and remarking, "For the first time in my life, I feel like I am normal. Everyone is like me. They understand me. Can I finish high school at Rift Valley?" Noah graduated from Rift Valley Academy in 2006. He played rugby and soccer and took school trips to the Kenyan coast and a game park. He even visited a camel farm in northern Kenya on one break. I remember another time he asked to spend a school break at the home of one of his friends. We thought that might be possible until we realized he was asking to fly to Zambia for a month. On another occasion, he pressed us to let him go to visit friends in Yemen. Because nearly all the time Noah spent in East Africa was in Kenya, he will put Kenya on his Facebook bio for the question, "Where are you from?" On occasion, Noah will start speaking English in a Kenyan accent or throw out a Swahili sentence. He avoids coffee but drinks hot tea several times a day. Noah instinctively gravitates to minorities, hungers for international cuisine, decorates his house with African artifacts he still has, and includes African music in his list of favorites. To this day, he has a keen sense of East African humor.

Natalie spent her first three years in Kitale, Kenya, but didn't really remember it or consider any place as "home" until she was living in Mbale, Uganda. Natalie grew up in a cooperative home school in Mbale and did only a few years of high school at Rift Valley Academy in Kenya. She overlapped with Noah for one year. Natalie's friends were in Uganda. She traveled with us to Fort Portal, Masaka, Mbarara, Kampala, Jinja, Sipi Falls, and many other places near the Nile River. We had lots of team retreats and meetings around Uganda. She spent very little time in Kenya. So when Natalie answers the question on Facebook about where she is from, she will answer Uganda. Natalie keeps up with lots of her Ugandan friends via social media. She texts, shares pictures, rejoices over someone's accomplishment and is saddened by someone's parents having problems. Her friends literally span the globe. Natalie loves to cook East African food, misses the days she could run around outside without shoes, and loves to host visitors in her home – just like her parents did in Uganda.

Linda and I will say we are from America. Noah says he is from Kenya, and Natalie calls Uganda home. We are a great example of a Third Culture Family. On one occasion, our family was "home" in America on a four-month visit. We spent a lot of time traveling to see "friends," and Noah and Natalie were miserable. Linda and I were enjoying ourselves and couldn't understand why the kids were not happy. At one point, I asked them why they were not enjoying our friends' house. Noah spoke up and said, "These people are your friends, not ours. You have known them for a long time. We have never met them before. Our friends are back in East Africa." An American female coworker in Mbale, Uganda, realized one time that she was the only one in her family who was looking forward to going "home" to America. Her kids wanted to stay in Uganda, where their friends were, and her husband, who had been born in Africa, actually preferred staying in Uganda rather than going "home." What she did not realize was that her children had become Third Culture Kids (TCK's).

Growing a Third Culture Family

There is no way for Western residents who dig deeply into their host culture to return home unchanged. The topics in this book, which only scratch the surface of East African culture, outline some of the ways in which Westerners will meet, struggle with, and be shaped by their host home. The changes will be dramatic at first, subtle later on, but life-changing in perspectives, values, customs, thought processes, and social responses. Any Westerner who lives cross-culturally for a long time becomes an oddity. Some struggle with their experience. Others embrace it proudly to the point of irritating those around them. Most struggle with the transformation into the host culture and then again and upon returning home. They will be forever changed.

Many Westerners who spend lengthy periods of time in East Africa may not realize it, but they are becoming a third culture family. Adults remain rooted in their home culture and adapt to their host culture (acculturation); they will have less of a problem returning "home." Western children have less "home" culture for a foundation. Instead, they grow up in and embrace their host culture as their "home" culture (enculturation), though it is mixed with some of their parents' beliefs, diet, values, traditions, and holidays observed as a family. Upon returning to their parents' home culture, children often feel like outsiders. They identify with other children who are on the social fringes of school or work. Both of my children took about four years to finally settle into American culture. I could literally track their progress by the kind of friends they associated with. There is not a one-size-fits-all formula for cultivating and shaping a third culture family. Personalities, length of stay, and the kinds of experiences all play a part in shaping TCKs and TCAs. Everyone's experience and response are unique.

The important thing to remember is that every decision a family makes concerning their work, housing, education for the kids, and social dynamics will impact everyone in the family. For example, many living in East Africa must choose between some form of homeschooling (either a single-family model or in a cooperative group), local schooling (not really an option because of low academic standards), or an international boarding school. If a family finds these options unacceptable, they may not stay long in East Africa. Homeschooling or a co-op is often more affordable and can handle elementary grades up to high school. However, to truly prepare a student for university studies, an international school may be a better option. Within East Africa, international schools offer a variety of educational models based on European, American, or International curricula. It can be expensive, but generally, such an education can be extremely beneficial. I remember Rift Valley Academy maintained more than a 92% success rate of their graduates entering university studies. Successful boarding school students learn how to develop good study habits away from home, making them better prepared for university life, and they find students who are also third-culture kids. They tend to bond well together.

So much more needs to be written about East African culture. This book could be volume one in a series. It is difficult to stop here, because there are more stories and insights to share, and I must confess I continue to learn. May this book be a help to all who visit, work, or live in East Africa. May you come to appreciate the people and land as much or more than I do, and because I am community-minded, share your insights with me, invite me over to tell you more stories or help you prepare for your move or project. I can remind us all of President Jomo Kenyatta's favorite political slogan –

Harambee (which means "let us pull together"). Finally, let me share with you a Swahili word for "welcome," which also means "come near" - *Karibu*.

Proverbs

"Travel teaches us how to see" – African Proverb
"One does not cross a river without getting wet" – Zulu Proverb
"Having a good discussion is like having riches" – Kenyan Proverb
"When the moon is not full, the stars shine more brightly" – Ugandan Proverb
"To the one who does not know, a small garden is a forest" – Ethiopian Proverb
"Knowledge is better than riches" – Cameroonian Proverb
"A traveler to distant places should make no enemies" – Nigerian Proverb
"The road does not tell the traveler what lies ahead" – Bantu Proverb
"The wise traveler leaves his heart at home" – African Proverb
"The person who has not traveled widely believes his mother is the best cook" – Ugandan Proverb

---

Additional Resources

There is no way in this chapter to cover all the points or needs of third-culture kids and adults. There are numerous resources offer more in-depth discussion on this often-unnoticed transformation of families living in a host culture. The following is only a starting list of books.

Third Culture Kids: Growing Up Among Worlds, David C. Pollock, Ruth E. Van Reken, and Michael V. Pollock, **ISBN** 978-1-47365-766-3

Third Culture Kids: A Gift to Care For, Ulrika Ernvik, **ISBN** 978-91-985480-0-6

Misunderstood: The Impact of growing Up Overseas in the 21ˢᵗ Century, Tanya Crossman, **ISBN** 978-1-909193-85-7

Finding Home: Third Culture Kids in the World, Ed. Rachel Pieh Jones, **ISBN** 9781731568625

The Global Nomad's Guide to University Transition, Tina L. Quick **ISBN** 978-1-904881-21-6

Belonging Everywhere & Nowhere: Insights into Counseling the Globally Mobile, Lois J. Bushong **ISBN** 978-0-615-69606-5

Unrooted Childhoods: Memoirs of Growing Up Global, Faith Eidse, Nina Sichel, ed. **ISBN** 13-978-1-85788-338-1

Children's Books providing insight into the world of children in East Africa

Rain School by James Rumford
The Marvelous Mud House by April Graney
ChirChir Is Singing by Kelly Cunnane and Jude Daly
My Name Is Blessing by Eric Walters
Beatrice's Goat by Page McBriar
One Hen by Katie Smith Milway

There is a whole series of East African children's books by Mwenye Hadithi and Adrienne Kennaway.

9 798330 524358